I0800511

IMAGES
of Rail

GREATER ERIE TROLLEYS

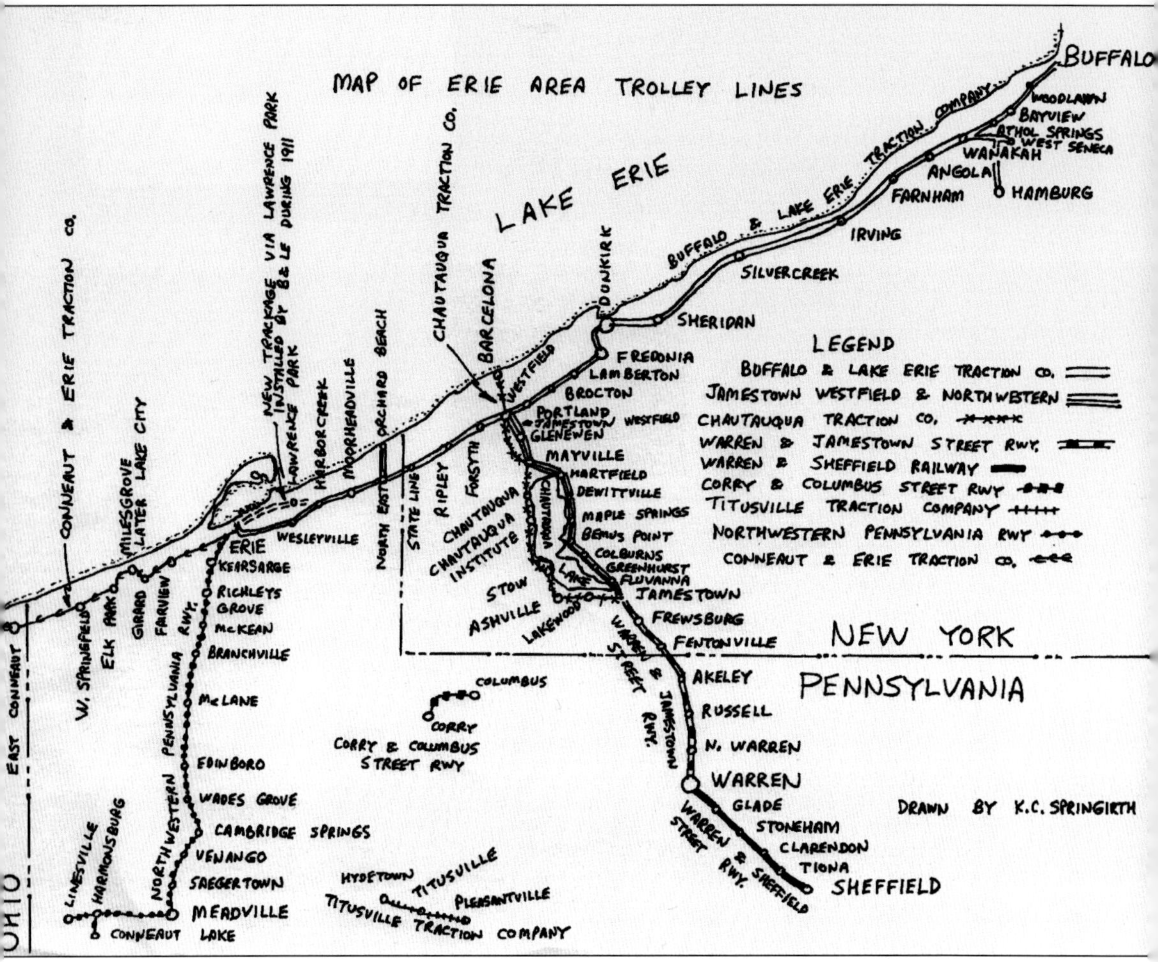

This map shows the connections Erie had by trolley car to Conneaut, Buffalo, Meadville, Conneaut Lake Park, and Linesville and from Westfield to Warren and Sheffield. These lines plus the isolated lines in Corry and Titusville totaled 401.41 miles served by 289 trolley cars, as follows: Buffalo and Lake Erie Traction Company including Erie city lines, 168 miles and 182 trolley cars; Chautauqua Traction Company, 26.73 miles and 19 trolley cars; Jamestown, Westfield and Northwestern Railroad, 40 miles and 13 trolley cars; Conneaut and Erie Traction Company, 31.29 miles and 8 trolley cars; Corry and Columbus Street Railway, 5 miles and 4 trolley cars; Northwestern Pennsylvania Railway Company, 71.5 miles and 28 trolley cars; Titusville Traction Company 16.71 miles and 10 trolley cars; Warren Street Railway including the line to Sheffield, 20.25 miles and 18 trolley cars; and Warren and Jamestown Street Railway, 21.93 miles and 7 trolley cars.

IMAGES
of Rail

GREATER ERIE TROLLEYS

Kenneth C. Springirth

ARCADIA
PUBLISHING

ISBN 978-0-7385-3938-6

Published by Arcadia Publishing
Charleston, South Carolina

Printed in the United States of America

Library of Congress Catalog Card Number: 2005933195

For all general information contact Arcadia Publishing at:
Telephone 843-853-2070
Fax 843-853-0044
E-mail sales@arcadiapublishing.com
For customer service and orders:
Toll-Free 1-888-313-2665

Visit us on the Internet at www.arcadiapublishing.com

This book is dedicated to Faith May Julia Turnbull,
our first granddaughter, whose energy and enthusiasm
acted as a catalyst to spur this book into reality.

On the cover: Elk Creek carbarn, located just west of Girard, Pennsylvania, was the midpoint and nerve center of the Conneaut and Erie Traction Company. This was the storage, repair center, and administrative office location of the system. These trolley cars were received by the company on Tuesday, August 11, 1903, and were placed in service on Saturday, August 15, 1903, on the section of the line completed from Erie to the Dobler Farm just east of Girard. (Florence Teller photograph.)

Contents

ACKNOWLEDGMENTS

My wife, Virginia Springirth, spent months meticulously going through Erie newspapers, including *Erie Observer*, *Erie Dispatch*, and *Erie Daily Times*, on microfilm and took copious notes at the Erie Public Library, covering the time period from 1866 to 1935. Over the years, we were able to interview former employees of the trolley companies. Studying issues of the *Electric Railway Journal* provided technical information and an insight into the transportation industry. Our daughters Grace and Kathleen and sons Peter, Philip, and Timothy have been a source of encouragement to put this book together. My parents, Clarence and Sallie Springirth, taught me an appreciation for public transit and the importance of handling details, which is a necessary part in writing a book. My father was a trolley car motorman in Philadelphia and went to work with his uniform cleaned and pressed, and his shoes always had a military shine. He, like his associates, served as a combination guide, host, salesman, and public relations professional during his outstanding years of guiding trolley cars through the labyrinth of city traffic. My mother was a very practical, resourceful person who would always have dinner ready to meet my father's work schedule. Lastly today's transit vehicle operators in Erie and throughout the country deserve recognition for providing accessibility to the riding public.

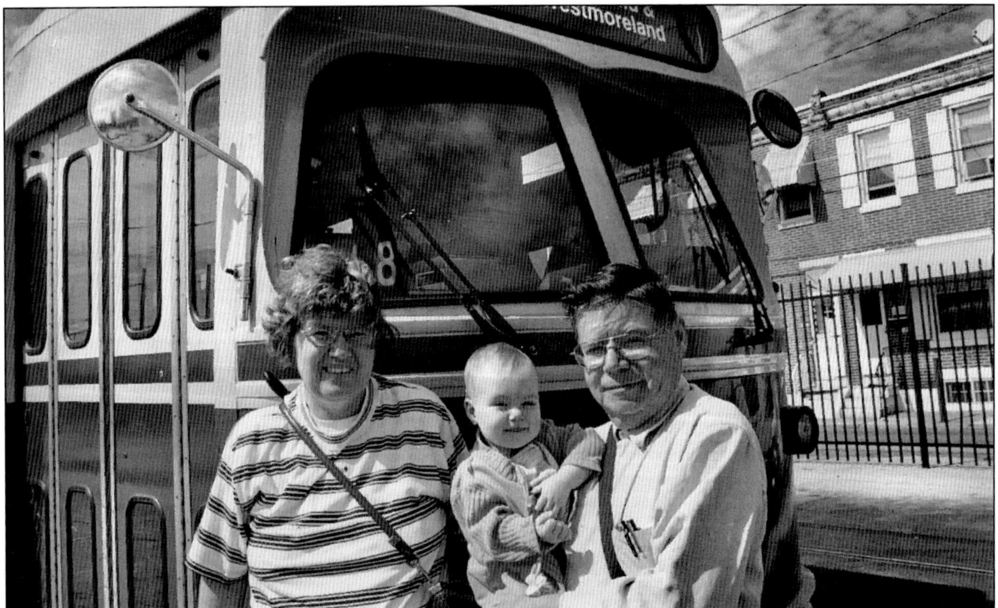

Virginia Springirth, who did the research, Faith May Julia Turnbull, whose enthusiasm inspired this book, and author Kenneth Springirth pose in front of a 1947 vintage refurbished trolley car No. 2326 at the Richmond and Westmoreland terminus of Route 15 in Philadelphia, returning to service as a trolley line on September 4, 2005, slightly more than 70 years after the last trolley operated in Erie. (Grace Turnbull photograph.)

INTRODUCTION

An Erie commercial traveler visiting Richmond, Virginia, during February 1888 became intrigued with an amazing new electric system designed by Frank Julian Sprague. A committee was dispatched to Richmond. Plans were quickly formulated for conversion of horsecar to electric streetcars. Thursday evening, June 25, 1889, the Erie Electric Motor Company operated the first electric trolley car in Erie. The company established an amusement park at Waldameer Park just west of Erie with service to the park by the West Eighth Street line. On December 24, 1906, the existing trolley systems between Erie and Buffalo, New York, were merged into the Buffalo and Lake Erie Traction Company. The Buffalo and Lake Erie Traction Company went into receivership on August 1, 1915. Ridership on the Erie city portion of the system decreased from 14,468,955 in 1922 to about 4 million by 1932. On May 12, 1935, Erie Railways trolley No. 171 left Perry Square at 12:20 a.m. operated by Harry Thunberg for the last run.

Effective January 1, 1909, the Buffalo and Lake Erie Traction Company began through service from Erie to Buffalo. The company had many years of hard times and was reorganized into the Buffalo and Erie Railway on July 1, 1924. Fourteen new cars were purchased from the Cincinnati Car Company, and for a while ridership improved, but the ever-increasing number of automobiles took its toll, and on December 1, 1932, service was discontinued from Erie to the New York state line and from Buffalo to Angola, New York. Service ended with car No. 50 operated by William S. Morgan from the New York state line to Angola on Saturday, January 28, 1933.

In 1901–1902, there were numerous stories about a steel mill to be built between Conneaut, Ohio, and western Erie County, Pennsylvania, which provided the impetus to build a trolley line from Erie to Conneaut. On Sunday, November 8, 1903, through service began between Erie and Conneaut by the Conneaut and Erie Traction Company. The steel mill was never built, and the company went into receivership and was sold and renamed Cleveland and Erie Railway on May 12, 1909. At the midpoint on the line, just west of Girard, Pennsylvania, the company built Elk Park. In the summertime, the trolley company hired bands to draw crowds via trolley to the Friday night dances. The company also sponsored the Elk Park baseball team, which drew riders to the park. With the advent of the automobile, trolley riding declined, and the company went into receivership. On September 15, 1922, the company was sold to the Buffalo Housewrecking Corporation for $75,000, and on September 16, 1922, service ended.

On Sunday, September 23, 1900, the Erie to Edinboro trolley line was opened by the Erie Traction Company. The Meadville to Cambridge Springs trolley line opened during 1903, and eventually there was through service from Erie to Meadville, Pennsylvania. On July 1, 1911, the Meadville and Cambridge Street Railway and the Erie Traction Company were reorganized into the Northwestern Pennsylvania Railway Company. On October 1, 1922, the system was reorganized into the Northwestern Electric Service Company of Pennsylvania. The last trolley operated from Erie to Meadville on September 28, 1928.

Beginning June 22, 1902, the Jamestown Chautauqua and Lake Erie Railway began train service from Westfield, New York, to Jamestown, New York. During 1907, the company was merged into the Buffalo and Lake Erie Traction Company. On October 15, 1913, S. B. Broadhead and A. N. Broadhead purchased the company. The line was renamed Jamestown, Westfield and Northwestern Railroad, and electric service began August 20, 1914. The company struggled through the Depression years. Car No. 302 made the last trip on Sunday night,

November 30, 1947, operated by veteran motorman Arthur L. Sheldon. This was the last interurban trolley line in New York State. Freight service was dieselized and operated until 1950.

On April 27, 1904, the Chautauqua Traction Company completed the line from Jamestown to Chautauqua, New York, on the west side of Lake Chautauqua and reached Westfield on Monday, September 24, 1906. Losing riders to the automobile, service ended on the Westfield to Mayville portion of the line in 1925, and the Mayville to Ashville section closed on March 26, 1926. The Ashville to Lakewood section was transferred to the Jamestown Street Railway. On October 6, 1927, the New York Public Service Commission approved the abandonment of the Lakewood streetcar line. Trolley service ended in Jamestown on January 29, 1938.

Construction of the Warren (Pennsylvania) Street Railway began April 20, 1892. The first test run was made Saturday afternoon, July 1, 1893 on Water Street from the Pennsylvania Railroad Depot to the Conewango Creek Bridge. In 1903, a 12-mile line was constructed along present-day U.S. Highway Route 6 from Warren to Sheffield, Pennsylvania. In December 1905, the Warren and Jamestown completed its line from North Warren, Pennsylvania, to Jamestown. With completion of the paved highway from Warren to Sheffield, ridership declined sharply, and the last trolley operated on March 31, 1928. The Warren and Jamestown Street Railway ended service December 2, 1929. On October 18, 1930, motorman Paul F. Egger operated car No. 47 for the final run in Warren.

Construction of the Corry and Columbus Street Railway began during July 1906 with completion during 1908. Business never reached expectations as the automobile siphoned off riders. On August 27, 1923, a transformer burned out at the powerhouse, and trolley service was immediately discontinued.

M. B. Dunham of Warren organized the Titusville Traction Company in 1897, which completed their line from Titusville to Pleasantville, Pennsylvania, on 1898. By 1901, the line was extended from Titusville to Hydetown. Twice a week, the company operated trolley freight service from the Pennsylvania Railroad in Titusville to Pleasantville. To generate riding, the company built Mystic Park near Hydetown. Jacob A. Lamenskie, who was involved in building the line back in 1898 and was its road master, made the last run on December 31, 1924.

One

Erie Trolley Cars

In 1891, the Erie Electric Motor Company had 23 miles of track, 38 trolley cars, and carried 2,636,620 passengers. On March 13, 1906, the Erie Electric Motor Company was merged into the Buffalo and Lake Erie Traction Company, and 10 new streetcars were purchased. The system was at its peak in 1911, and considerable improvements had been made under the Buffalo and Lake Erie Traction Company, with the system expanded to 65 miles of track and 115 trolley cars. In the early years of the company, there were 12 cars, number series 100 to 111, that were double-truck, double-end, deck roof, steel-sided cars built by J. G. Brill, and 15 cars of number series 150 to 164 that were double-truck, double-end, arch-roof, steel cars built by the Cincinnati Car Company. On April 9, 1916, 10 new cars were placed in service from the Southern Car Company, and eventually there were 30 cars in this series, 165 to 194. Cars numbered 201 to 206 and 210 to 230 were double-truck, double-end Peter Witt–style cars built by Kuhlman. During World War I, the U. S. government, for the emergency war transportation effort, purchased cars numbered 231 to 236 and 265 to 269 for the Buffalo and Lake Erie Traction Company. There were also five cars numbered 260 to 264 that were double-truck, Peter Witt–style cars built by Kuhlman. The first batch of new one-man Birney Safety cars as part of an order for 25 cars numbered 325 to 349, each costing $6,500, arrived April 26, 1922. Built by J. G. Brill, the cars had 2-GE264-A motors, General Electric air brakes, and Brill 79E-1 trucks. Car doors could not be opened until the brakes were applied, and the brakes could not be released until the doors were closed.

As the automobile came on the scene, ridership dropped. The company made many attempts to attract ridership. On May 23, 1922, a new universal transfer was adopted allowing passengers to change from one line to another provided they did not go back in the direction they came. The transfer was free upon payment of the regular fare. Effective Sunday, February 5, 1923, a 20 percent increase in service was made on the West Twenty-sixth Street line with cars every 8 minutes instead of 10 minutes. A new brilliant green paint scheme with bright trimming was adopted in place of the former dark olive green. The system reorganized October 1, 1924, with the Buffalo and Erie Railway Company taking over the line from Erie to Buffalo and local ownership under the Erie Street Railway Company operating the city system. With hard economic times, ridership was only 4 million in 1932, compared to 14,468,955 in 1922, and the last run was made May 12, 1935.

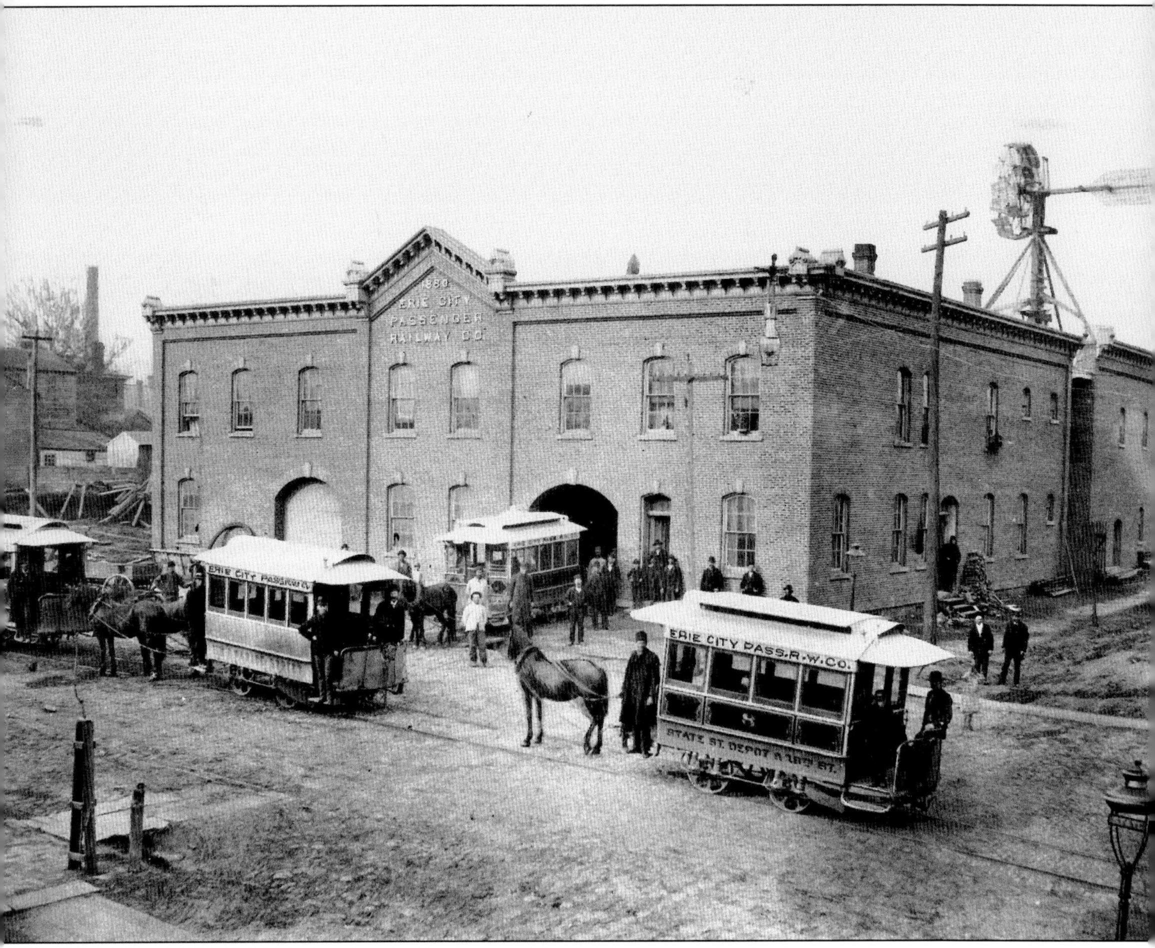

Erie City Passenger Railway horsecars appear at the Second and State Streets stable in Erie in 1885. During the mid-1860s, William Loesch began an omnibus line from Perry Square to Twenty-sixth and Peach Streets. On March 1, 1867, the Erie City Passenger Railway was chartered. By 1888, the system had eight and a half miles of track, 20 vehicles, and 103 horses and mules providing the motive power.

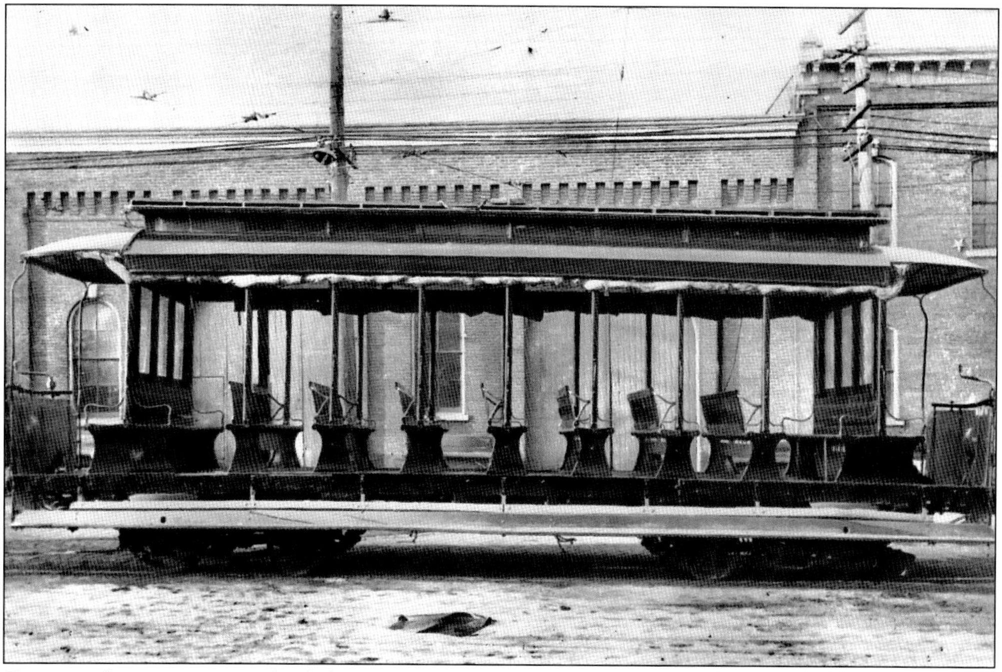

Open trolley car No. 20, built by J. G. Brill Company in 1905, was parked at the Second and State Streets carbarn. This type of car was heavily used during the summertime on the lines that served Waldameer Park west of Erie and Four Mile Creek Park in Lawrence Park just east of Erie. On a hot summer day, these cars were a treat to ride.

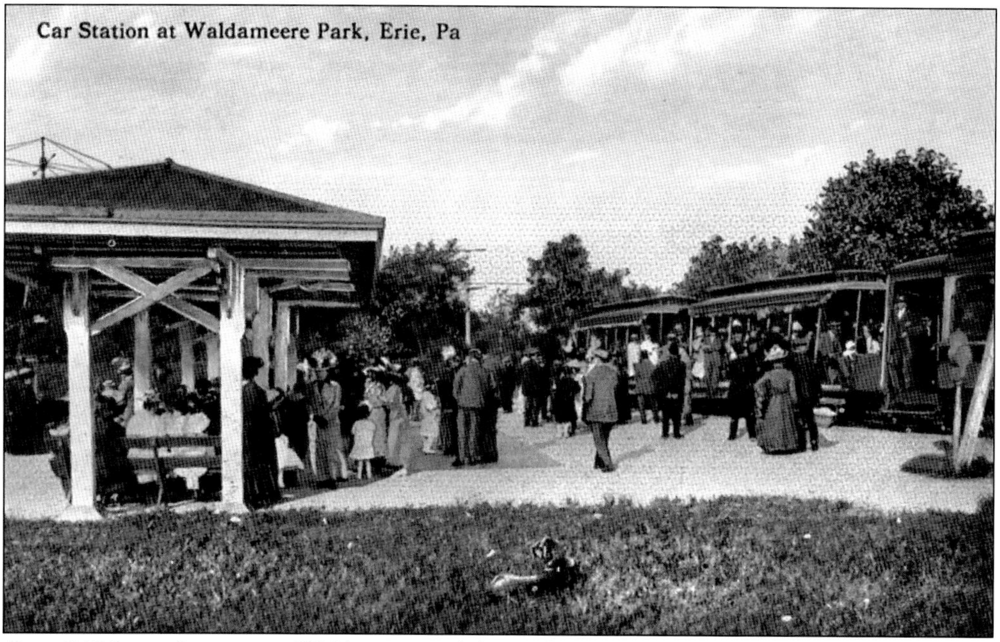

Over 5,000 people came to Waldameer Park by trolley car on May 11, 1903. The Erie Electric Motor Company provided extra service as people were anxious to get out of the hot Erie downtown area. The West Eighth Street line originally served the park, and in later years, the West Twelfth Street line also served the park.

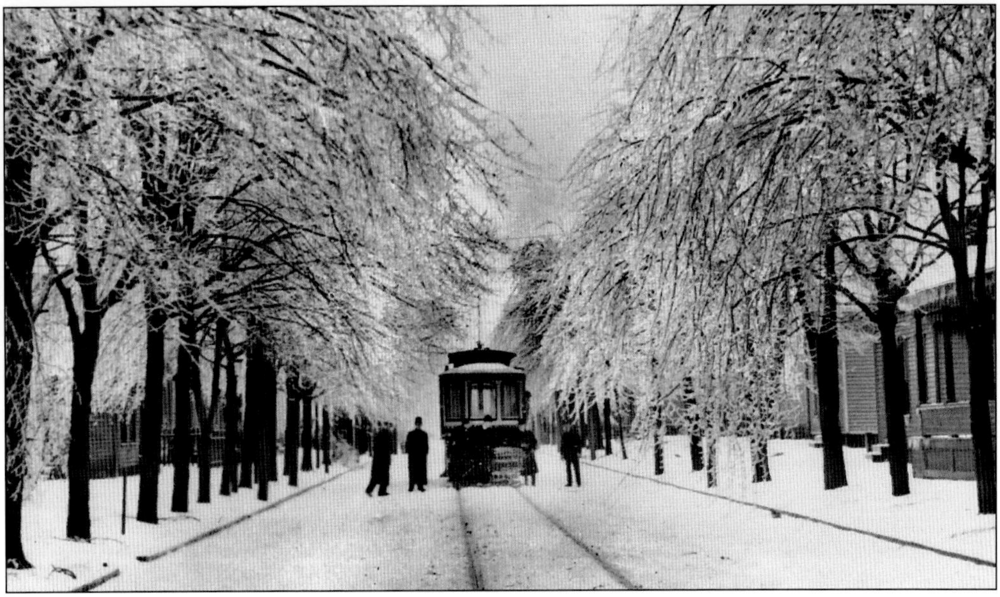

Snow has fallen in this winter scene along the East Eleventh Street trolley line in Erie. The East Eleventh Street trolley line operated from State Street east on Eleventh Street to East Avenue, south on East Avenue to Twelfth Street, and east on Twelfth Street to the city limits. Tracks were later relocated onto East Twelfth Street, which became a major east-west trolley line in Erie.

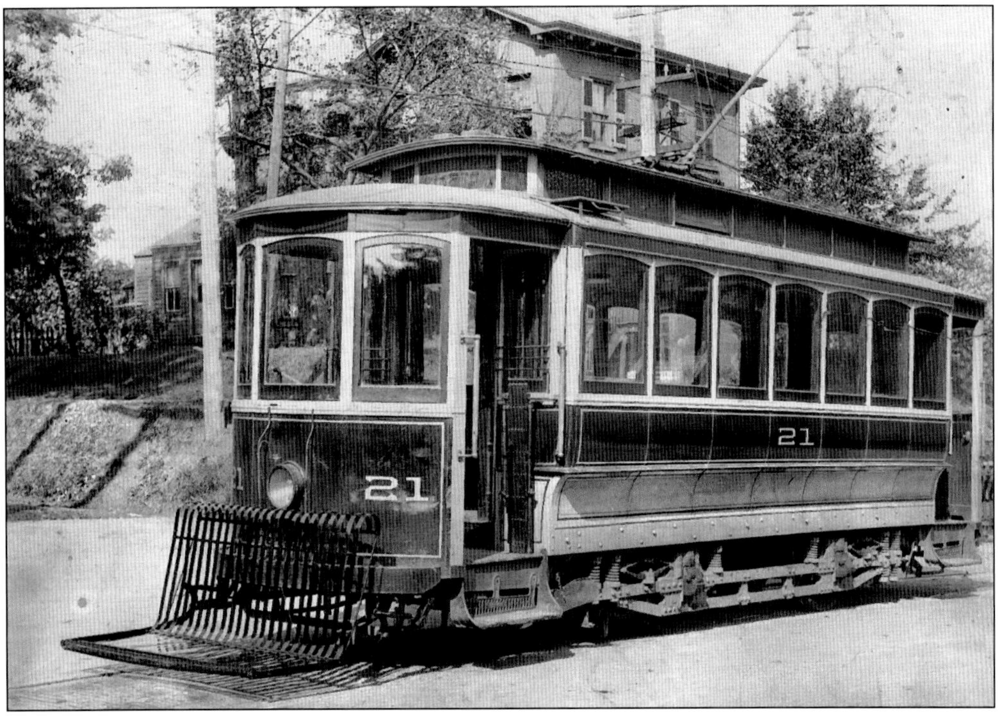

Erie Electric Motor Company car No. 21 was in prosperous times as the West Eighteenth Street line opened November 18, 1889. The West Twelfth Street line opened November 16, 1891, the West Twenty-sixth Street line opened November 19, 1891, and on June 4, 1899, the line was completed on East Lake Road to Four Mile Creek Park.

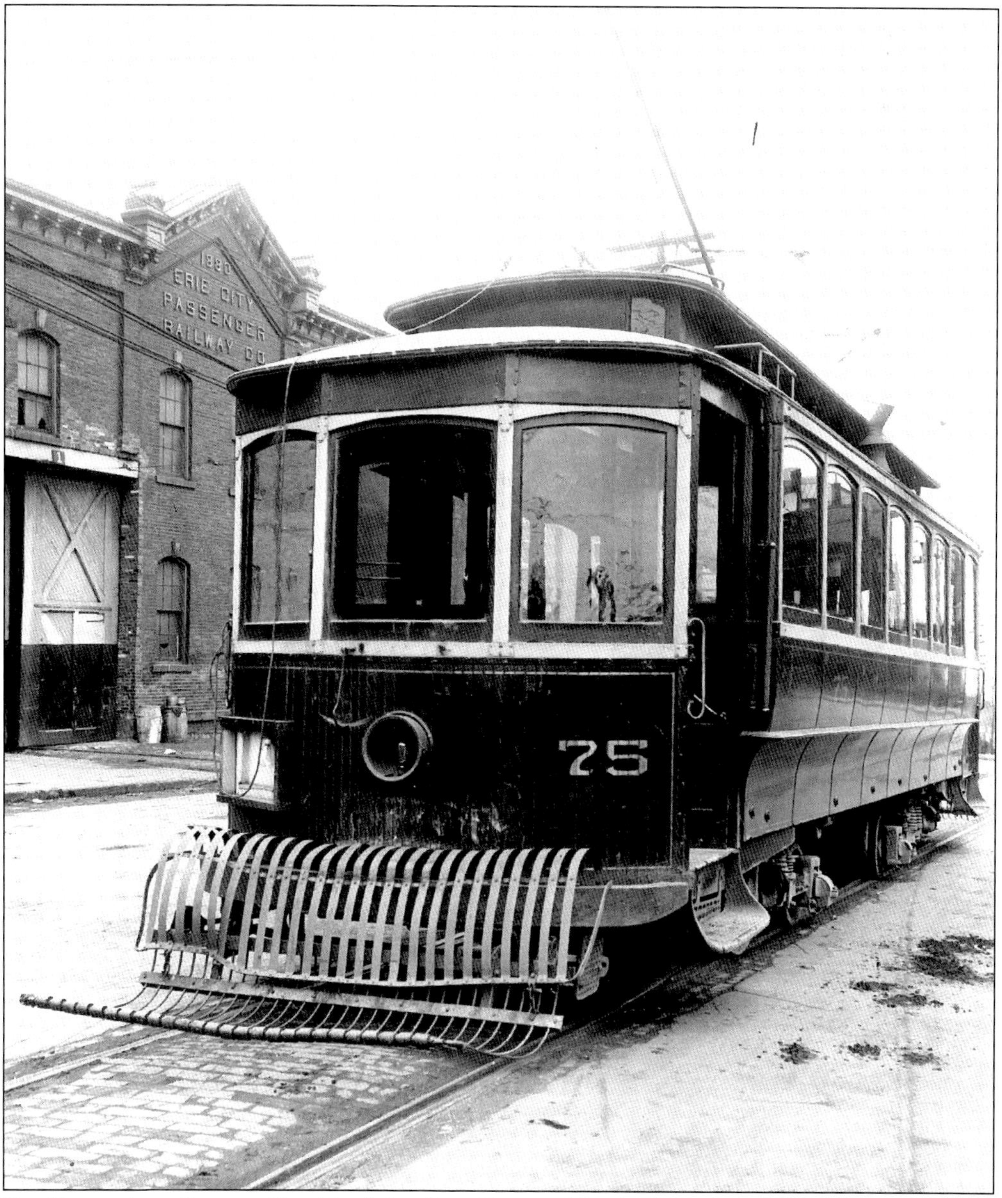

Double-truck trolley car No. 75 of the Erie Electric Motor Company was ready for the next run in front of the Second and State Streets carbarn in Erie. By 1902, trolley car lines reached most sections of Erie. On April 18, 1906, the Erie Electric Motor Company was merged into the Buffalo and Lake Erie Traction Company. Beginning January 1, 1909, trolley service was operated from Erie to Buffalo with the completion of the 1,100-foot-long bridge over Chautauqua Creek at Westfield, New York.

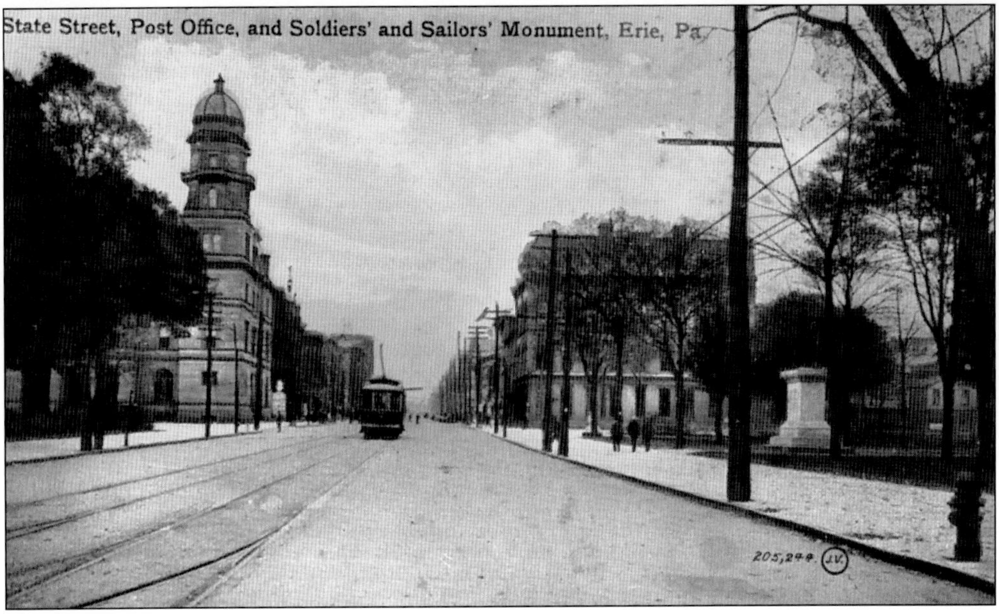

State Street at Perry Square with a southbound trolley car ready to pass the post office is shown here. The first electric trolley operated in Erie at this spot on June 25, 1889. By the end of 1892, the Erie Electric Motor Company had 23 miles of track, 71 trolley cars, and 16 trailer cars. Probably the best compliment the company had during 1892 was when a resident named Mr. Carr, who was very delighted with the trolley line, had his firstborn son christened Trolley Carr.

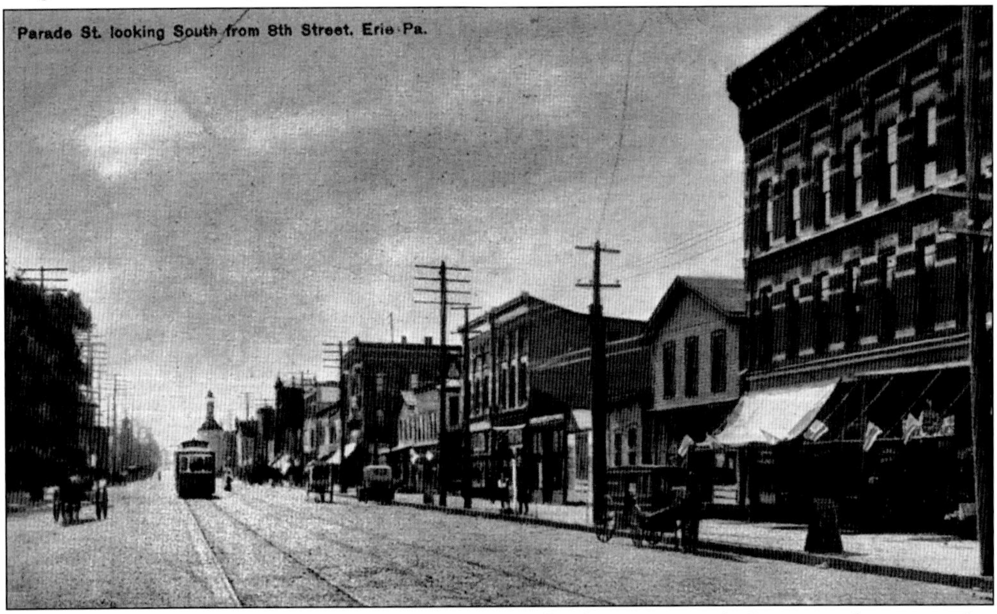

On June 24, 1901, plans were revealed for a new trolley line on Parade Street, and opening day for the Parade Street trolley line was October 26, 1903, with service every 10 minutes. The Parade Street trolley line was the only line that did not operate on State Street but crossed State Street at Fourth Street. Parade Street has changed over the years since this scene was taken, looking south from Eighth Street, but the building on the right still survives as Kraus Department Store.

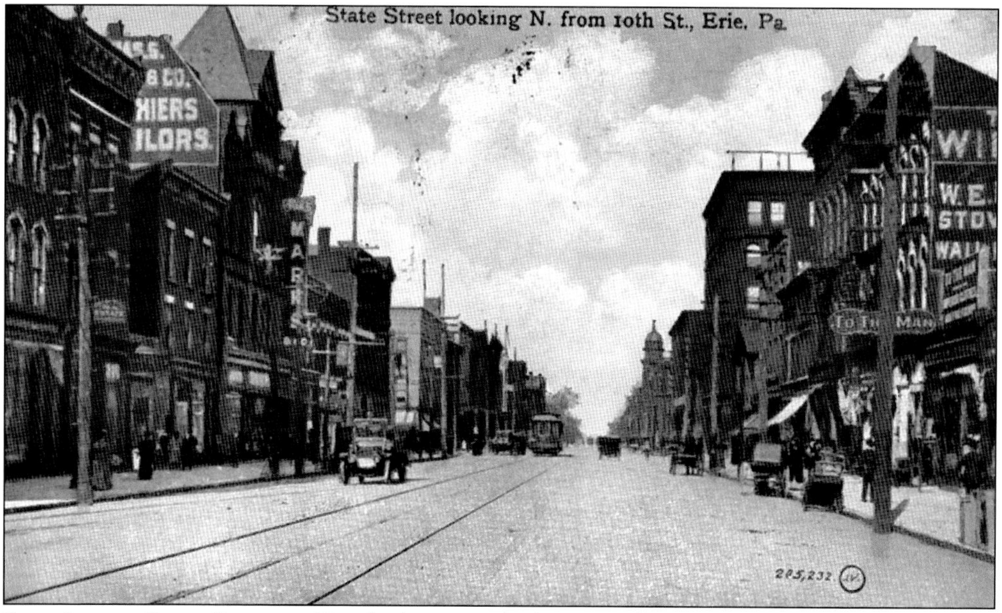

Seen here is State Street in Erie looking north from Tenth Street in 1908. This section of State Street had the Conneaut and Erie Traction Company service to Conneaut, Ohio, and the Northwestern Pennsylvania Railway service to Meadville. All of the city trolley routes, with the exception of the Parade Street line, operated on State Street. The Parade Street line operated on West Fourth Street from Cascade Street to East Fourth Street and turned south on Parade Street to East Eighteenth Street.

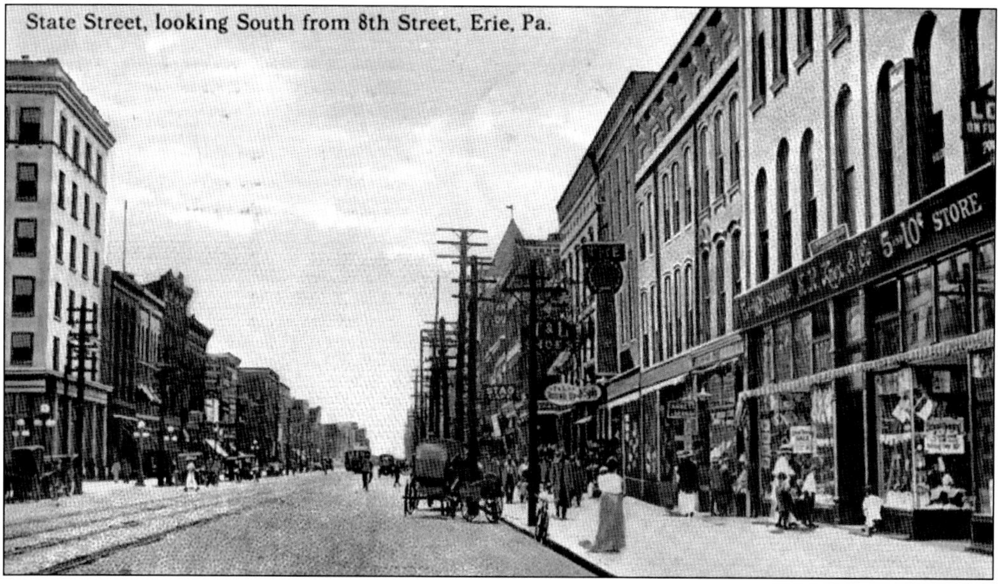

With very little automobile traffic in view, this is State Street looking south from Eighth Street in 1910. There were less than 40,000 people when electric streetcar service was introduced in Erie in 1889, but by 1910, Erie's population reached 66,000. The trolley car made it convenient for workers and shoppers to live in outlying areas and channeled commercial development along State Street. New housing developments were built along the trolley lines and listed the trolley line as a reason to buy a home in that area.

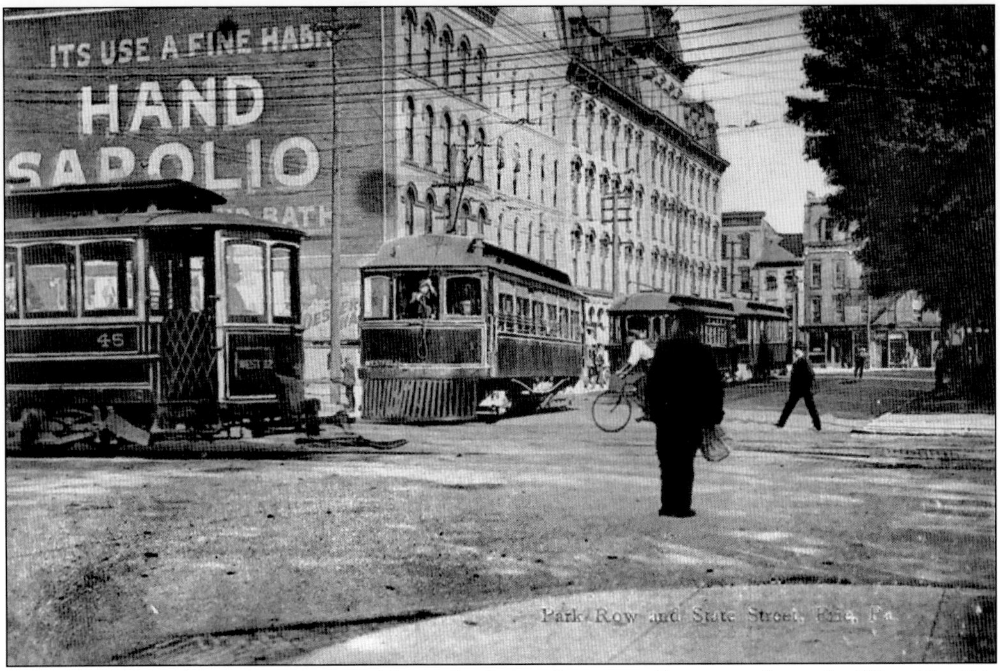

Erie Railways trolley car No. 45, southbound at Perry Square in Erie, is working the West Twelfth Street line. The three trolley cars waiting to turn south on State Street are Buffalo and Lake Erie Traction Company for Buffalo, New York; Conneaut and Erie Traction Company for Conneaut, Ohio; and Northwestern Pennsylvania Railway for Edinboro and Meadville, Pennsylvania.

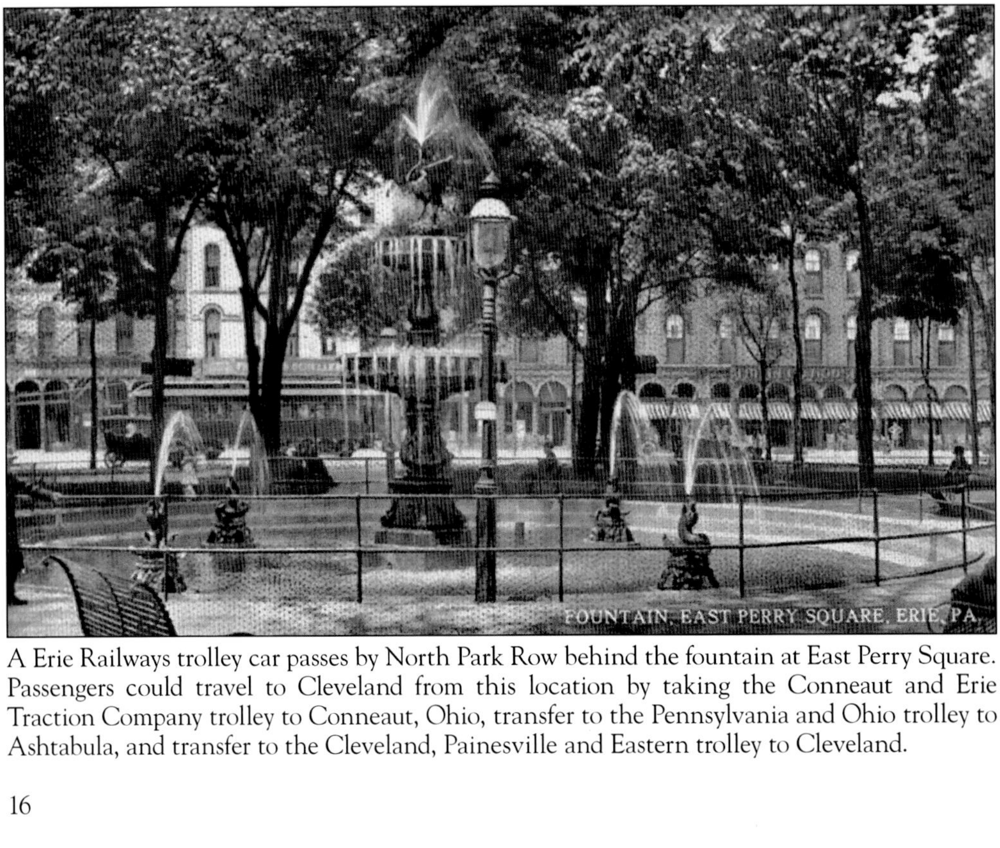

A Erie Railways trolley car passes by North Park Row behind the fountain at East Perry Square. Passengers could travel to Cleveland from this location by taking the Conneaut and Erie Traction Company trolley to Conneaut, Ohio, transfer to the Pennsylvania and Ohio trolley to Ashtabula, and transfer to the Cleveland, Painesville and Eastern trolley to Cleveland.

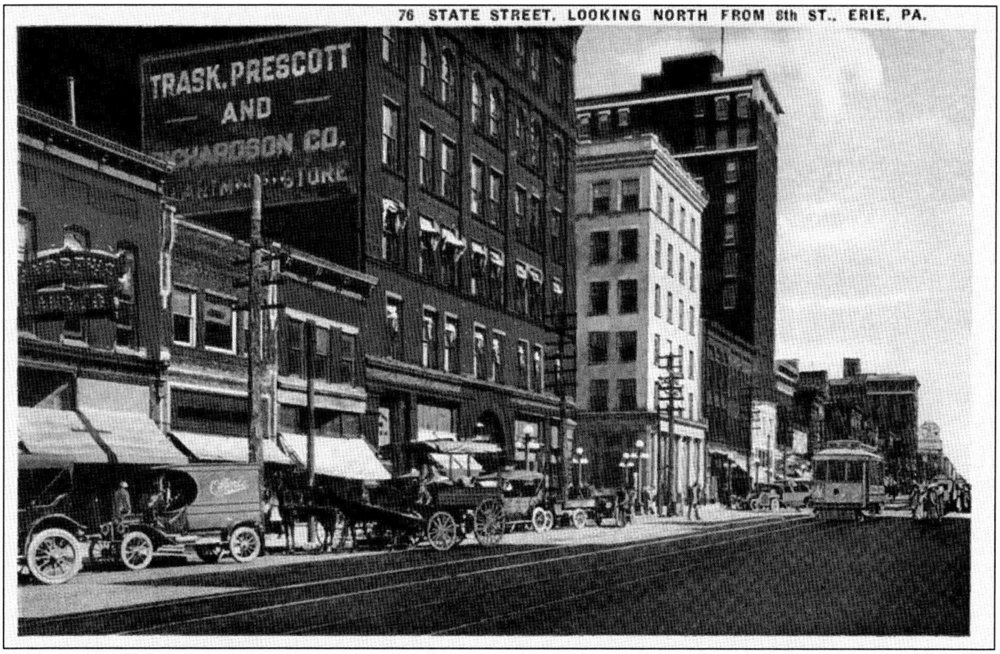

In this 1910 postcard scene, an Erie trolley is about to pass the Trask Prescott and Richardson Store on State Street in the main commercial district of Erie. In 1911, trolley car motormen were paid 19¢ per hour, advancing 1¢ per hour per year to a maximum of 22¢ per hour. The fare was 5¢ or six tickets for 25¢.

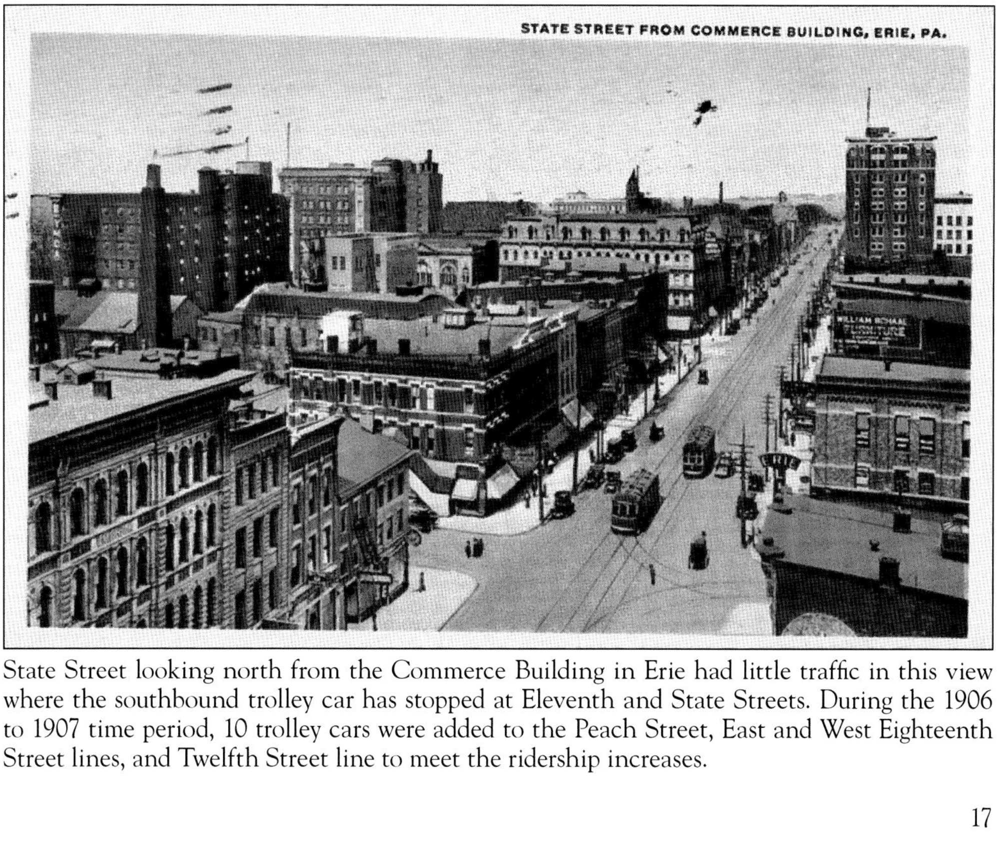

State Street looking north from the Commerce Building in Erie had little traffic in this view where the southbound trolley car has stopped at Eleventh and State Streets. During the 1906 to 1907 time period, 10 trolley cars were added to the Peach Street, East and West Eighteenth Street lines, and Twelfth Street line to meet the ridership increases.

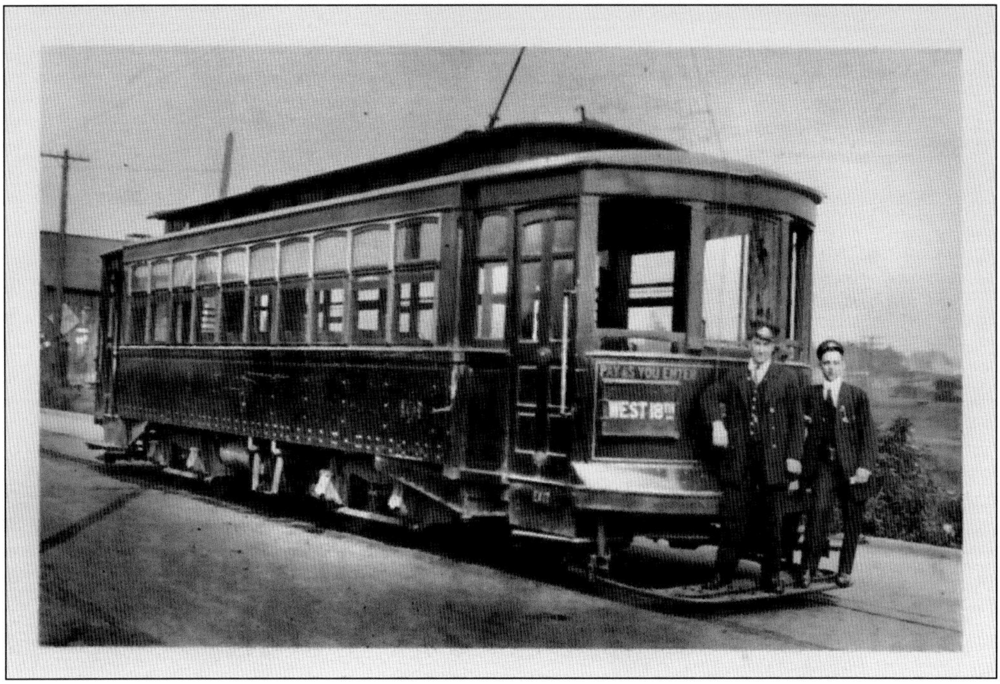

Erie trolley No. 401 pauses on West Eighteenth Street near Cranberry Street. Carl Anthony (left) and Frank Seider get ready for the return trip to downtown Erie. This was open country, and within a few years, this would become a densely populated area. Development was channeled along Erie's trolley lines.

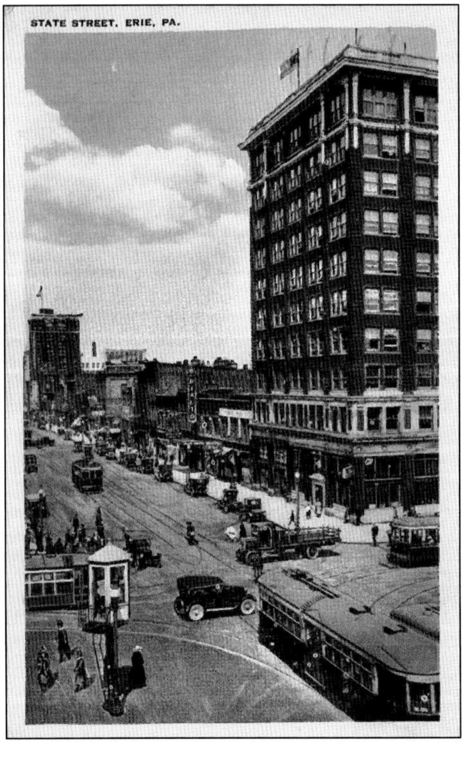

The Buda Steel Company of Hawey, Illinois, fabricated a grand union for the intersection of Twelfth and State Streets at a cost of $22,000 to permit a trolley car to make a right or left turn or go straight from any approach track at the intersection. Installation was completed by the end of June 1918 at a cost of $15,000.

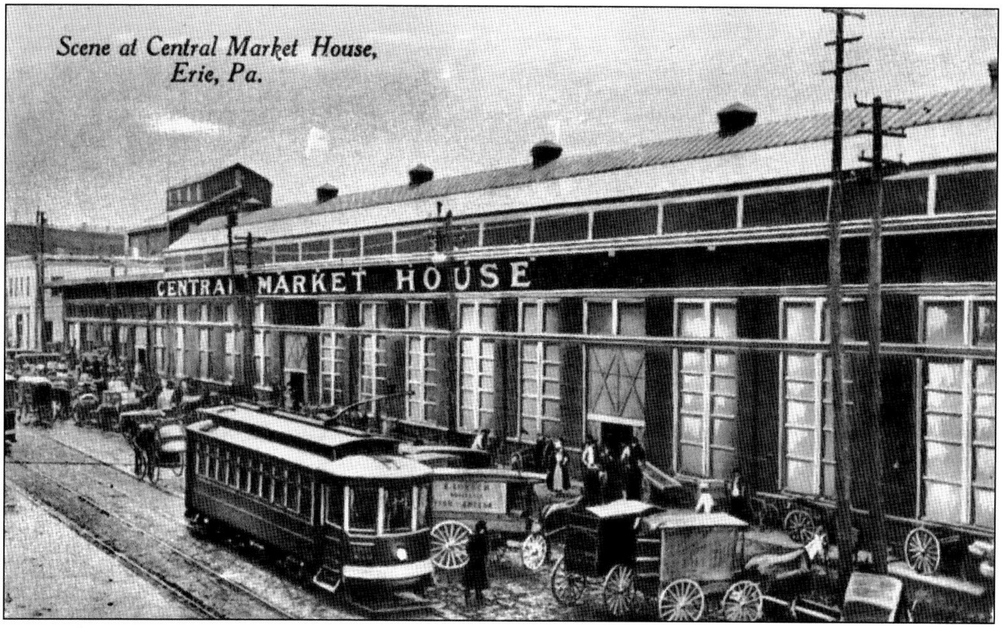

Central Market House located on State Street between Fifteenth and Sixteenth Streets was a very busy place on the Wednesday and Saturday market days. People would come from all over the city via the many trolley routes that served this location to purchase beef, sides of pork, butter, eggs, poultry (both live and dressed), fresh vegetables and fruits, honey, and even live hogs and calves.

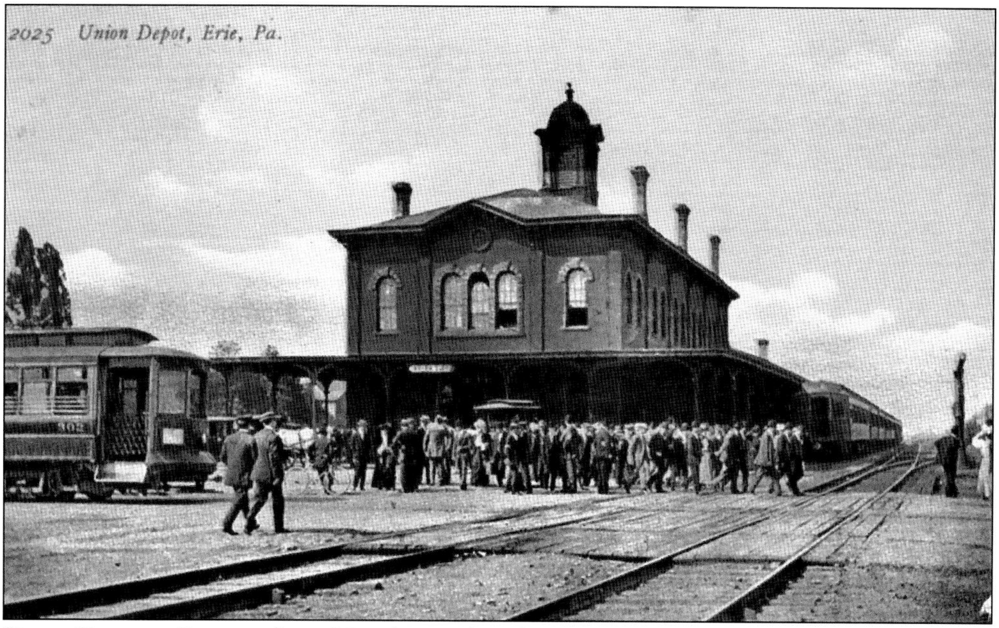

Union Depot at Fourteenth and Peach was directly served by the Peach Street trolley line, the Conneaut and Erie Traction Company line to Conneaut, and the Northwestern Pennsylvania Railway line to Meadville and Conneaut Lake Park. This station linked Erie to the outside world with the Pennsylvania Railroad providing direct passenger train service to Pittsburgh and Philadelphia. The New York Central Railroad provided direct service to Buffalo, Cleveland, and Chicago.

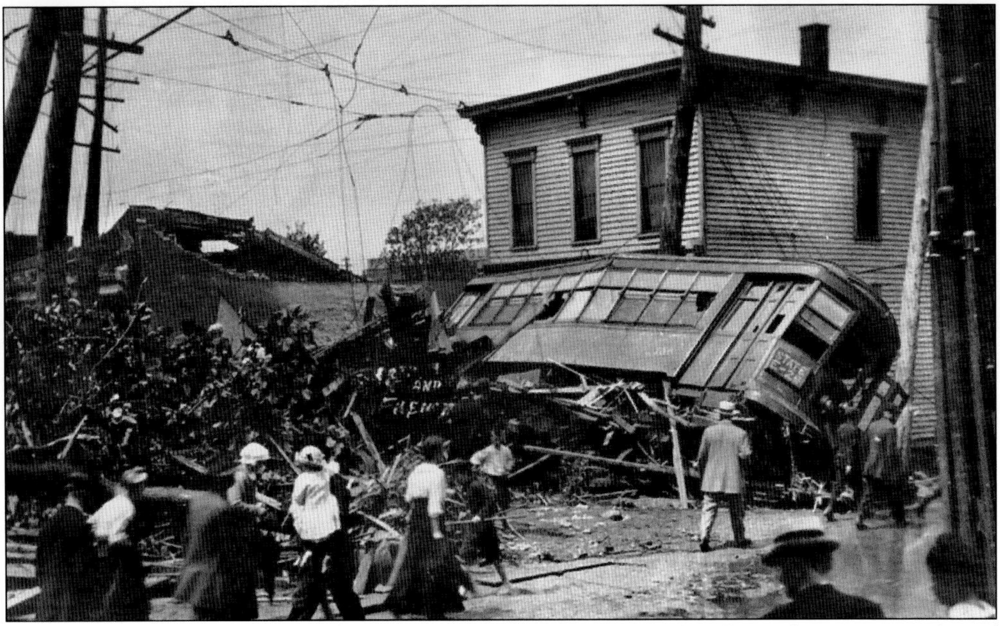

On August 3, 1915, almost five inches of rain fell in six hours, and Mill Creek in Erie overflowed its banks and began picking up debris. A logjam developed behind the culvert at Twenty-sixth and State Streets, creating a lake that extended south beyond Twenty-ninth Street. At 8:30 p.m., the logjam burst, and the water surged north leaving a path of destruction and overturning the trolley car at Eighteenth and French Streets.

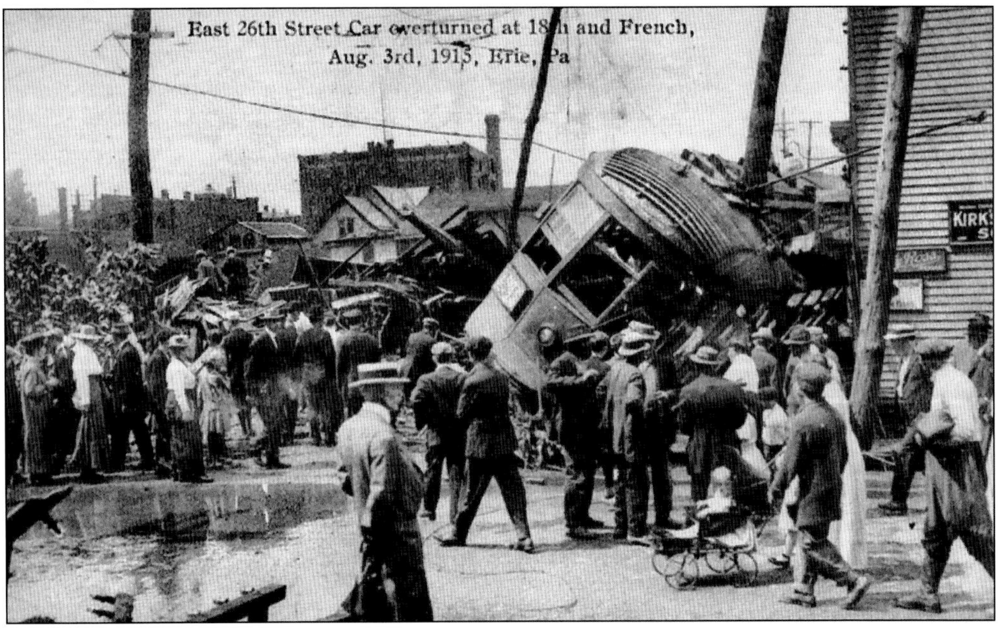

One can only imagine the shock of seeing 100 buildings totally destroyed and 36 lives lost when Mill Creek overflowed in Erie. The overturned trolley car was a prime example of the power of nature. The flood affected trolley service on a number of lines, and East Eighteenth Street trolleys had to use Parade Street trackage to access the eastern part of the line until the area was cleared.

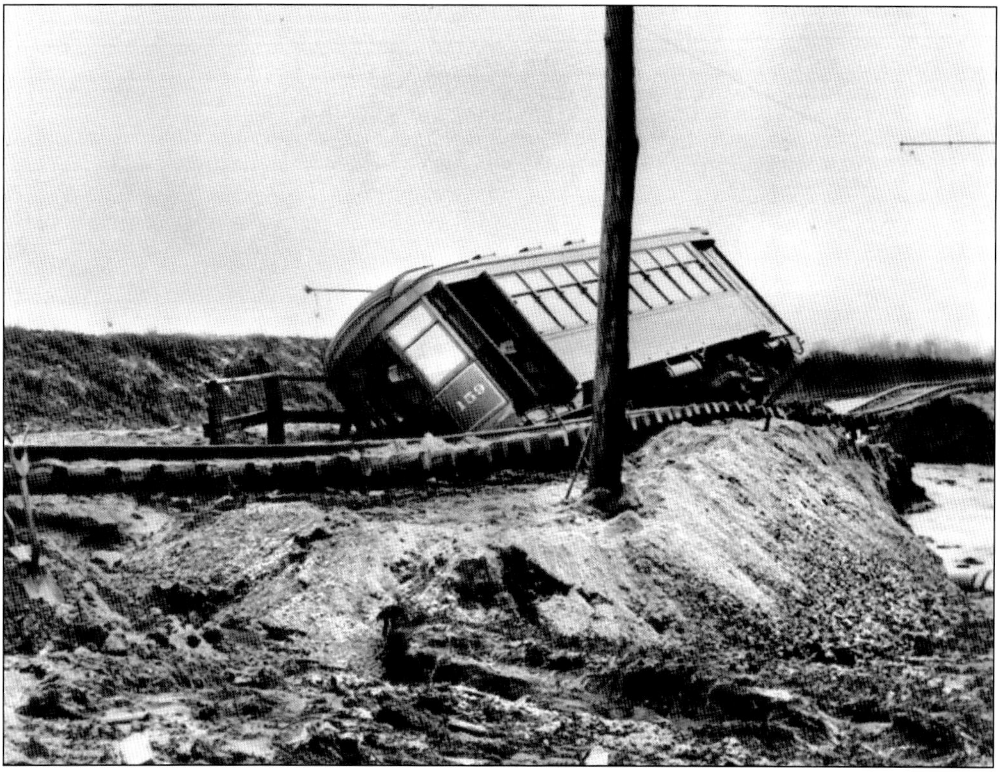

The heavy rain of August 3, 1915, overturned the trolley and undermined the track at Four Mile Creek Park in Lawrence Park, which is a suburban area just east of Erie. In the lower scene, four ladies in their Sunday best pose on the trolley track at the Four Mile Creek Bridge.

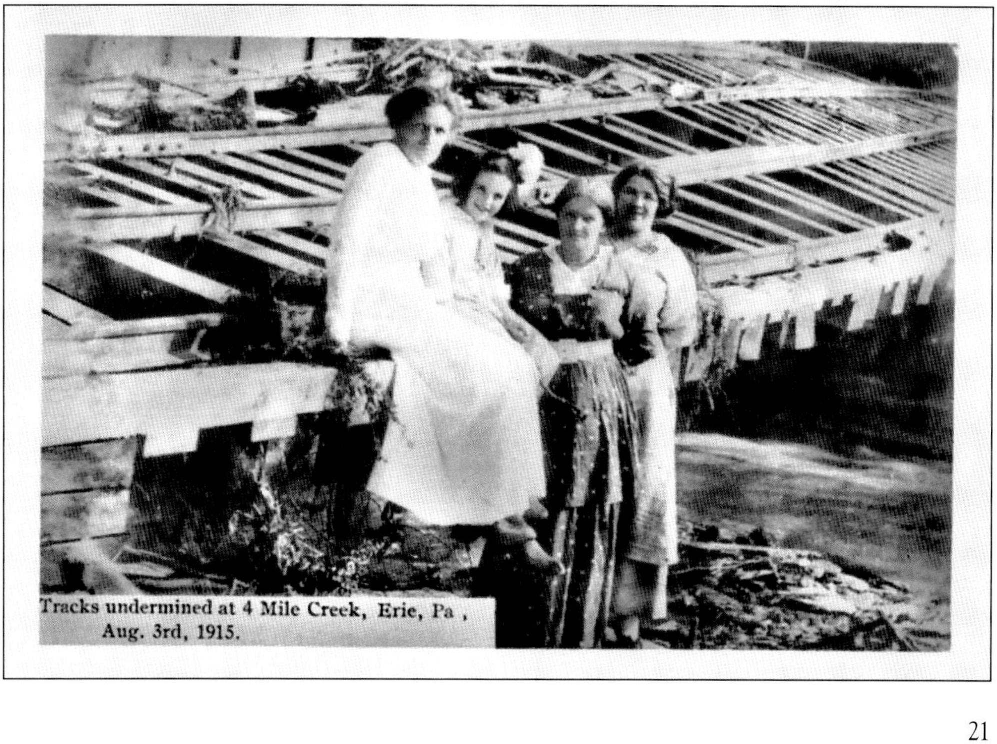

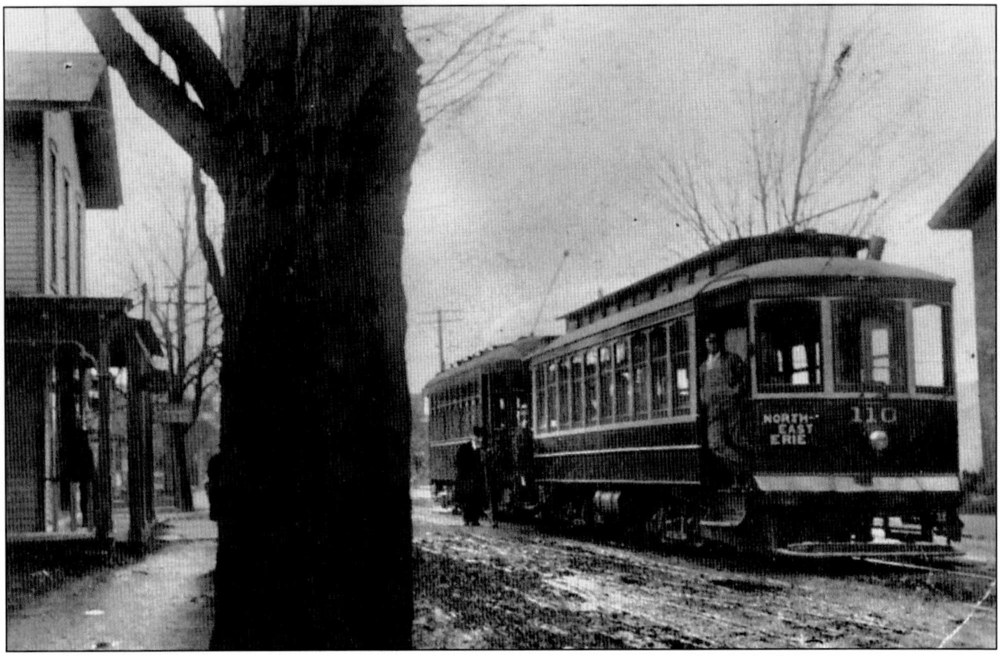

Car No. 110 of the Erie to North East Trolley Line, also known as the Lake Erie Fast Line, meets an Erie city trolley at Buffalo Road and Station Road in Wesleyville. The Erie to Wesleyville trolley line was completed in September 1, 1901, and on November 27, 1901, the line was completed to North East, Pennsylvania. The Lake Erie Fast Line was merged into the Buffalo and Lake Erie Traction Company on August 19, 1906.

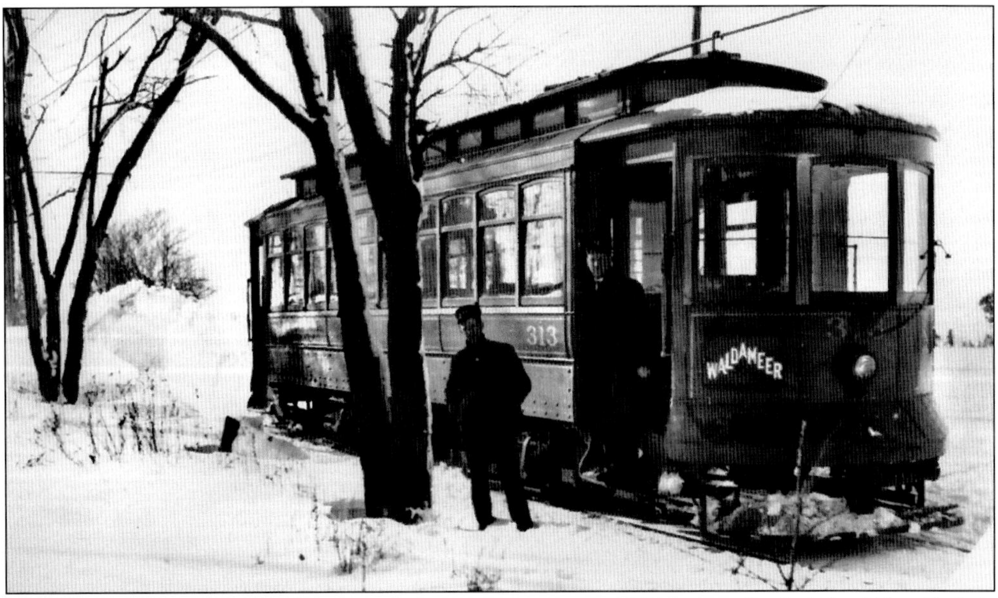

Erie Street Railway car No. 313 is in the winter snow at Waldameer Park. The West Eighth Street line served the park, and effective May 24, 1908, the West Twelfth Street line also began serving the park with service on State Street from Second to Twelfth Streets, west on Twelfth Street to Union Avenue, north on Union Avenue to Eighth, and west on Eighth Street to Waldameer Park.

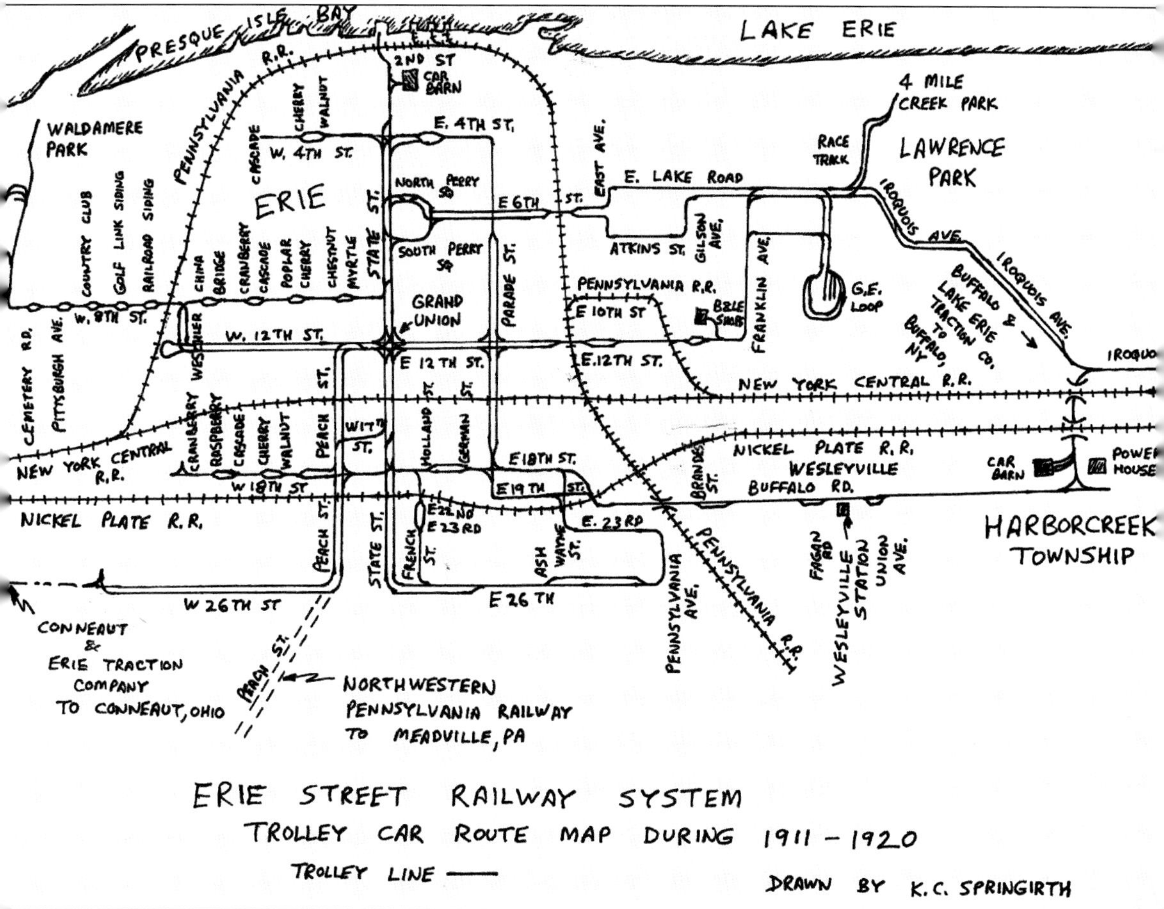

Erie Street Railway system at its peak operated 115 trolley cars on 65 miles of track. As shown by the map, the trolley lines covered the major parts of Erie. The suburban areas were served by the Conneaut and Erie Traction Company west on West Twenty-sixth Street, the Northwestern Pennsylvania Railway Company south on Peach Street, and the Buffalo and Lake Erie Traction Company east on Iroquois Avenue.

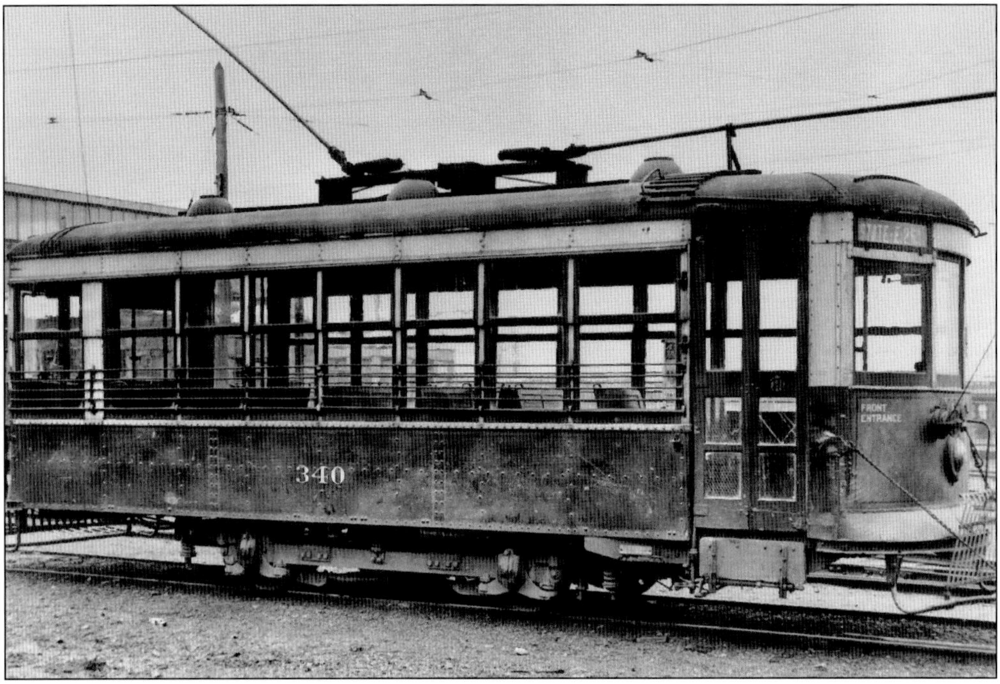

Erie Railways car No. 340, waiting for the next assignment at the Franklin Avenue carbarn on December 10, 1923, was one of 25 cars purchased from the J. G. Brill Company in 1922 numbered 325 to 349. Known as a Birney Safety car for one-man operation, it featured a safety device that would stop the car and open the door if the operator became incapacitated.

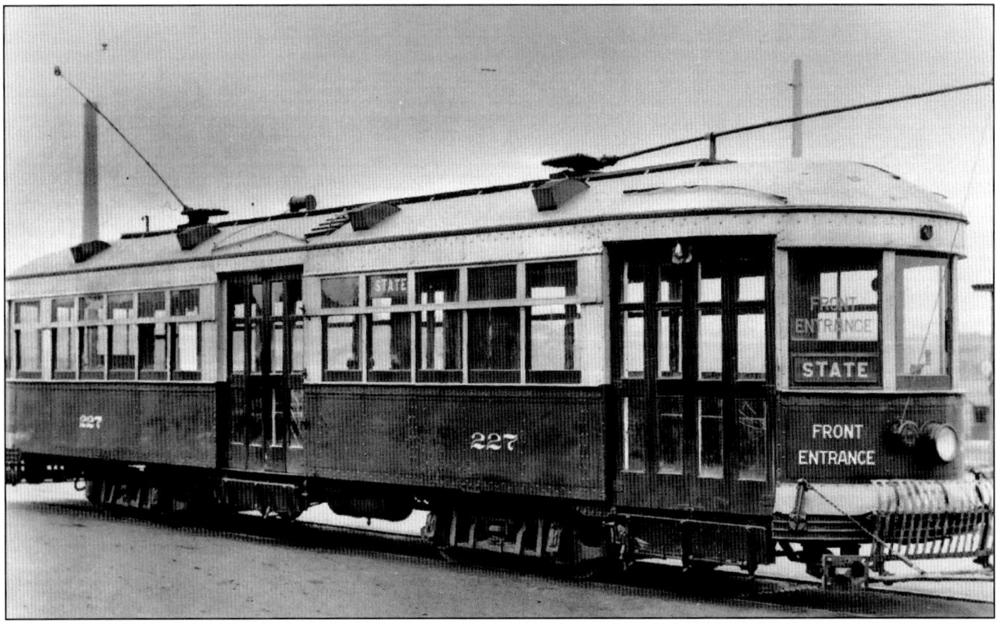

Car No. 227, at the Public Dock in Erie on March 14, 1924, was one of 21 cars numbered 210 to 230 purchased from the Kuhlman Car Company for the Buffalo and Lake Erie Traction Company by the U.S. government for the emergency war transportation effort. This was a Peter Witt–type car named after the designer Peter Witt.

An Erie Railways trolley car, built by Southern Car Company, has just passed under the New York Central Railroad bridge and is heading south on State Street approaching Sixteenth Street in Erie during 1928. Many of the buildings on the east side of State Street in this area are still in place. The automobile was already very prominent in this scene.

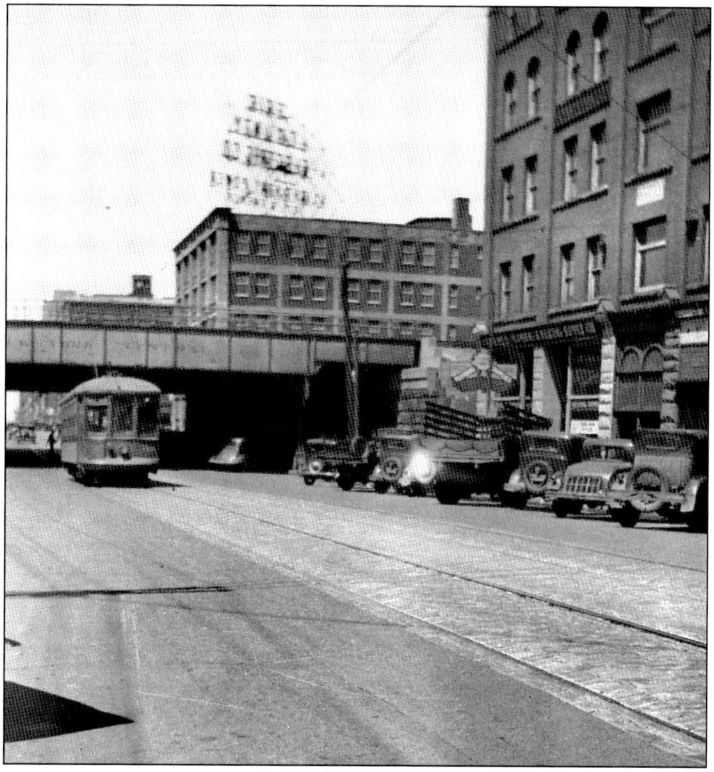

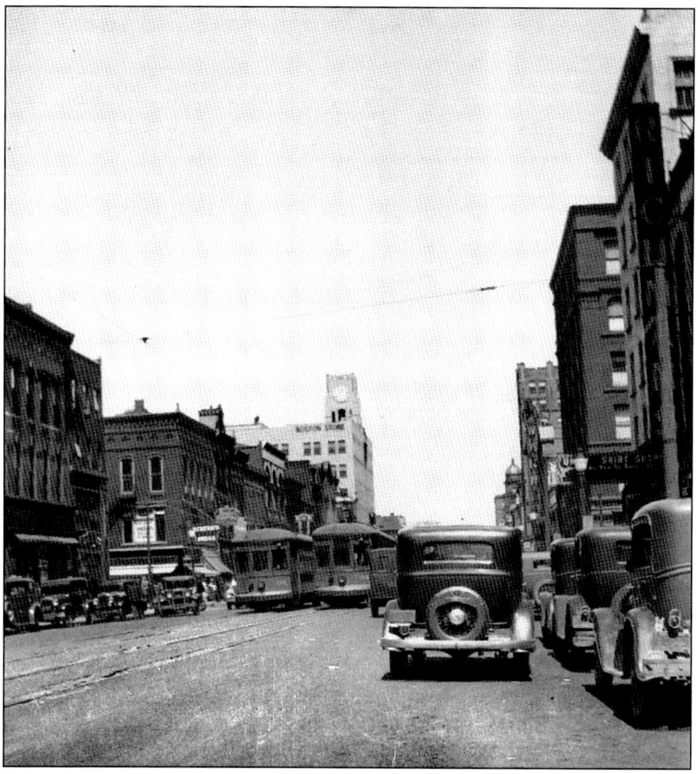

Two Southern Car Company–built trolleys pass by State Street between Ninth and Tenth Streets in downtown Erie in this 1928 scene. This was the heart of the downtown retail area, but the increasing number of automobiles resulted in a significant decline in trolley ridership from 12 million in 1929 to 4 million by 1932.

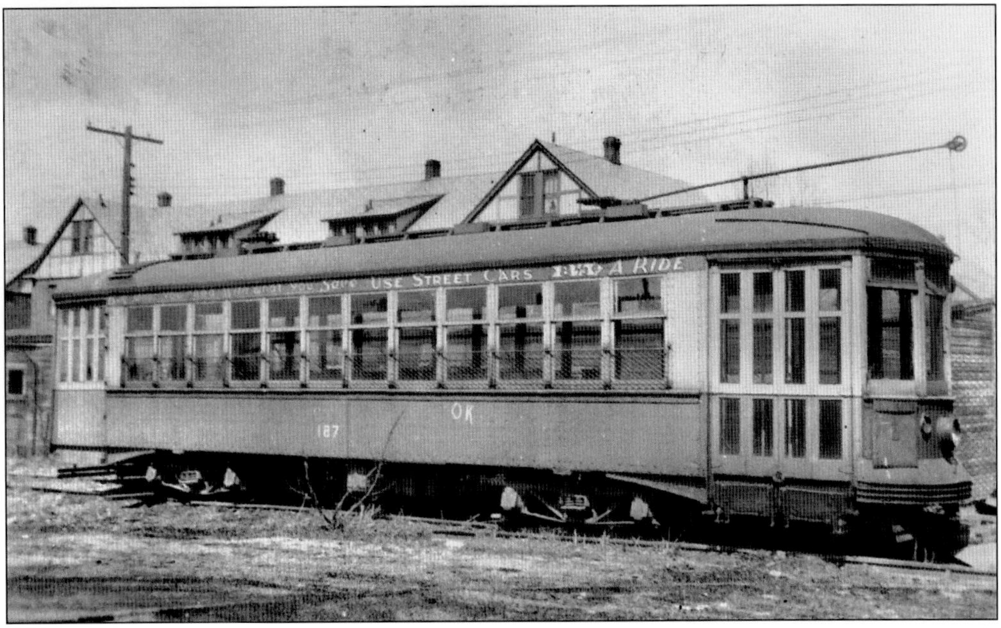

Car No. 187, at the Franklin Avenue carbarn, was built by the Southern Car Company in High Point, North Carolina. The first 10 of these cars were placed in service on April 9, 1916. Car length was 45 feet 1.5 inches. This was a double-truck, double-ended car with controls at both ends so the car could be operated at either end.

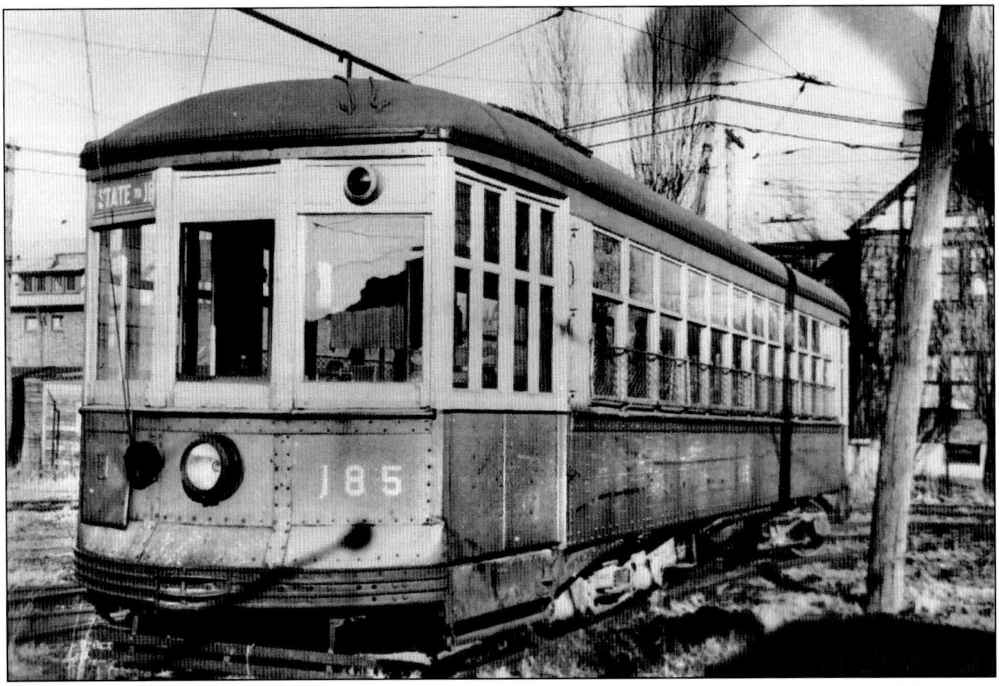

Car No. 185 at the Franklin Avenue carbarn was part of a 30-car series numbered 165 to 194 built by the Southern Car Company. Seating 48 passengers, the car had a flush platform with an all-steel low floor design and weighed 31,750 pounds. This type of trolley had widespread use throughout the United States.

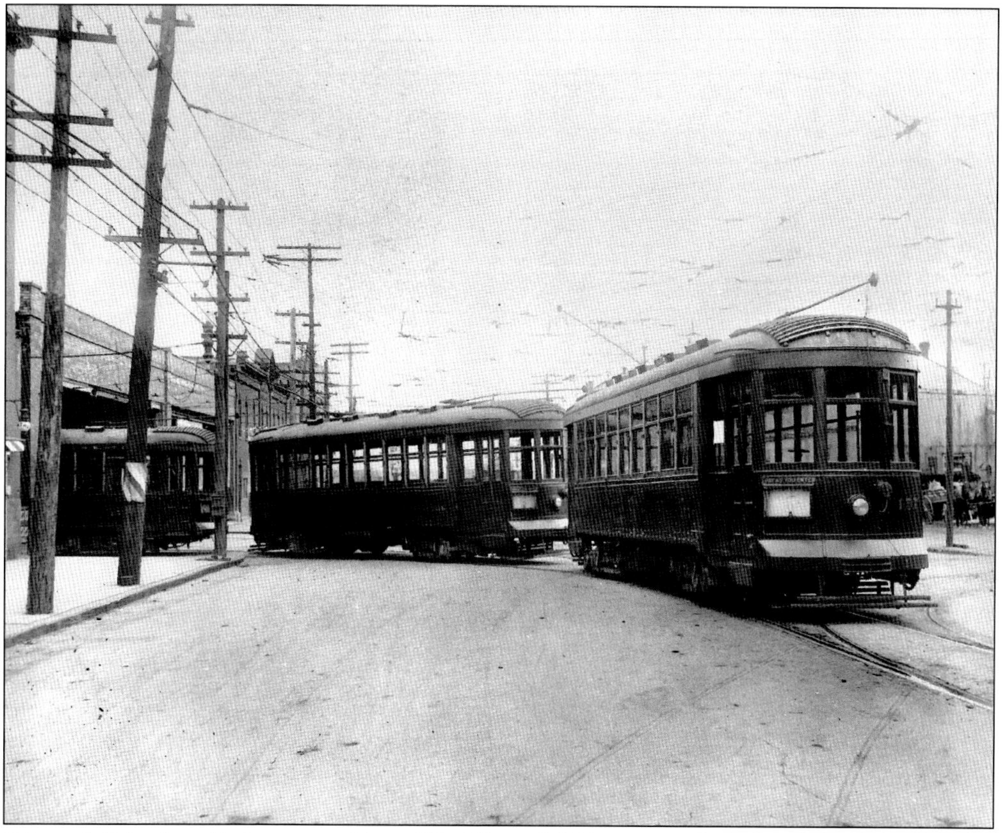

Erie and Suburban Railway cars Nos. 157, 168, and 156 were ready to head out for rush hour service at the Second and State Streets carbarn in Erie on January 28, 1913. Cars series 150 to 164 were built by the Cincinnati Car Company. Cars series 165 to 194 were built by the Southern Car Company, and dimensions are shown in the drawing below.

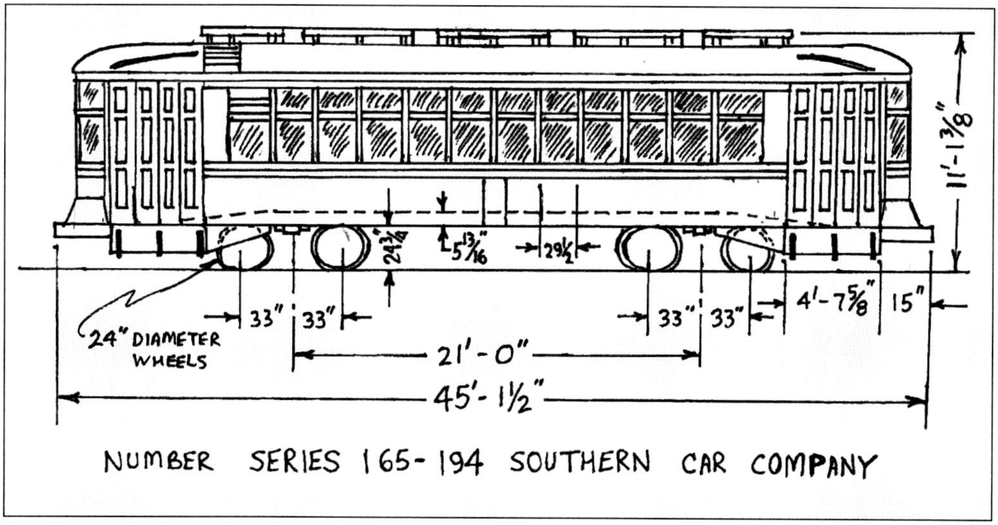

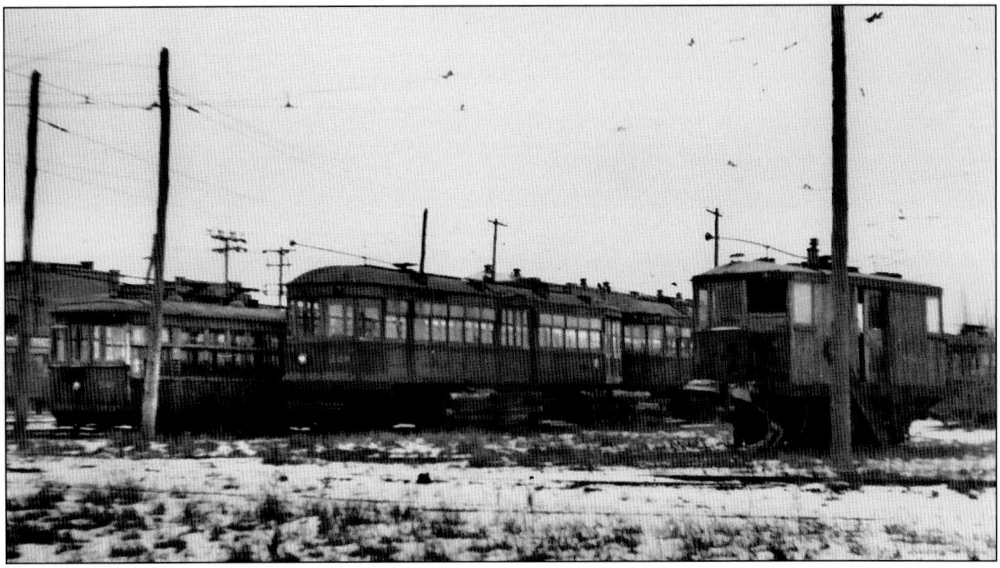

Construction of a new carbarn for the Buffalo and Lake Erie Traction Company at Twelfth Street near Franklin Avenue began on April 24, 1916. Henry Shenk Company was awarded the $100,000 contract for the building, which had nine tracks and a machine shop, carpenter shop, armature rooms, blacksmith, wheel and axle room, paint shop, and a repair shop. In less than 20 years, the trolley system was abandoned.

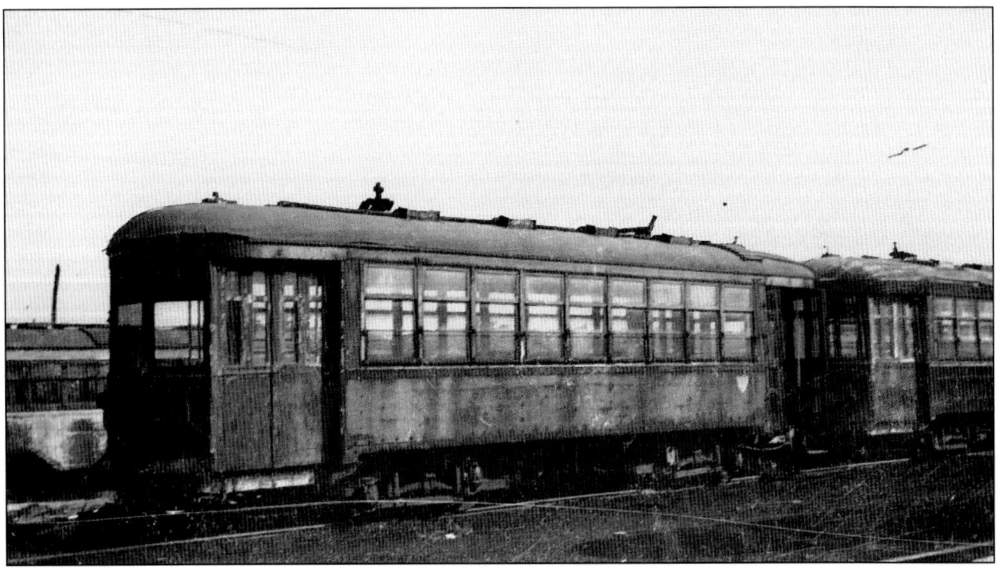

After trolley car service ended in Erie on May 12, 1935, the cars were lined up at the Franklin Avenue carbarn. Most of the cars were scrapped, but some were purchased and used as homes. None of the Erie trolley cars were preserved in operating condition. There are modern trolley systems in nearby Cleveland, Buffalo, Pittsburgh, and Toronto.

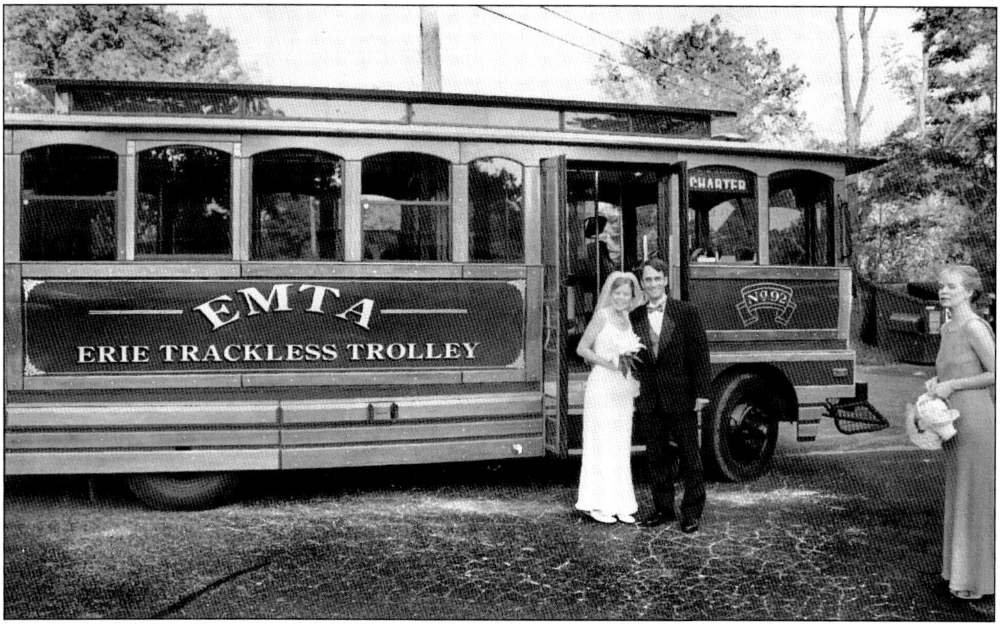

The Erie Metropolitan Transit Authority 20-passenger bus No. 92, styled as a trolley car, was built by the Chance Company in 1992. Kathleen and Michael Ruggio chartered the vehicle for their September 6, 2003, wedding with matron of honor Grace Sallie Turnbull on the far right. The continued popularity of this vehicle demonstrates the sentimental appeal of the trolley car. (Kenneth Springirth photograph.)

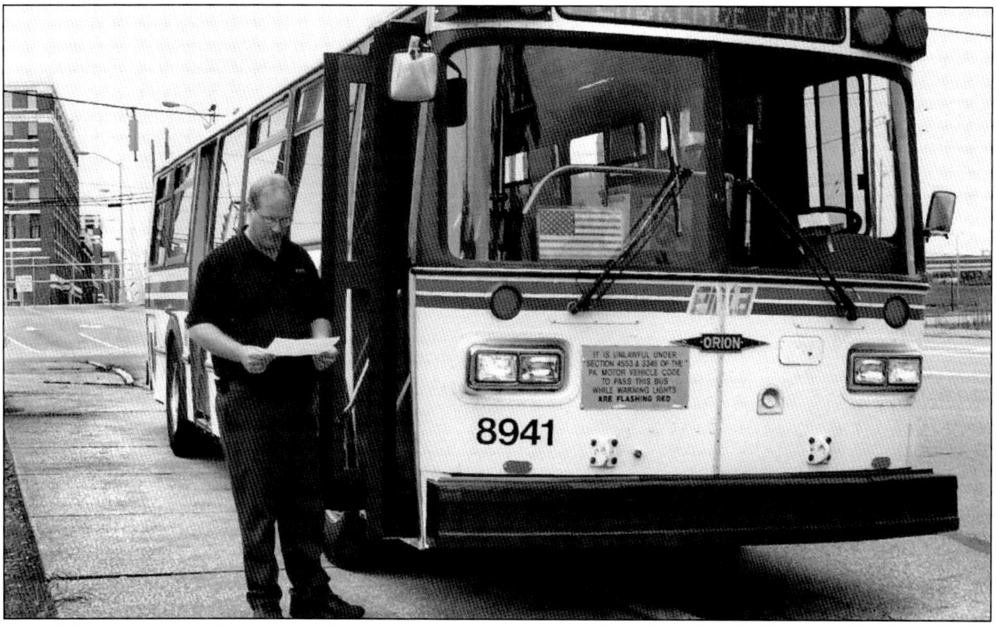

Erie Metropolitan Transit Authority bus operator Kurt Kesselring continues the custom of trolley car operators in checking the departure time for Route 4 at Main and Water Streets in Lawrence Park, which was a trolley line until May 12, 1935. Bus No. 8941 was built in August 1989 by Bus Industries of Americana Inc. and had 443,649 miles on the odometer on August 13, 2005. (Kenneth Springirth photograph.)

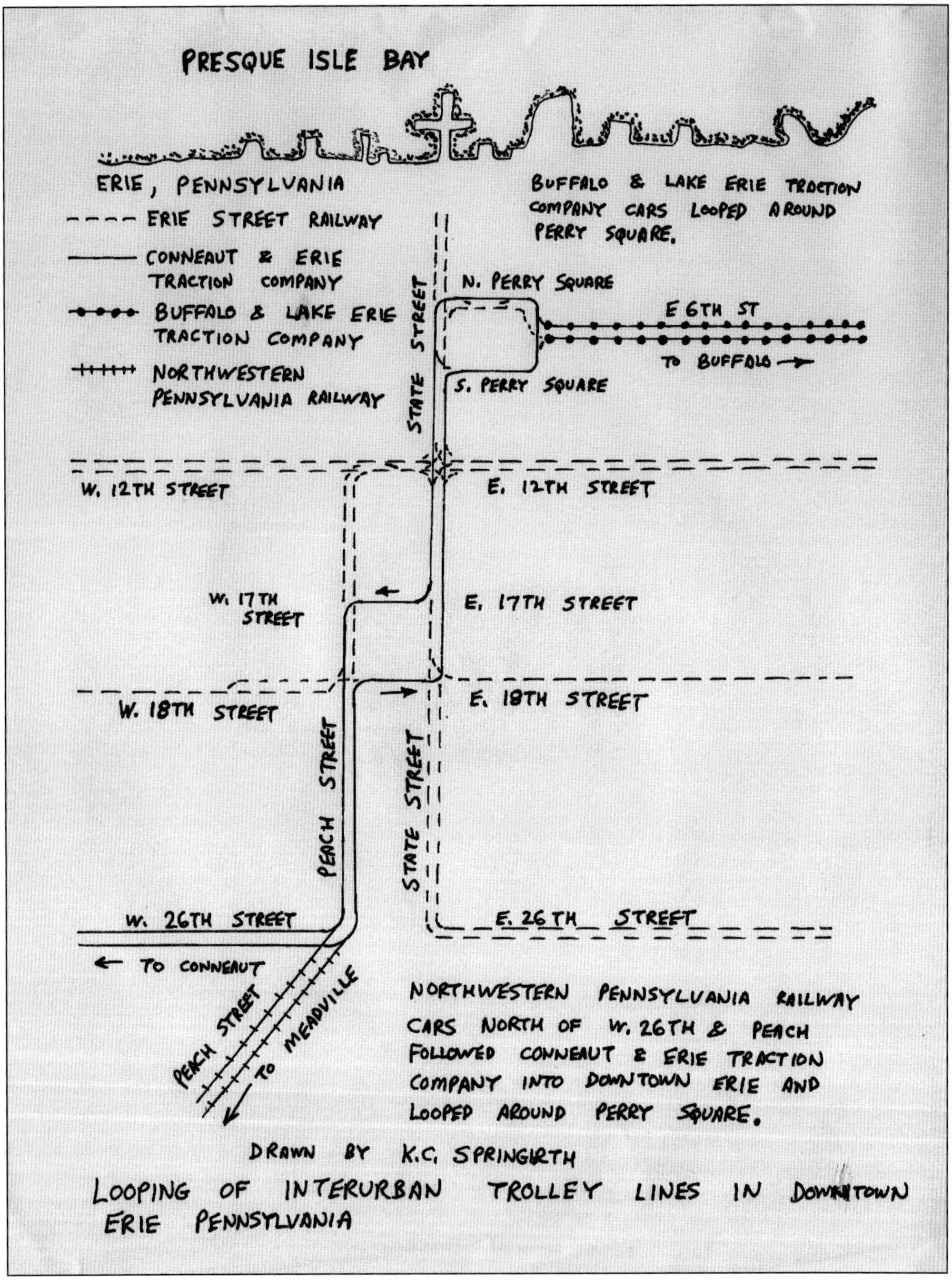

As shown by the map the Buffalo and Lake Erie Traction Company, cars used East Sixth and looped around Perry Square. Conneaut and Erie cars used West Twenty-sixth, north on Peach Street to Eighteenth Street, east on Eighteenth Street to State Street (cars to Conneaut went west on West Seventeenth Street) and north on State Street to Perry Square. Northwestern Pennsylvania Railway cars used Peach Street and followed the Conneaut and Erie routing to Perry Square.

Two

Conneaut and Erie Traction Company

The Conneaut and Erie Traction Company was built under the premise that there was going to be great industrial expansion at Conneaut, Ohio, and nearby northwestern Pennsylvania. A state-of-the-art car house was built at Elk Park just west of Girard, Pennsylvania. As noted by the *Street Railway Journal* of February 6, 1904, it was 127 feet 4 inches long, 78 feet 8 inches wide, and 16 feet high to the bottom of the horizontal roof trusses. It contained a repair shop, storage room for 12 cars, a stock storeroom, lounging room for the men, and two offices. The foundations were of stone, the walls were brick, the framing and trusses were wood, and the wooden roof was covered with slag. In one half of the building there were three tracks, one of which had a pit along its entire length. A fourth track on the right of the centerline of the car house extended into the repair shop where there was a short pit. The repair shop, measuring 43 feet by 37 feet 10 inches, was equipped with the following tools: a 28-inch Cincinnati drill press, a 34-inch Porter lathe, a 14-inch Reed lathe, a 20-inch Steptoe shaper, a 36-inch 60-ton wheel press, a Buffalo forge, and a complete assortment of small tools, all driven by a 5-horsepower motor. One of the repair pits featured a pneumatic hoist for raising the motors into position on the trucks, and a Barrett armature lifter for use when it was only necessary to remove that part of the motor. One point of the large pit was arranged such that the car wheels could be lowered without lifting the car body. The needed ridership never materialized. On May 12, 1909, the company was sold for $200,000 and became the Cleveland and Erie Railway Company. On March 11, 1914, the first of the newly repainted trolleys was on display at Conneaut, and all six regular cars were repainted to encourage ridership. During 1914, there were special rates from Conneaut to Erie providing a round-trip for just 75¢. Two new center-entrance trolleys, No. 207 and No. 208, were purchased from Niles Car Company during 1915. A heavy sleet storm hit the lake region on March 6, 1916, and severely damaged the overhead wire. The line crew diligently repaired the damage and service was restored.

In spite of the heavy inroads made by the automobile into the line's ridership, it was remarkable that service was only slightly reduced. While the March 1, 1907, timetable had 13 through westbound trips and 14 through eastbound trips, the March 30, 1919, timetable showed 12 through westbound trips and 13 through eastbound trips. In spite of overwhelming odds, the company was doing everything possible to increase ridership.

With a depleted cash balance, the company was not able to make its payments to the Buffalo and Lake Traction Company for use of its trackage over the local Erie Street Railway to downtown Erie and in 1920 was in receivership. The winter of 1920 was rough. From February 5 to February 19, 1920, trolley service was virtually halted by ice covering the rails. The company was in such bad financial condition that it did not have the necessary funds to dig out the line. Cleveland and Erie workers were joined by a shoveling party of citizens and tackled three- and four-foot snowdrifts in West Springfield around stop 117. During the afternoon of March 11, 1920, a trolley got through to West Springfield and then jumped the tracks. Local townspeople, anxious to have service restored rallied to aid the crew, and after a four-hour struggle amid the polar winds of Lake Erie were able to get the car back on the rails. A public plea was made by the receiver, which appeared in the *Girard Cosmopolite Herald* on Thursday, December 9, 1920, as follows:

> Are you interested in the continuance of service over the Cleveland & Erie Railway Company or must this road be abandoned and the property salvaged? This is entirely a question for you to decide. You must in order to warrant continuance of operation, not only give this road your patronage by riding and by express business, but you must become a booster for business. You should look upon this road as a personal asset to you, because it really does increase the value of your property, which may be adjacent to the line. Since my appointment as receiver of the Cleveland & Erie Railway Co. operating between Erie, Pa and Conneaut, Ohio, I find that the present earnings are not sufficient to meet even operating expenses. By request, on November 1, the service was increased, although it was not justified by present patronage. I believe that the public in the territory served will appreciate this benefit to the extent where simple earnings for operation would be received and permit me in the near future to reduce the present rate of fare which will be done as soon as conditions will allow.

The letter continued, "No dividends have been paid and this line is solely operated for the benefit of the public and unless it is given sufficient support to the extent that it will be self-sustaining, operation will cease. Only by your liberal support will continuous operation be insured. Do you want it?" Signed A. O. Chapin, Receiver.

Over in Conneaut, the High Level Bridge was reported to be in poor condition. The Cleveland and Erie was given permission to continue using the bridge, but all other traffic was excluded. During the summer of 1922, the Cleveland and Erie was diligently trying to bolster revenue by conducting special excursions.

The Cleveland and Erie was sold for $75,000 at a receivers' sale to the Buffalo Housewrecking Corporation. No other bids were received. The line was turned over to the new owners on September 15, 1922, and service ended September 16, 1922.

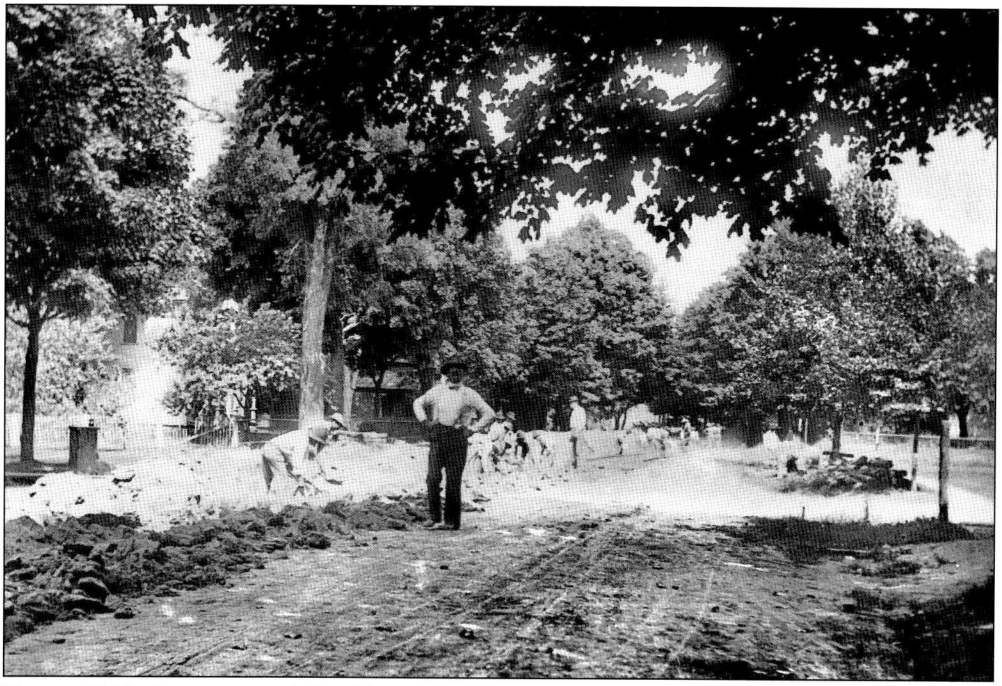

During 1902, Conneaut and Erie Traction Company crews distributed ties and poles along the route from Conneaut to Erie. Half the rail came in November 1902, and the balance was delivered during February 1903. In this 1903 scene, track is being laid in East Springfield, Pennsylvania, and the line was rapidly taking shape.

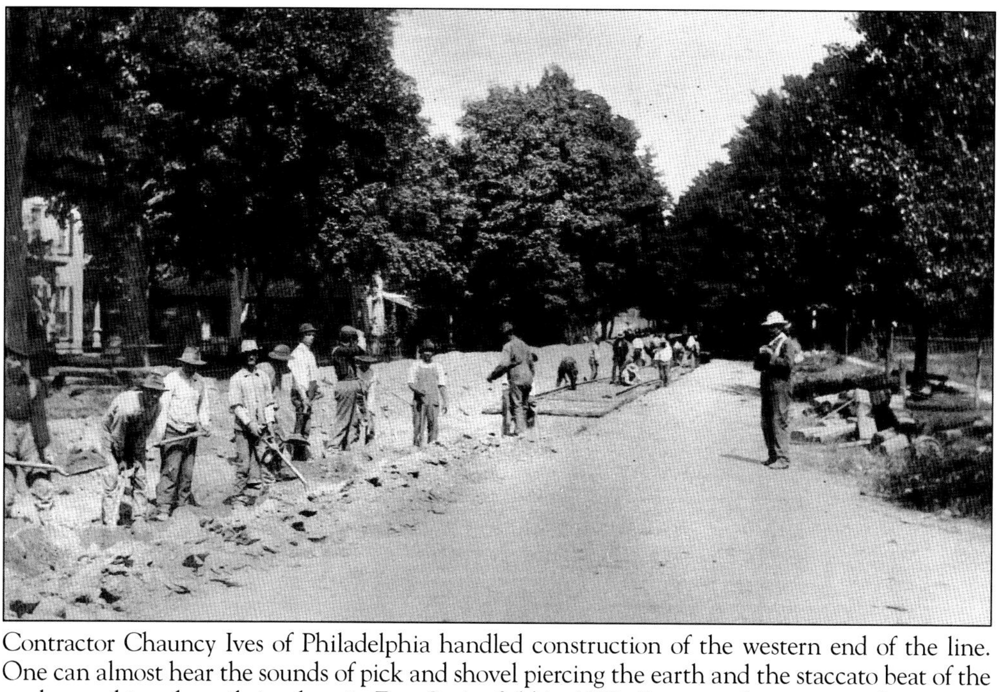

Contractor Chauncy Ives of Philadelphia handled construction of the western end of the line. One can almost hear the sounds of pick and shovel piercing the earth and the staccato beat of the workers spiking the rails in place in East Springfield in 1903. One can also envision the anxious faces of the townspeople wondering when they might see the first trolley come through town.

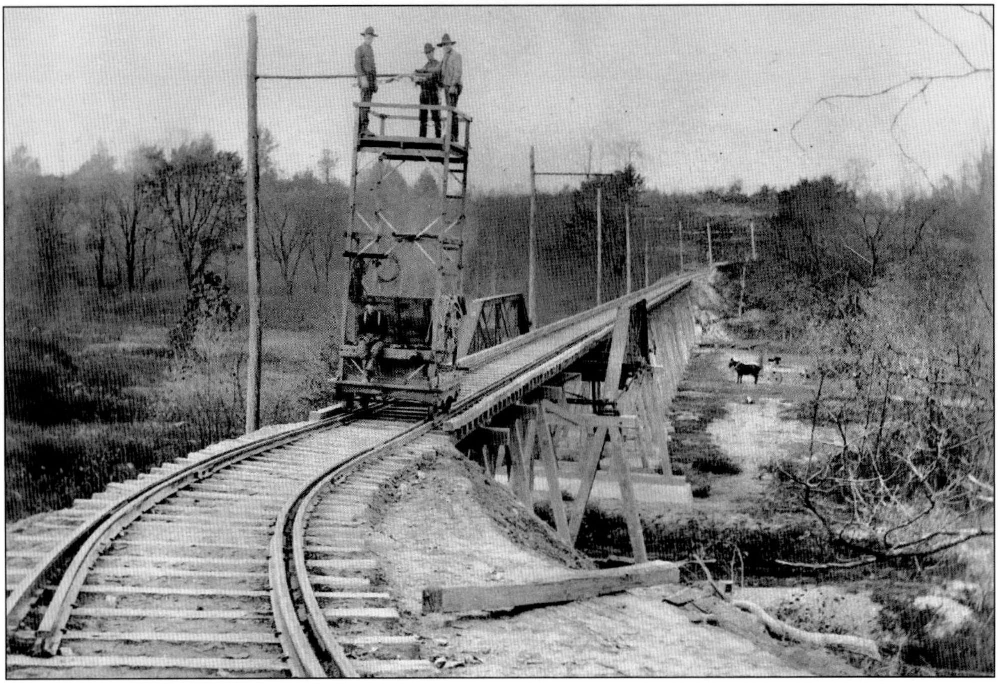

Construction of the Conneaut and Erie Traction Company line began at the state line between Pennsylvania and Ohio on Friday June 27, 1902, and proceeded eastward into Pennsylvania. The once-quiet Crooked Creek Valley became alive with workers in 1903 placing ties to support the rails. Next came the pole crew digging the holes and dropping the wooden poles, and this crew was hanging the overhead wire. (B. J. Miller photograph.)

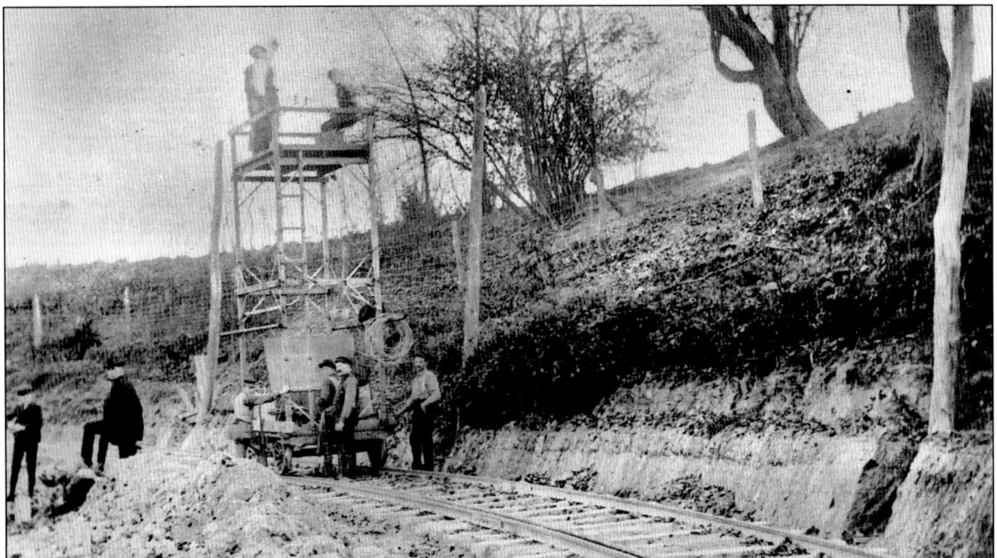

In this 1903 scene near Crooked Creek, the line crew rolled their 4-wheel decked hand car along side each pole and bolted a two-and-a-half-inch diameter pipe bracket to the wooden pole, and a steel cable was installed to act as a truss rod from the end of the pipe to the pole. Below the pipe bracket, the trolley wire was hung. (B. J. Miller photograph.)

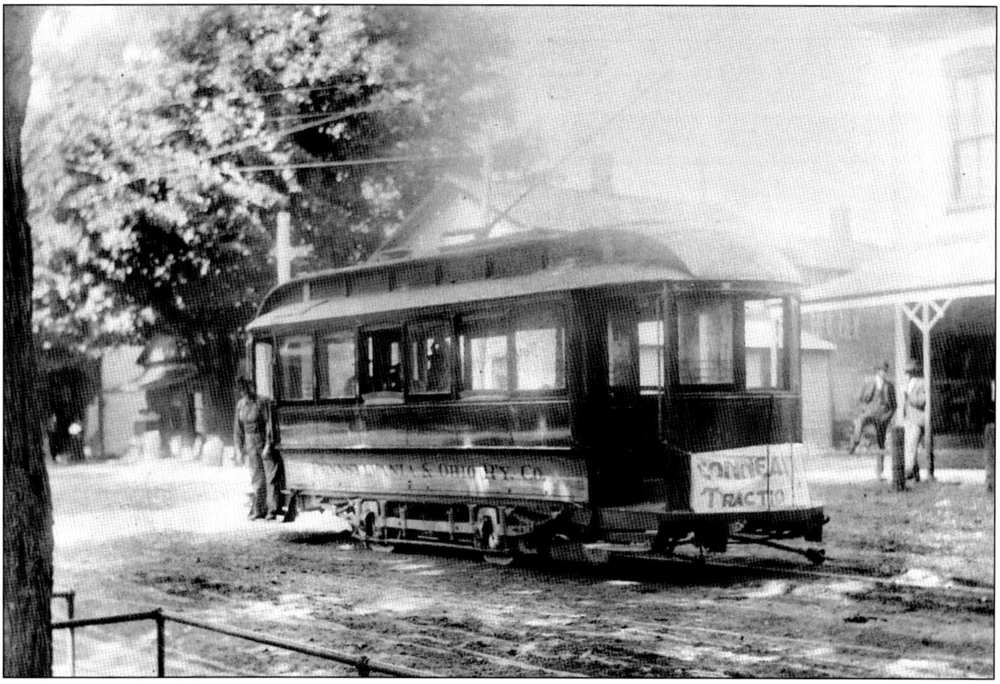

The Conneaut and Erie Traction Company borrowed Pennsylvania and Ohio Railway car No. 1 for the first run on September 25, 1903, leaving East Conneaut, Ohio, at 7:00 a.m. for East Springfield, Pennsylvania, and arriving back at the High Level Bridge in East Conneaut at 11:50 a.m. Regular service began that day with cars leaving East Conneaut eastbound at 6:00 a.m., 8:00 a.m., 10:00 a.m., noon, 2:00 p.m., 4:00 p.m., 6:00 p.m., and 8:00 p.m. (B. J. Miller photograph.)

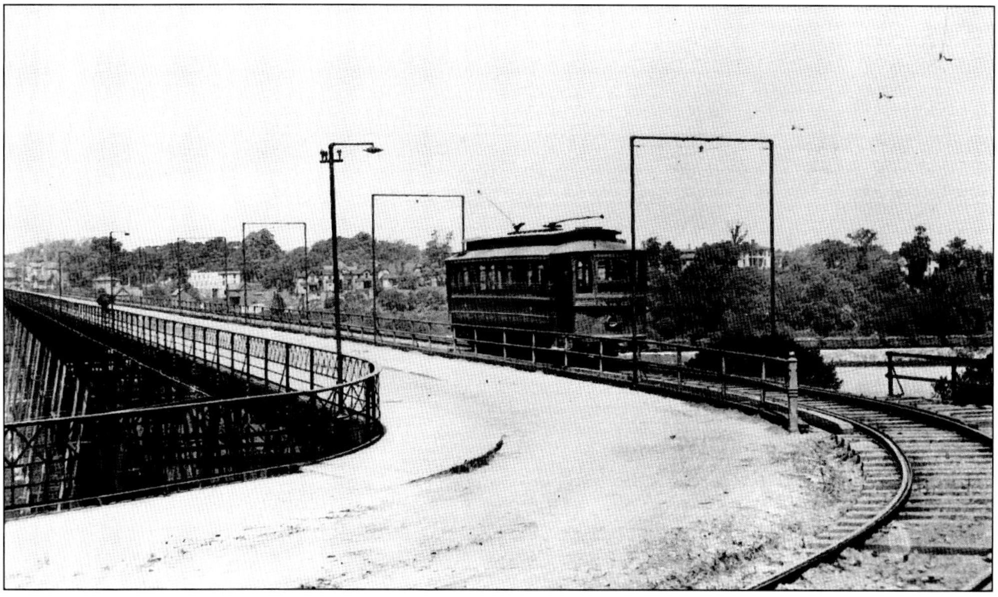

On June 13, 1903, the 2,128-foot-long High Level Bridge was completed, spanning the Bessemer Railroad, Conneaut Creek, and a wide ravine between East Conneaut and Conneaut. The Conneaut and Erie Traction Company built its track on the north side of the bridge. Trolley No. 4 is eastbound for Erie. (J. A. Tyler photograph.)

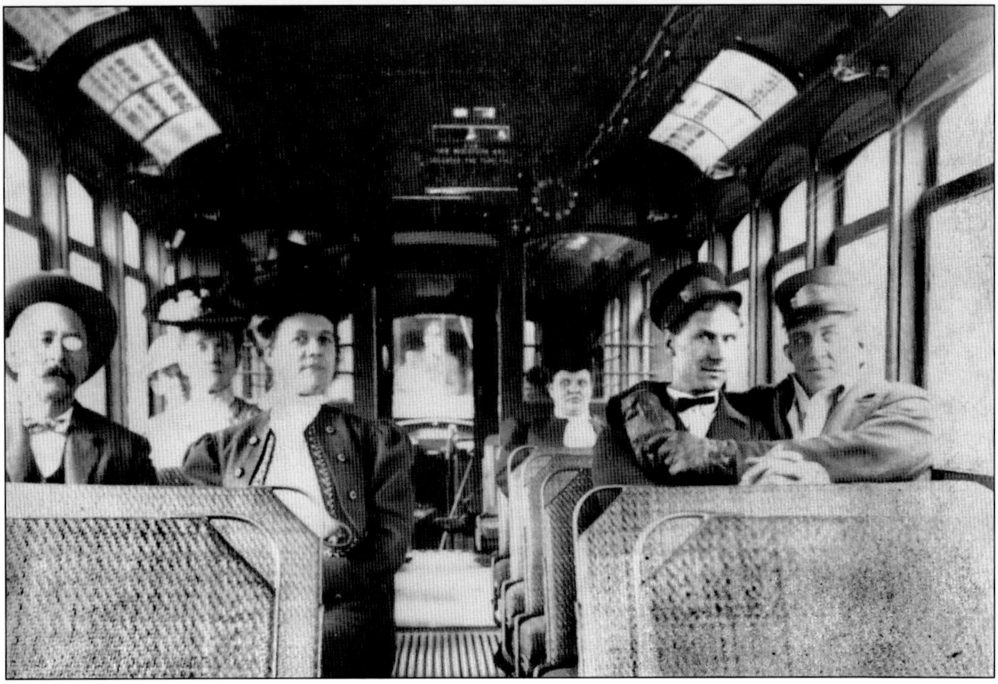

When the Conneaut and Erie Traction Company began trolley service on the entire line from Erie to Conneaut on November 8, 1903, ridership was good. As noted in this interior view of car No. 3, passengers put on their best clothes to ride the trolley. A new era was born that revolutionized traveling habits.

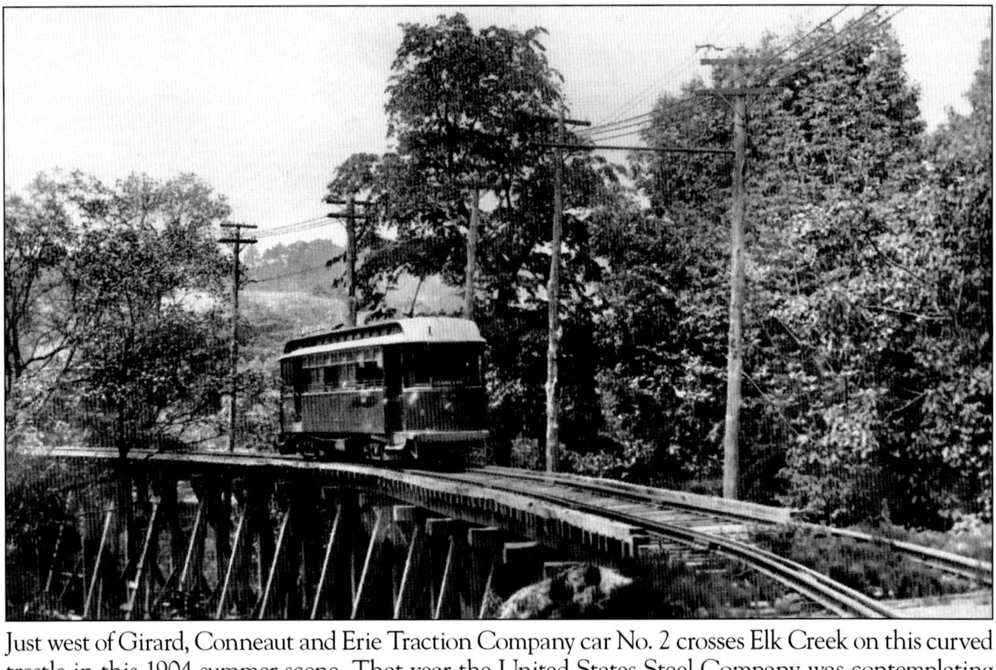

Just west of Girard, Conneaut and Erie Traction Company car No. 2 crosses Elk Creek on this curved trestle in this 1904 summer scene. That year the United States Steel Company was contemplating the purchase of property at Elk Creek Harbor to handle the increasing cargoes of ore and coal. The Conneaut and Erie was doing its part to make the area attractive for industrial development.

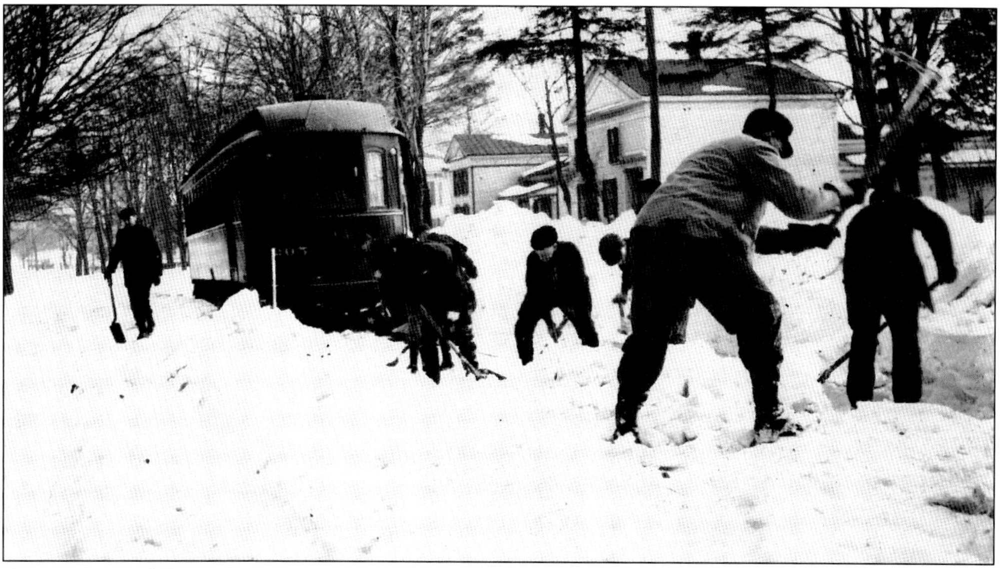

Conneaut and Erie Traction Company trolley No. 205 in East Springfield waits as a group of men shoveled the snow. By Wednesday, December 16, 1903, the entire line was out of service. On December 20, 1903, service was restored from Erie to East Springfield, and one week later, the entire line was reopened. (R. Evans photograph.)

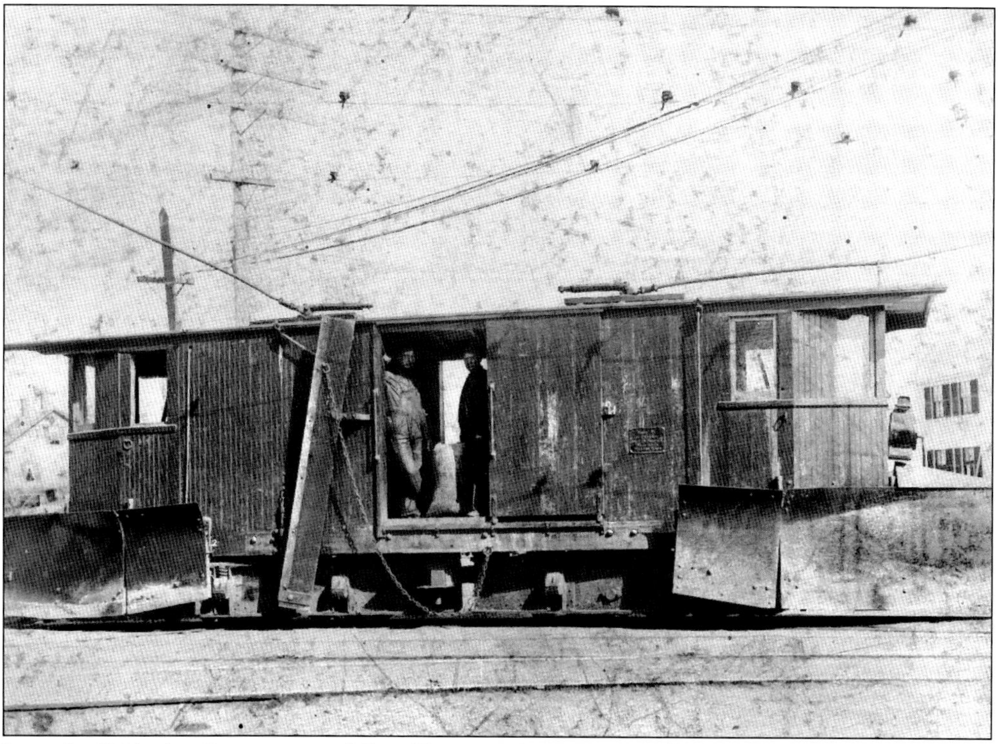

In early 1904, the Conneaut and Erie Traction Company purchased a snow sweeper, but the snowdrifts were so deep during January 1904 that for two weeks there was no trolley service from Conneaut to Girard. Even with the heavy lake-effect snowstorms, it can be noted that the Conneaut and Erie management kept the crews working to maintain some service.

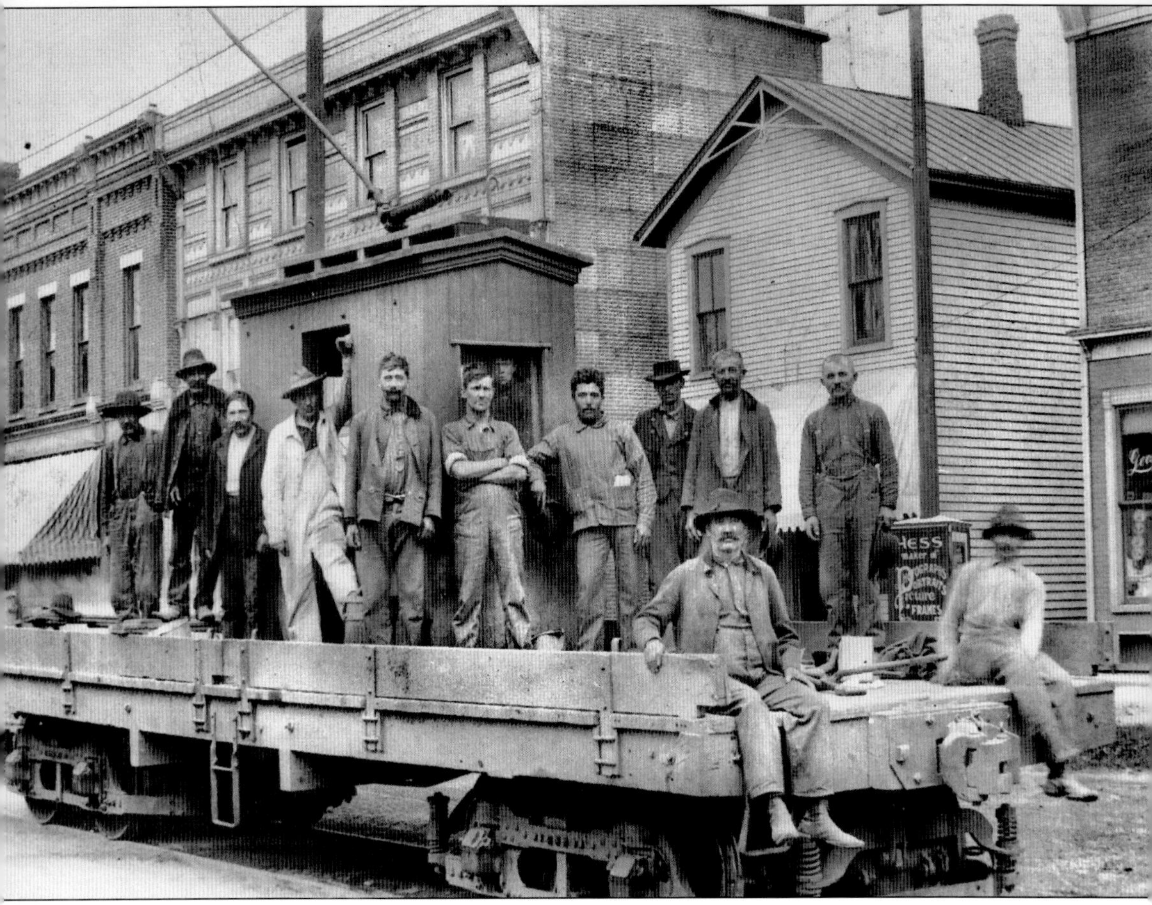

The Conneaut and Erie Traction Company work crew pauses on Main Street in downtown Girard in April 1904 on the work car affectionately known as the "mudhen." Full service on the line from Erie to Conneaut began November 8, 1903. The work crew was busy at the end of the first winter repairing the right-of-way that had been damaged by the 1904 spring thaw that resulted in 200 yards of track covered by mud and gravel west of Miles Grove, Pennsylvania (Lake City today).

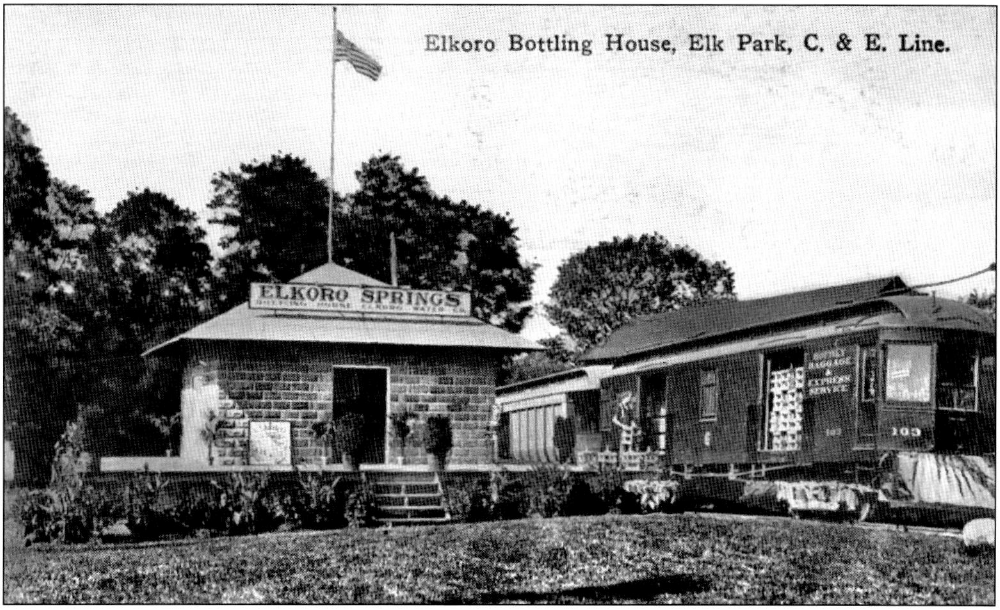

Elkoro Bottling House at Elk Park west of Girard finds Conneaut and Erie Traction Company trolley freight car No. 103 loading up with Elkoro Spring Water, which, according the postcard, was rated by Allen Rogers, New York chemist, as "one of the purest natural water I have ever examined." The trolley line had daily freight service that delivered and picked up various items at numerous stops from Erie to Conneaut.

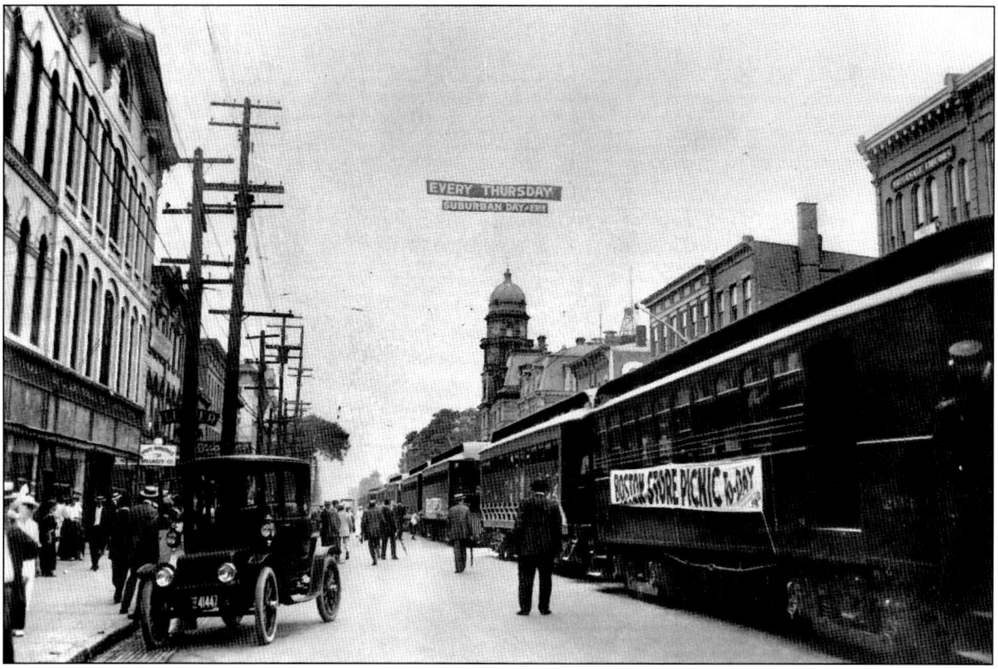

The Boston Store in downtown Erie chartered Conneaut and Erie Traction Company trolley cars for its annual employee picnic at Elk Park. The store closed at 1:00 p.m., and employees boarded trolley cars for the park. In this July 1917 scene, there were also picnics for the general public with the cars lined up on State Street receiving passengers for this popular event.

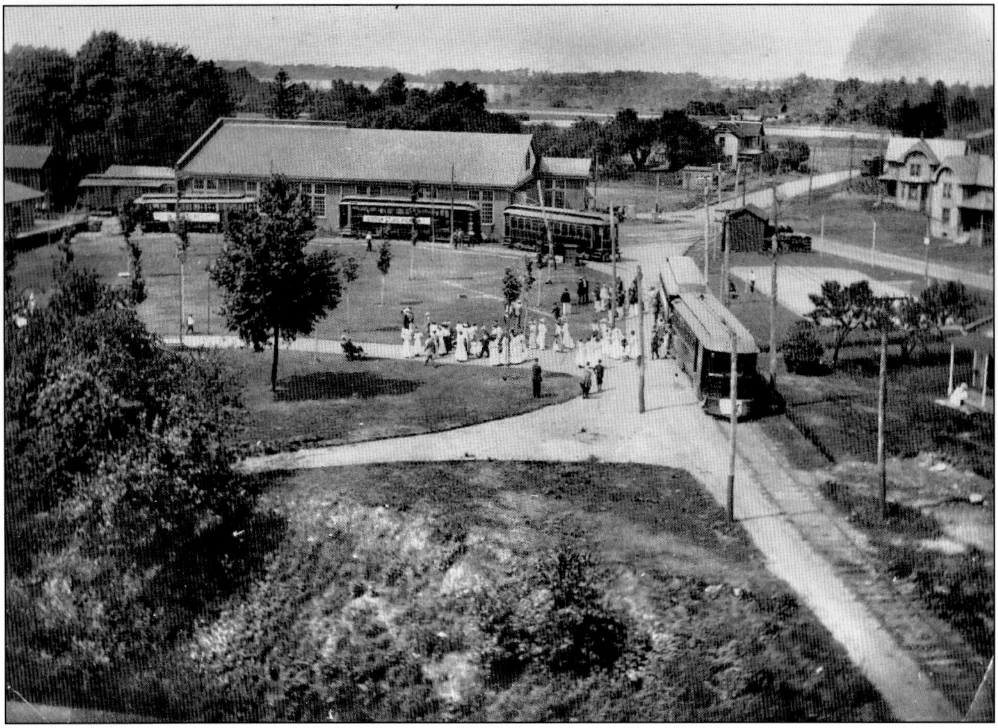

An annual summer event was the Boston Store Picnic. This typically involved five trolleys each seating 60 so that 300 passengers would be taken to Elk Park to enjoy the free boating on the lake, a breath of fresh country air, and a taste of the park's pure spring water. The Cleveland and Erie sold Elkoro Spring Water, bottled at Elk Park, for 25¢ for a five-gallon bottle.

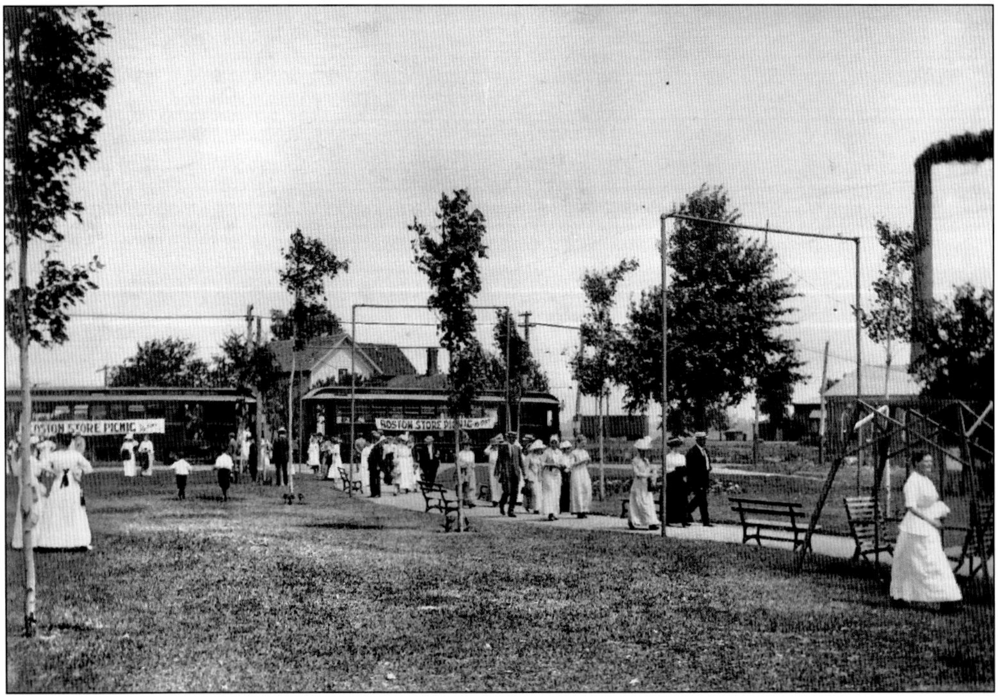

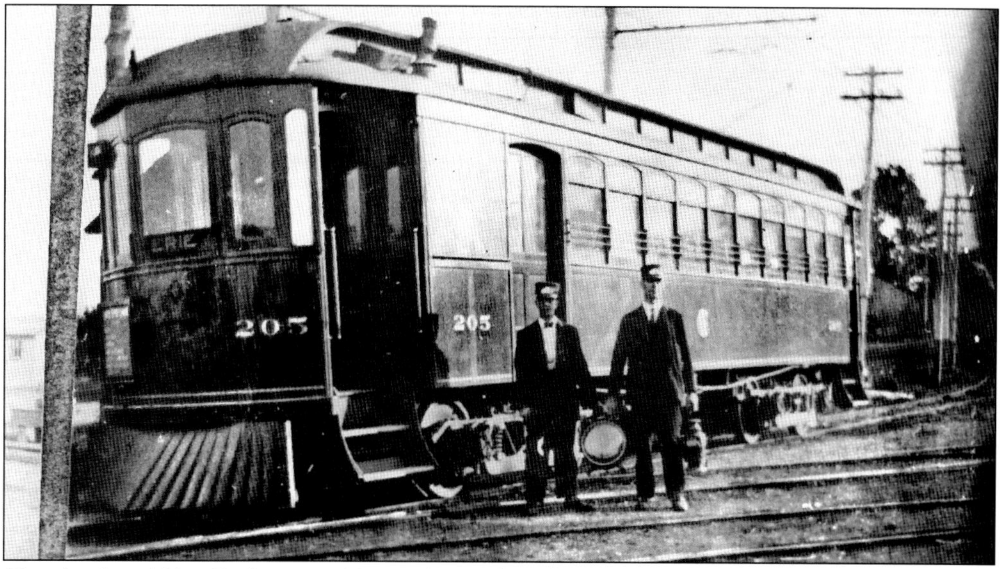

Cleveland and Erie Railway car No. 205 is at the Elk Park carbarn, and the employees are Ed Platz (left) and F. Wright. The line and equipment were generally well maintained up to the very end. A year before the line closed, new rail was laid on Main Street in Girard from the Rice Avenue intersection in the center of the highway to the edge of town.

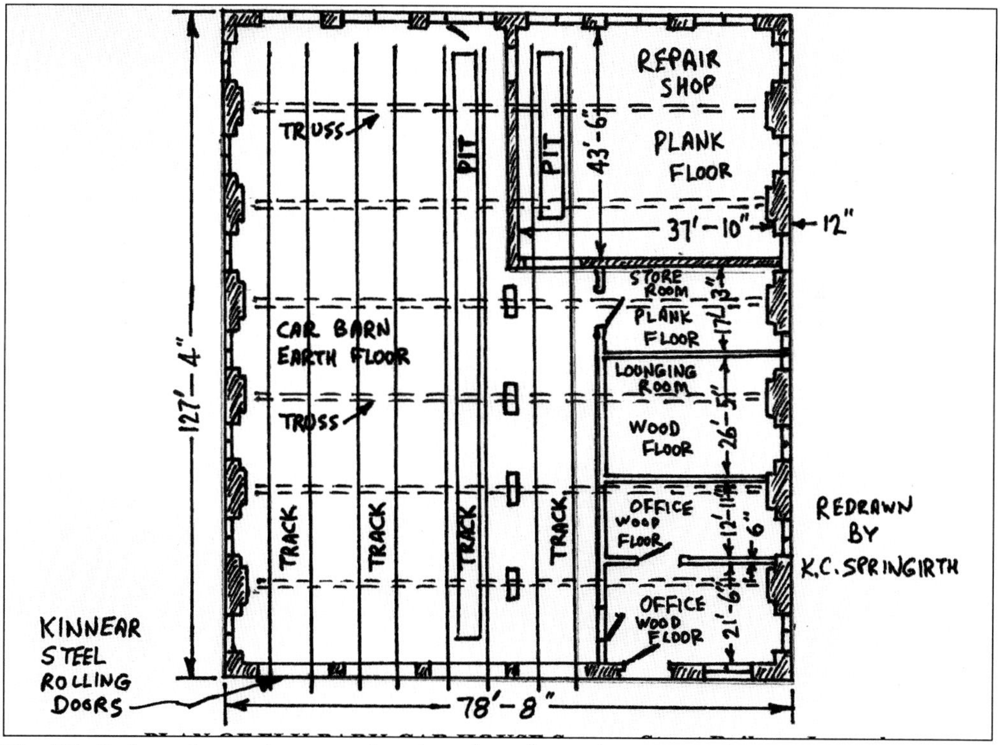

The Elk Park car house shown in the plan above housed 12 cars and contained a repair shop, storeroom, lounging room for the employees, and two offices. The repair shop was equipped with a 28-inch Cincinnati drill press, a 34-inch Porter lathe, a 14-inch Reed lathe, a 20-inch Steptoe shaper, a 36-inch 60-ton wheel press, a Buffalo forge, and a complete assortment of tools.

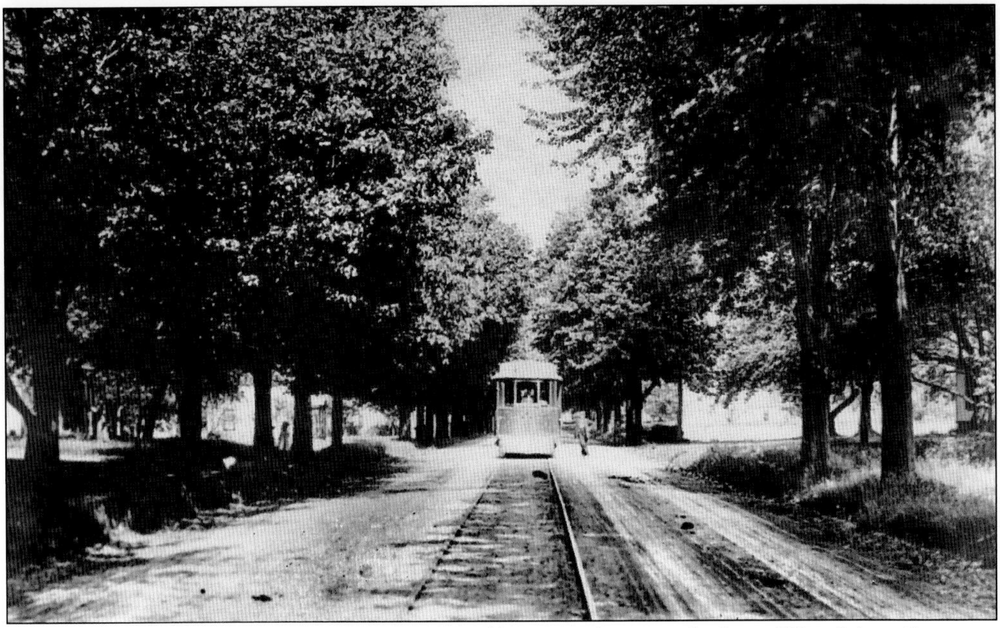

A Conneaut and Erie Traction Company trolley was photographed on West Main Street at stop 116 in West Springfield in 1905. Most of the communities along the 33-mile route from Erie to Conneaut were small, and the trolley provided hourly service throughout the day to communities that were off the steam railroad routes. (E. C. Blick photograph.)

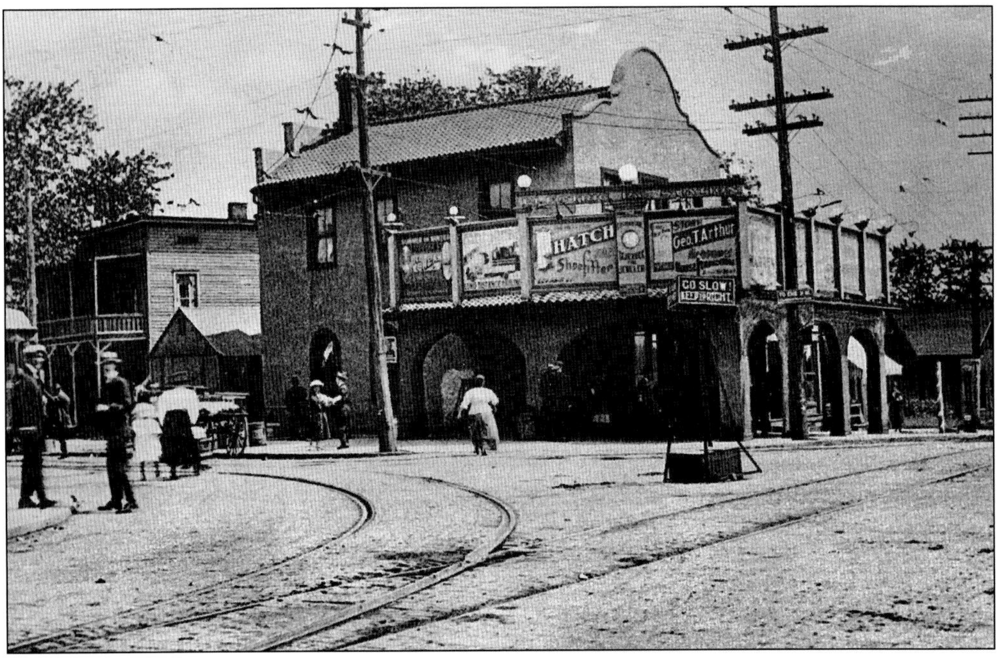

On June 12, 1907, the Conneaut and Erie Traction Company and Pennsylvania and Ohio Railway established a joint waiting station in Conneaut with ticket agent A. B. Crittenden. Both companies adjusted their schedules for better transfer connections. The trolley lines connecting Cleveland and Erie were beginning to lure passengers from the paralleling steam railroads. (J. A. Tyler photograph.)

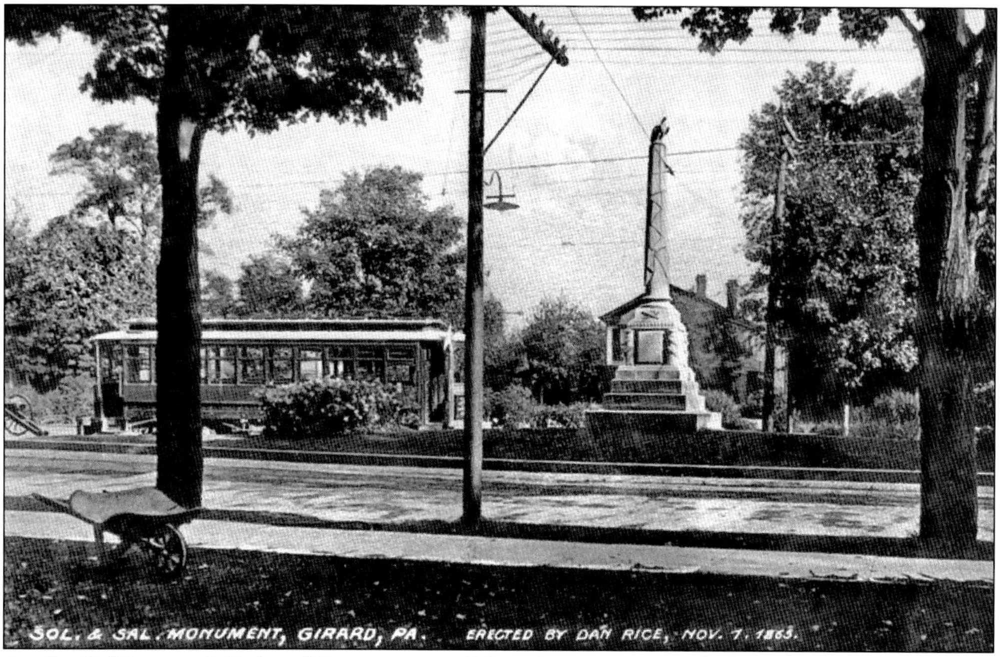

At the Soldiers and Sailors Monument on Main Street in Girard there was a passing siding on the single-track Conneaut and Erie Traction Company line. The March 1, 1907, timetable showed the first westbound trip Monday through Saturday left Erie at 7:05 a.m. and arrived at Girard at 8:15 a.m. with arrival at Conneaut at 9:15 a.m. Sunday service began one hour later. Service was hourly.

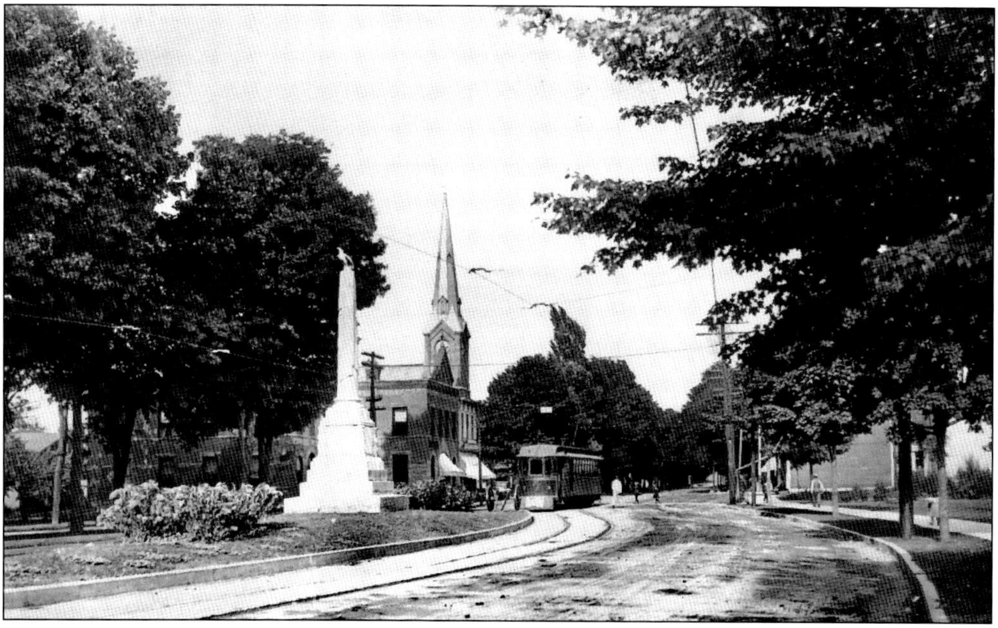

Car No. 3 is westbound for Conneaut by the Soldiers and Sailors Monument on Main Street in Girard. Five cars were originally needed to maintain the hourly service, but after November 15, 1908, travel time from Erie to Conneaut was reduced by 15 to 20 minutes, and four cars could then maintain the hourly service.

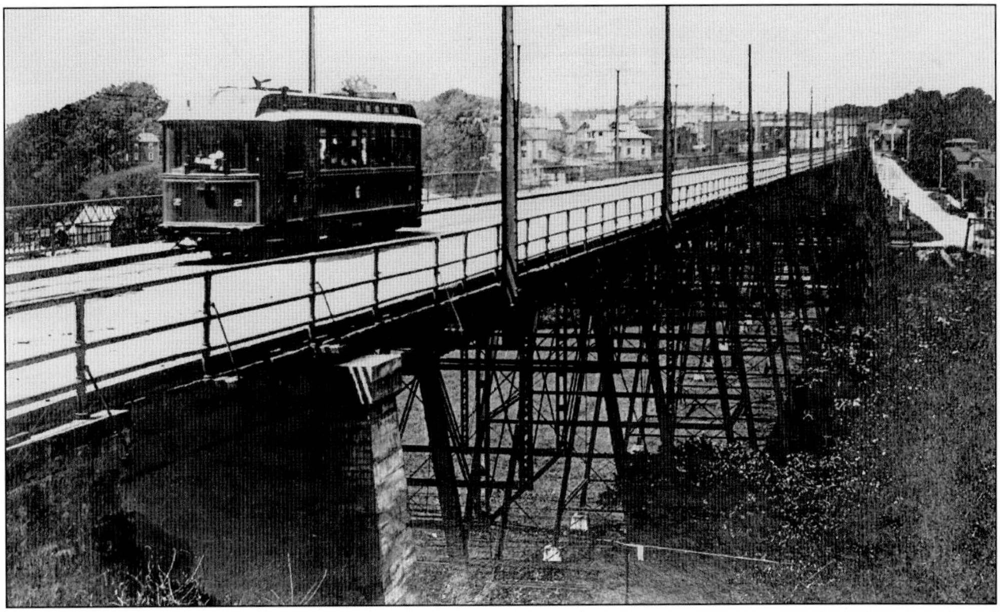

On Wednesday May 12, 1909, the company was sold for $200,000 and became the Cleveland and Erie Railway as trolley No. 2 headed eastbound to Erie on the High Level Bridge at Conneaut. During July 1909, the line carried 12,200 passengers, the largest total since the line began, but the industrial expansion never materialized. (J. A. Tyler photograph.)

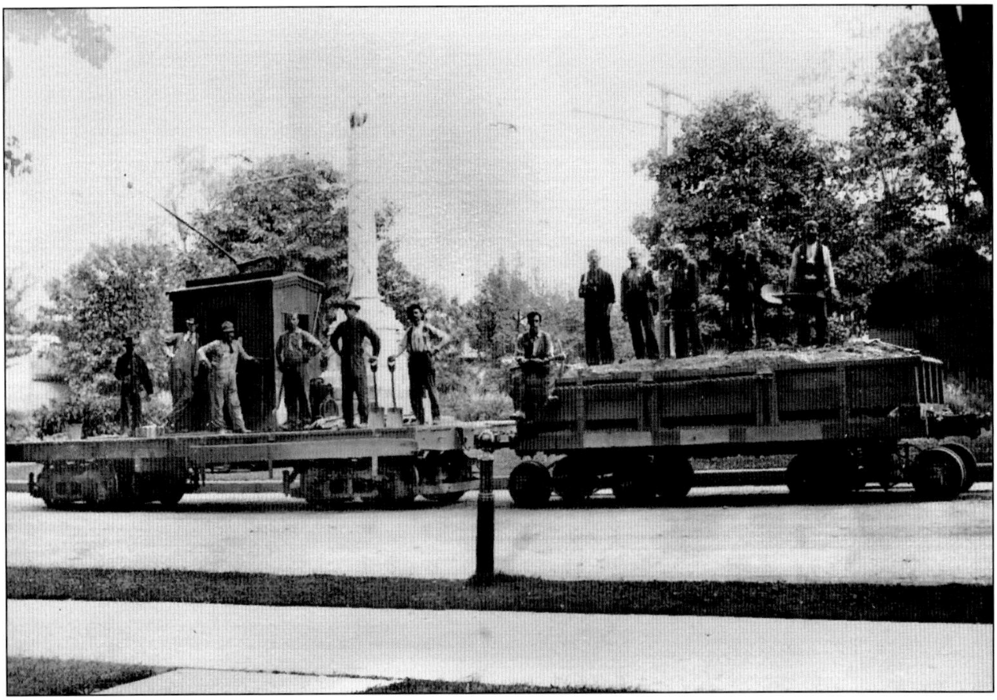

Even though the Cleveland and Erie Railway had limited revenues, their work crews were constantly improving the line. The crew on the work car known as the "mudhen," pulling a flatcar, pauses at the Dan Rice Monument in Girard. Service was hourly on the line, which meant the work car would have to get to a siding to let the regular service car pass.

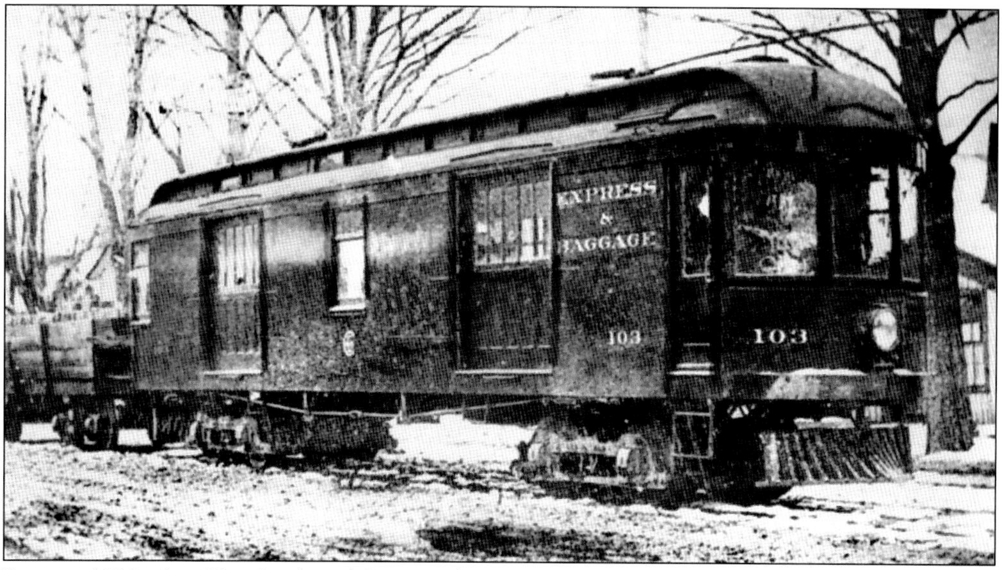

During 1909, the Cleveland and Erie Railway purchased a new trolley freight car, No. 103. At 4:00 a.m., the car would load up at Perry Square in Erie with boxes of bread from Firch's Bakery and would make the westbound trip to Conneaut, picking up and delivering various commodities at local stops along the way.

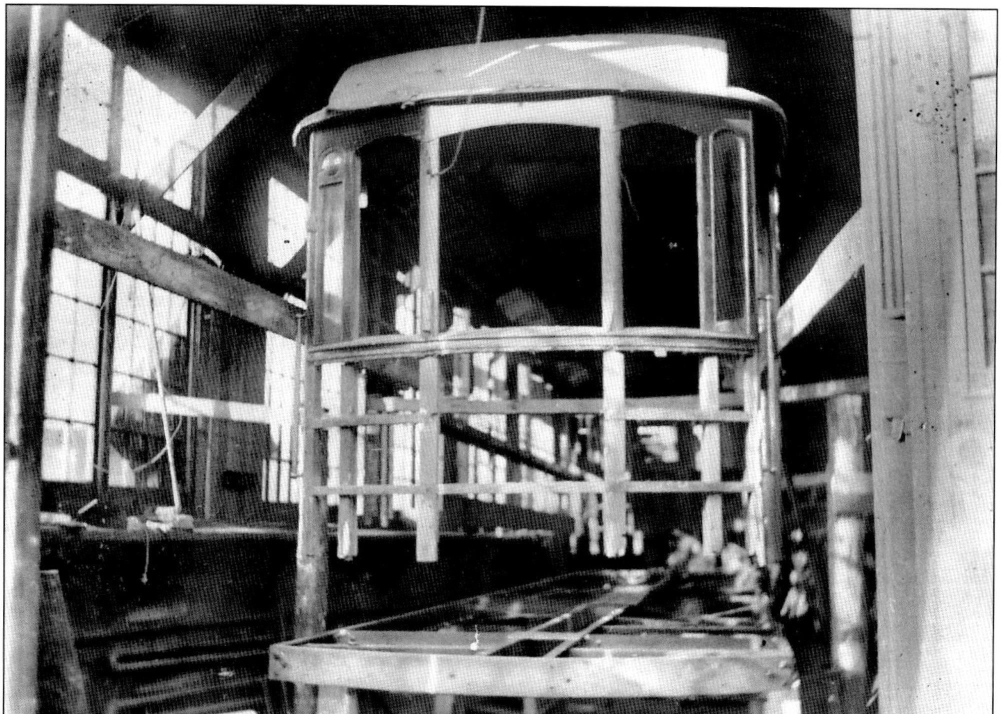

Henry Shenk of Erie built the Elk Park carbarn and shops in 1903 at a cost of $12,000. This was a well-equipped repair facility that could completely rebuild trolley cars. On February 14, 1902, the *Conneaut Daily Post-Herald* reported that United States Steel at Conneaut would build a $12 million tube plant. This facility was never built, but the trolley company was prepared to handle expansion.

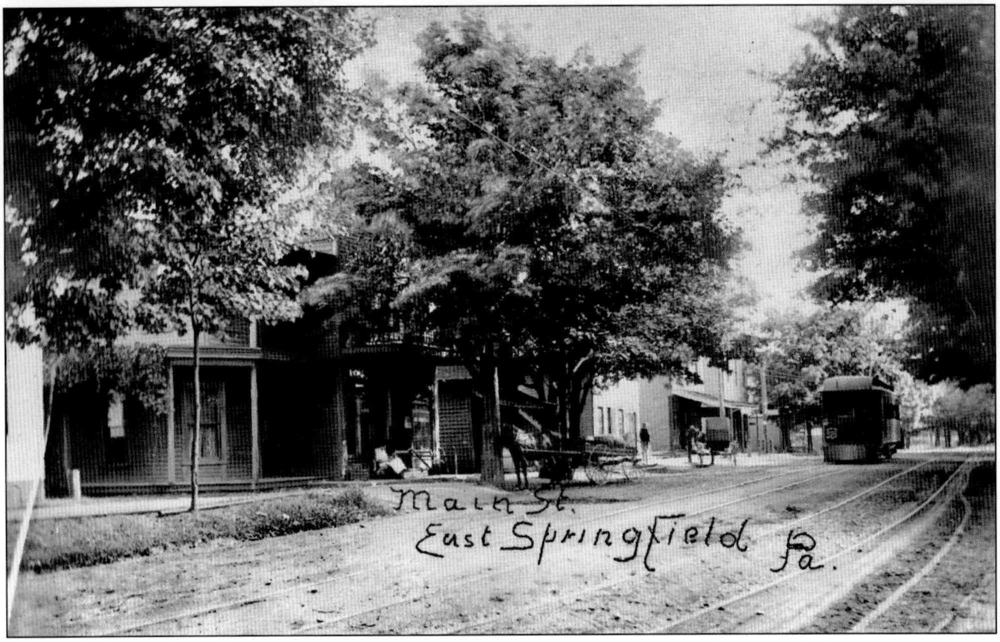

Cleveland and Erie Railway car No. 6 appears at car stop 99 in East Springfield during a summer day in 1911. The March 1, 1907, timetable showed the first eastbound car Monday through Saturday left East Springfield for Erie at 8:02 a.m. Eastbound Sunday service began two hours later. (B. J. Miller photograph.)

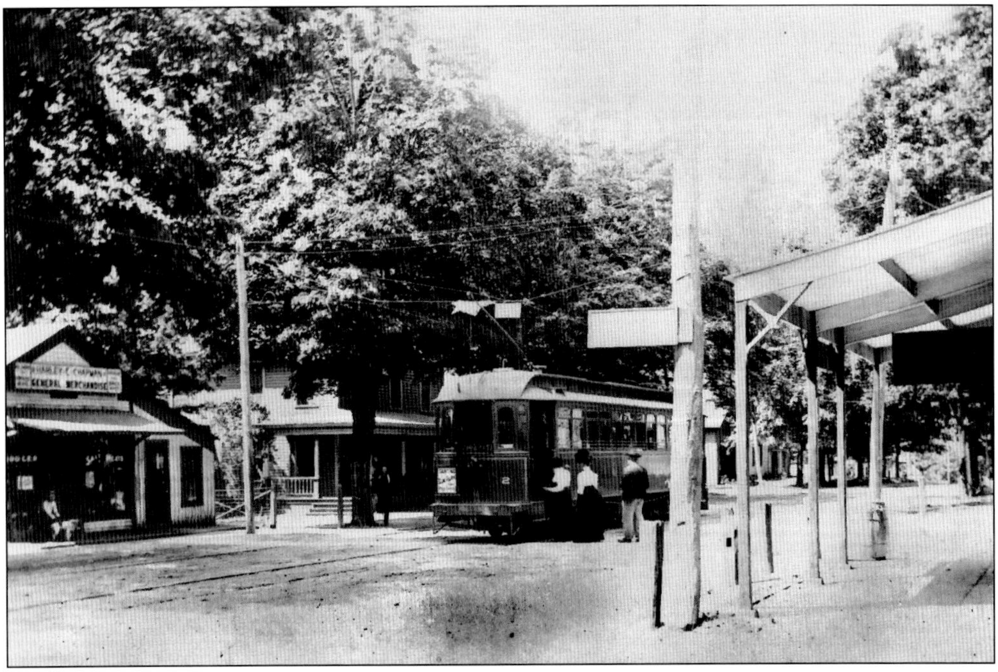

At car stop 99 in East Springfield in 1911, Cleveland and Erie Railway car No. 2 was westbound for Conneaut. The March 1, 1907, timetable showed the first westbound car Monday through Saturday left East Springfield for Conneaut at 6:49 a.m. Westbound service on Sunday began two hours later. Service was hourly. (B. J. Miller photograph.)

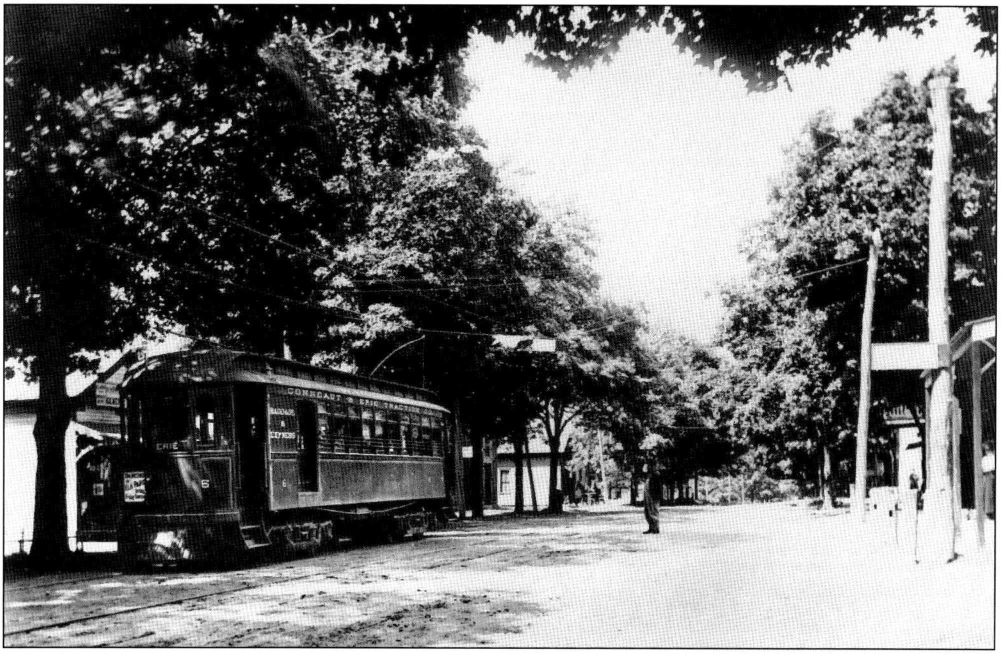

Cleveland and Erie Railway car No. 6 was eastbound for Erie at car stop 99 in East Springfield. The March 1, 1907, timetable showed 15 eastbound and 15 westbound trips Monday through Saturday passing through East Springfield. On Sunday, there were 13 eastbound and 13 westbound trips through East Springfield. (B. J. Miller photograph.)

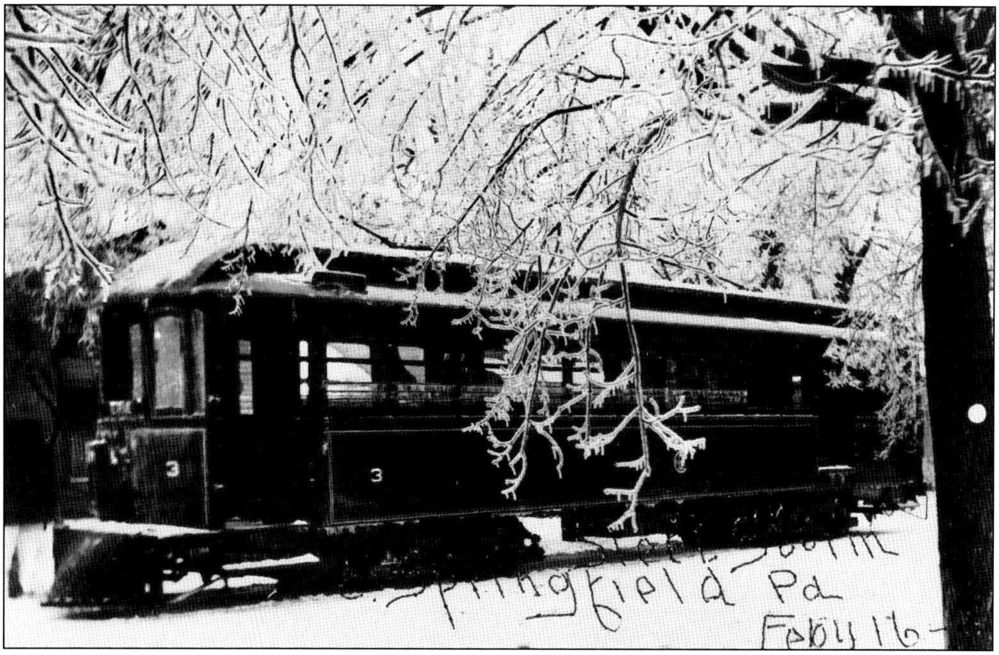

Car No. 3 was in a sleet storm on February 16, 1909, in East Springfield. Bad weather resulted in service disruptions, which affected ridership and revenue. The company went into receivership in 1907, and on January 10, 1909, a proposal was made to reorganize as the Cleveland and Erie Railway. New money was raised from new $100,000 first mortgage bonds. (B. J. Miller photograph.)

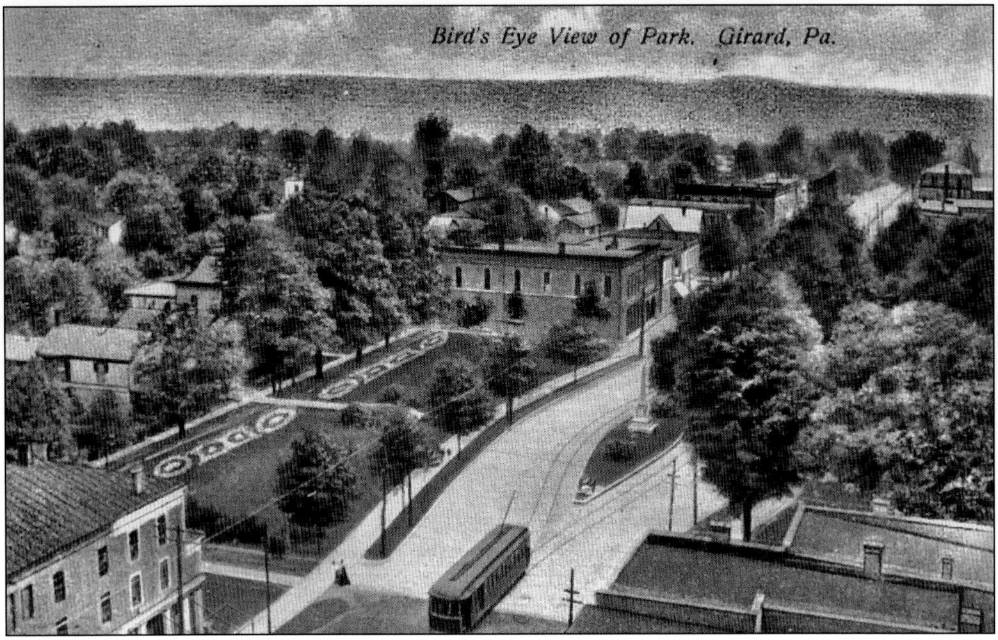

In this postcard of a bird's-eye view of the Soldiers and Sailors Monument on Main Street in Girard, a Conneaut and Erie Traction Company trolley has just cleared the siding heading westbound for Conneaut. This was a pleasant trip from the crowded city through the picturesque towns of western Erie County.

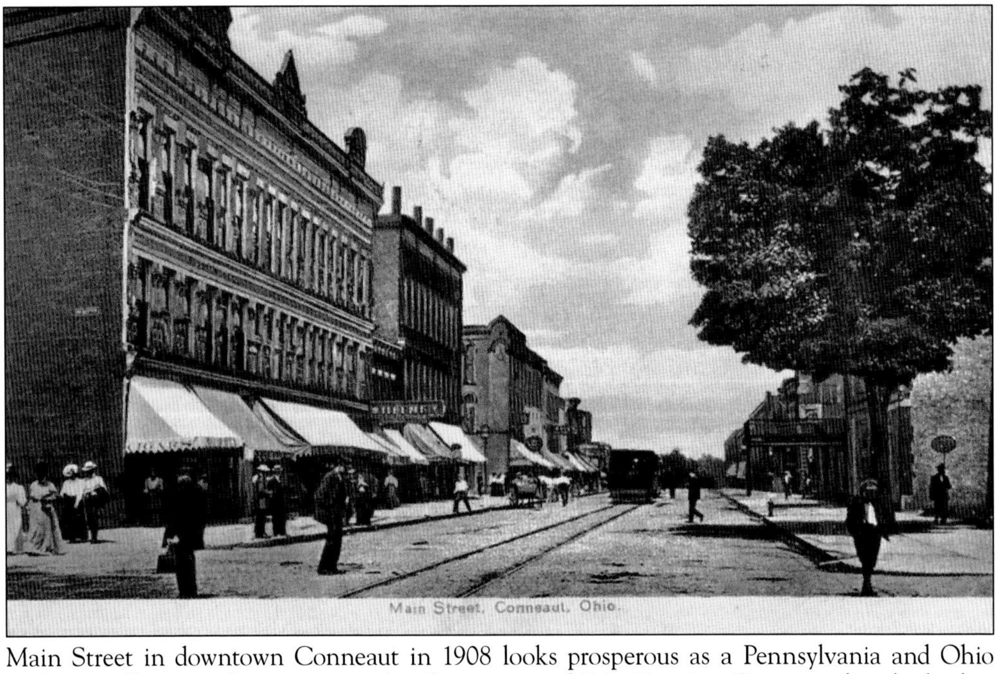

Main Street in downtown Conneaut in 1908 looks prosperous as a Pennsylvania and Ohio Railway trolley provides service to the Conneaut and Erie Traction Company line by both a local line to the Conneaut harbor and an interurban line to Ashtabula and Jefferson, Ohio. At Ashtabula, connections could be made with the Cleveland Painesville and Eastern, which went to Cleveland.

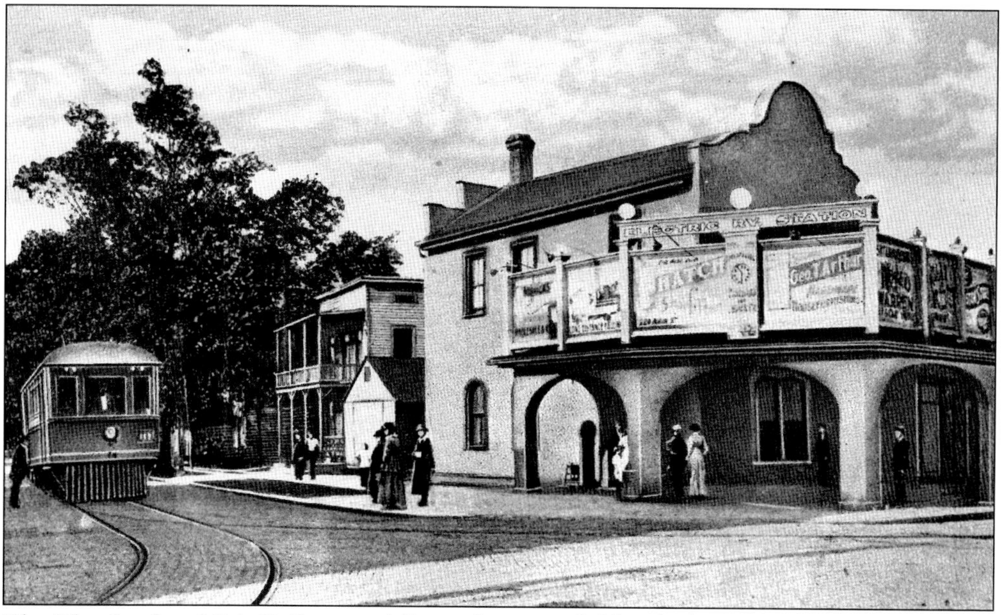

The Cleveland and Erie Railway and Pennsylvania and Ohio had a joint interurban station at Main and Harbor in Conneaut. In the photograph above, a Pennsylvania and Ohio trolley was on Harbor Street at the Main Street intersection. Both companies worked together to provide better connections, as they were striving to enlarge their customer base.

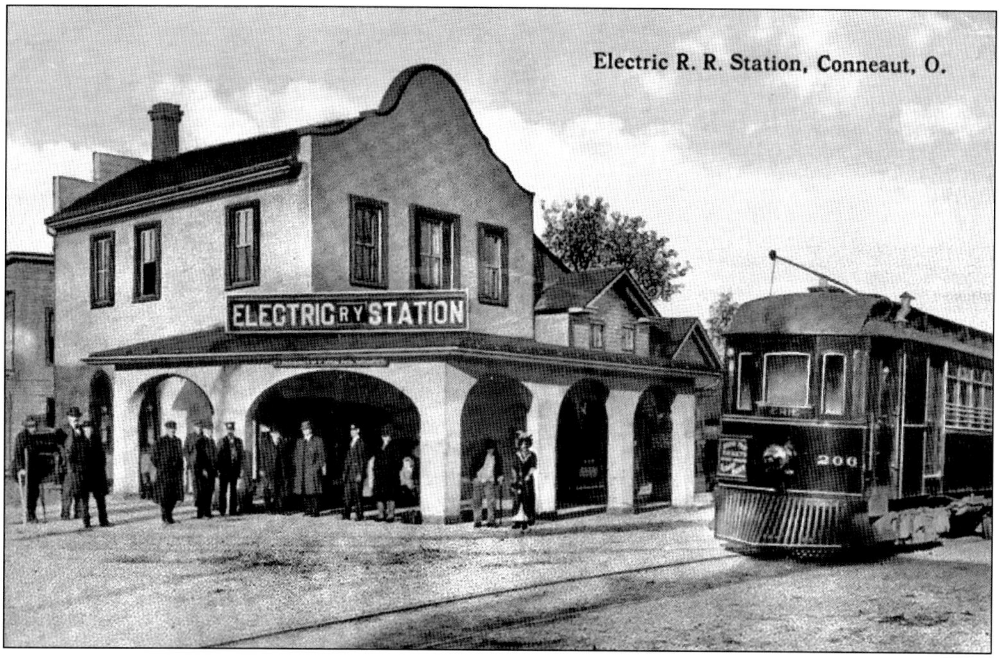

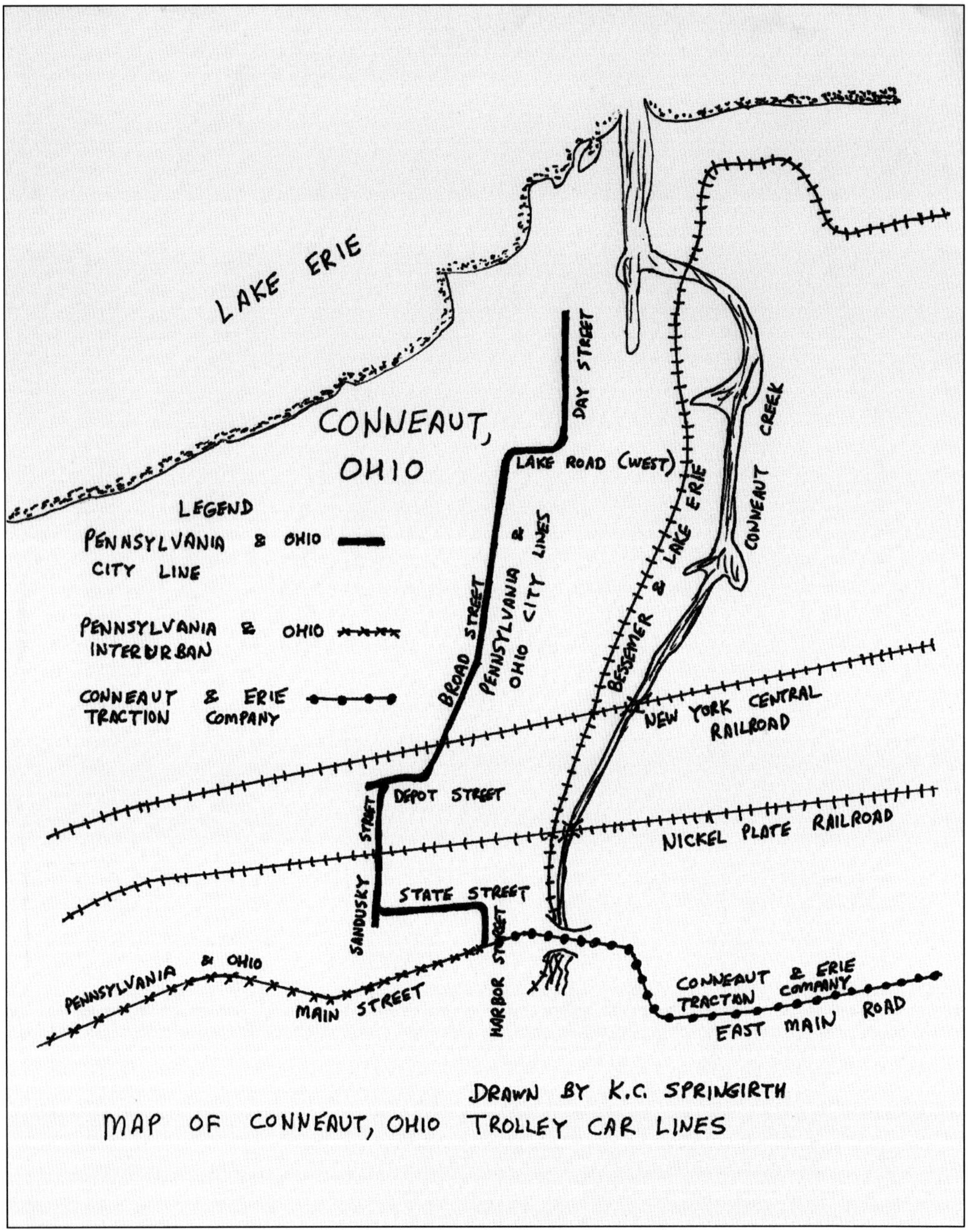

As shown on the above map of Conneaut at Main and Harbor Streets, connections could be made with the Pennsylvania and Ohio Railway for Ashtabula and for the local Conneaut line, which was also operated by the Pennsylvania and Ohio Railway. At Ashtabula, the Cleveland, Painesville and Eastern Railroad Company provided service to Cleveland.

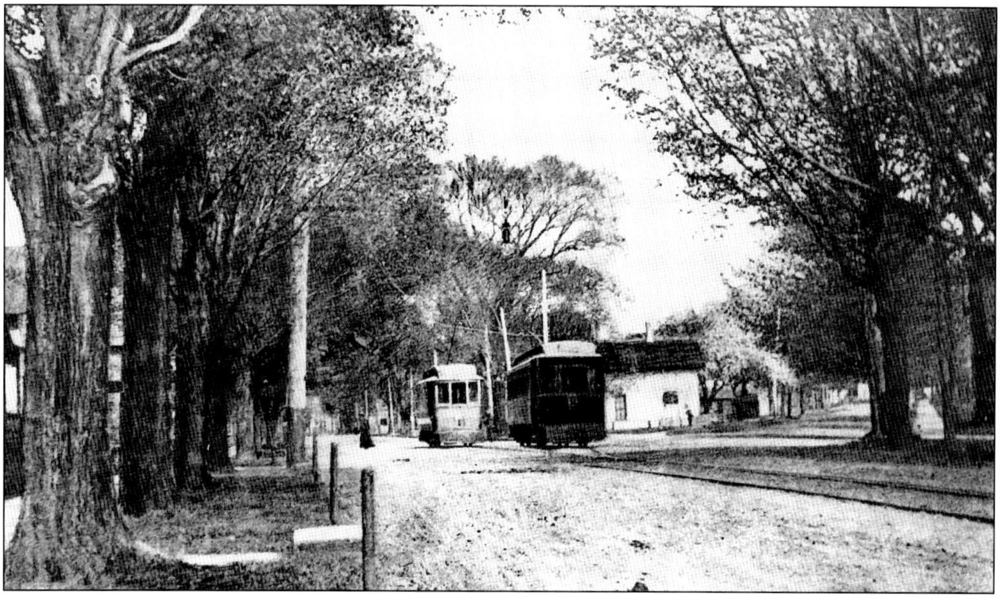

The Pennsylvania and Ohio completed its route from Ashtabula to Conneaut in 1901 and south to Jefferson, Ohio, during 1902. The McGraw Electric Railway List for August 1918 showed the company had 26 miles of track and 16 cars, but the 1924 McGraw Electric Railway Directory showed 24 miles of track and 5 cars. (J. A. Tyler photograph.)

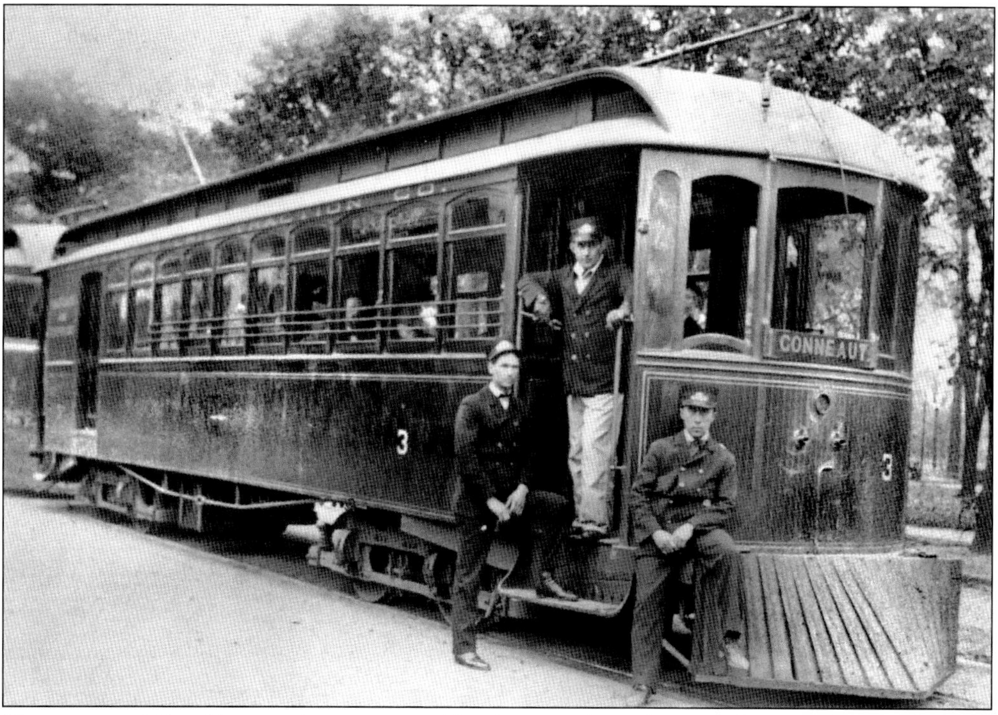

Conneaut and Erie Traction Company car No. 3 pauses for a photograph stop on Main Street in Girard with employees, from left to right, Paul Hathaway, George Calaway, and Jerrold Batchelor. It was a neat sight to see the motormen and conductors on duty, professionally dressed in the company uniform.

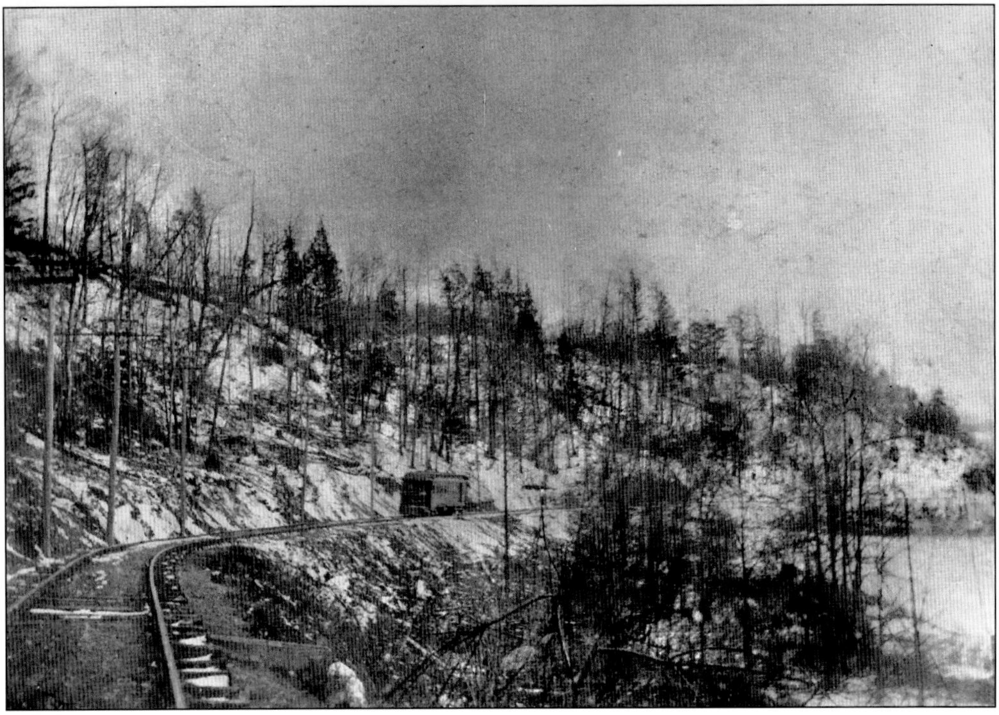

Wintertime for the Cleveland and Erie Railway could mean a dusting of snow like shown in this picture, or it could be a massive blizzard. With meager revenues and mounting expenses, the company made every effort to maintain service, but there were significant periods where drifts of snow caused a halt to service. (H. Miller photograph.)

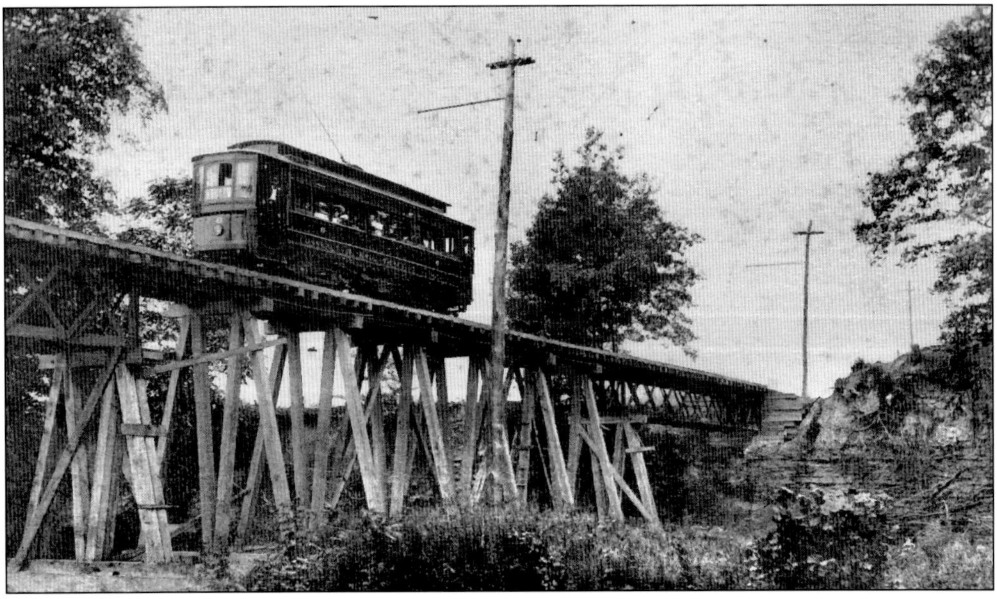

Cleveland and Erie Railway Company car No. 6 thundered across the Walnut Creek trestle near Fairview, Pennsylvania. The line traversed many streams and valleys, which required many bridges and added to maintenance expenses. Most of the communities between Erie and Conneaut were small and did not generate the ridership needed for financial solvency. (Florence Teller photograph.)

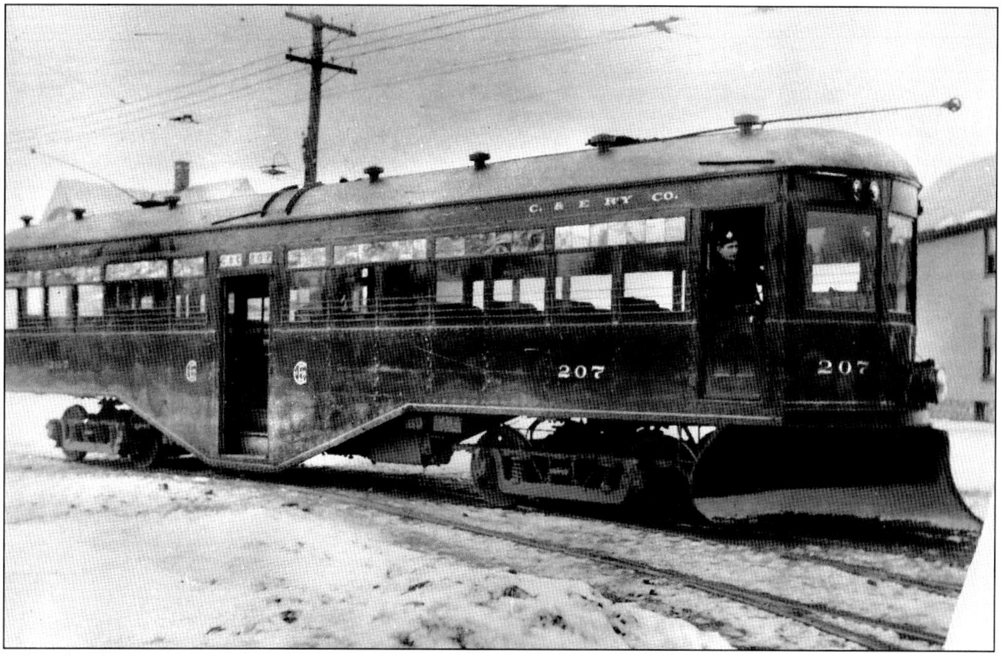

Cleveland and Erie Railway car No. 207, pictured in this 1916 snow scene, is heading into the Elk Park carbarn. This car, which arrived September 3, 1915, was built by Niles Car Company with Westinghouse motors, controls, and brakes. The center entranceway footboard was only six inches from the ground, which made it more accessible for passengers with disabilities.

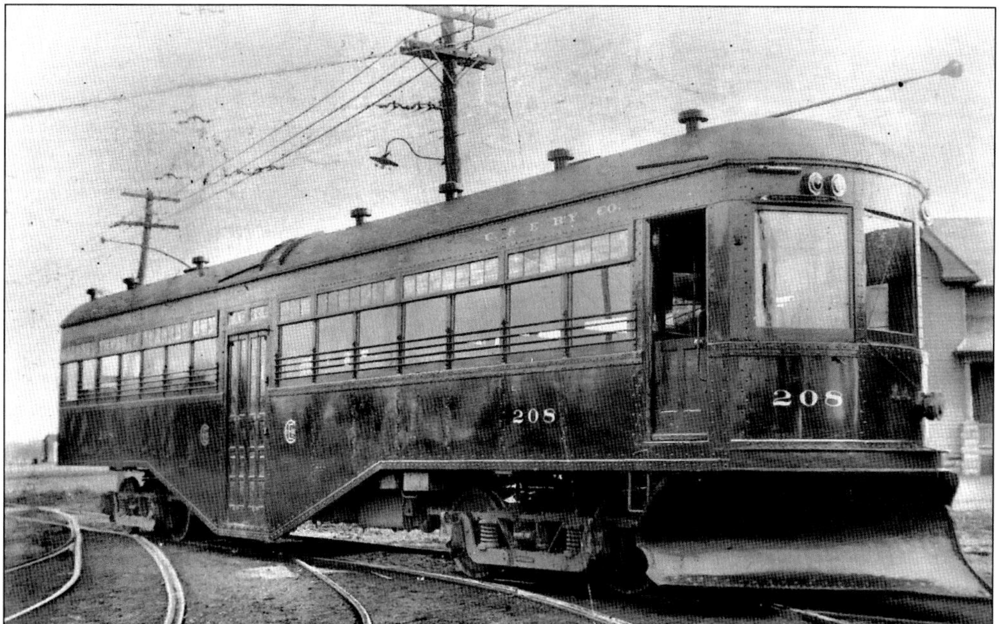

Car No. 208 was on the approach track to Elk Park carbarn. This 51-foot-long car was identical to No. 207. Struggling to meet automobile competition, the company adopted a special bargain rate for special events. For example, for the county fair of August 1921, a round-trip ticket could be purchased at a one-way ticket price.

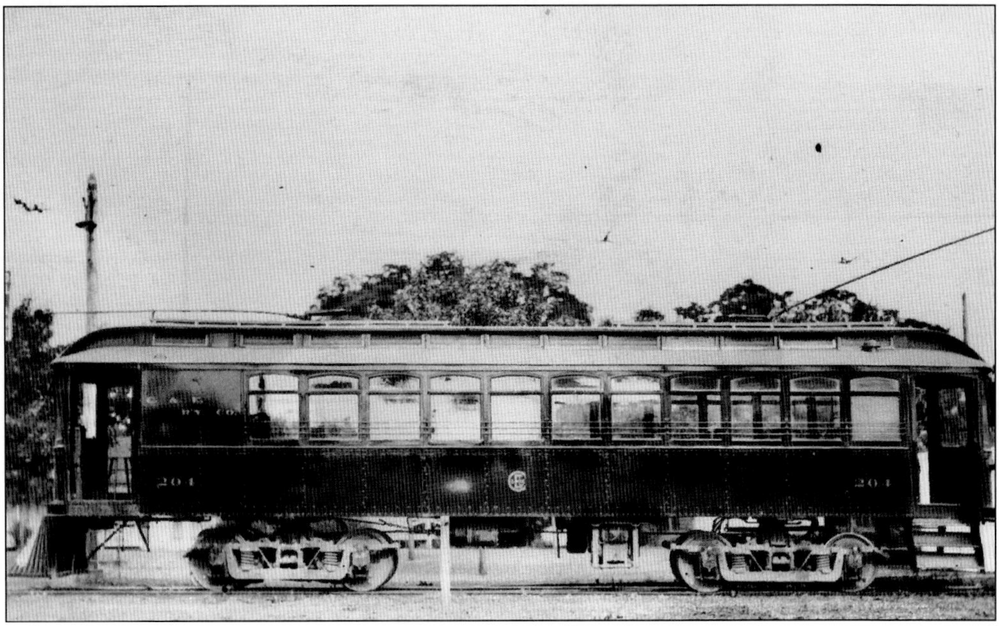

Cleveland and Erie Railway car No. 204, pictured at Elk Park, was a combination passenger and baggage car. It had a rebuilt steel body to the window rail and was equipped with General Electric 57 Quadruple motors, Westinghouse K14 controls, Westinghouse brakes, and Baldwin trucks. The company was doing everything it could to have attractive equipment to encourage riding.

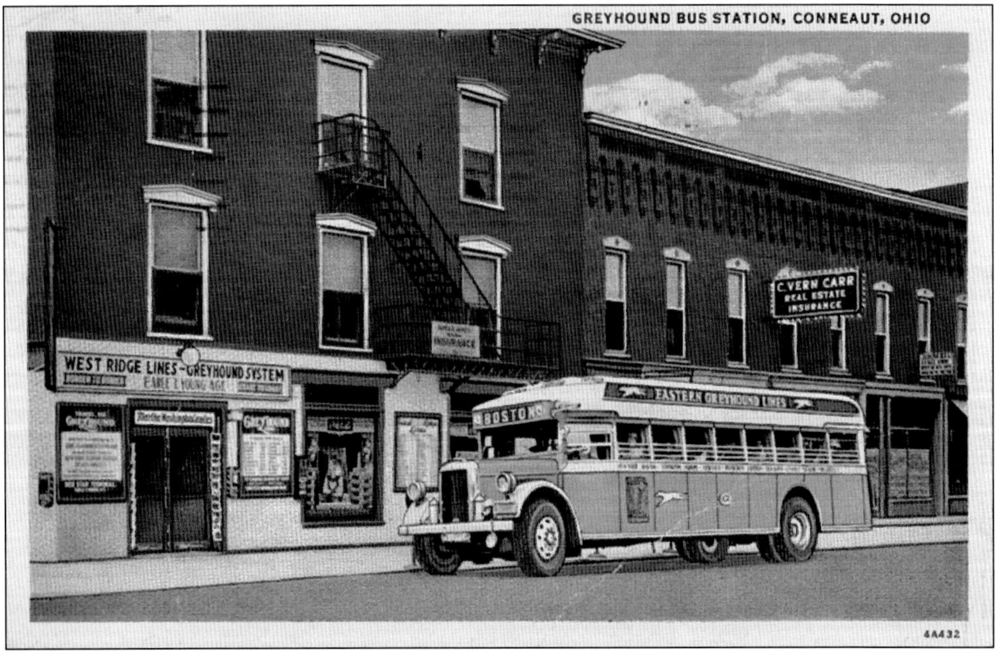

The Cleveland and Erie Railway was sold for $75,000 to the Buffalo Housewrecking Corporation. On September 16, 1922, trolley service ended. In later years, as shown on the postcard, Greyhound Bus Lines operated local service on its Cleveland to Erie route. The January 1969 schedule showed four westbound and three eastbound trips stopping at Conneaut with flag stops at Girard and Fairview.

Three

Buffalo and Lake Erie Traction Company

On September 1, 1901, the first section of the Erie–North East trolley line opened from Erie to Wesleyville. The first trolley car left Erie for North East, Pennsylvania, on November 27, 1901. Starting from Erie's Union terminal on Peach Street at noon, the special Erie Electric Motor Company car transferred passengers to a new Erie Rapid Transit Company (also known as the Lake Erie Fast Line) car at the end of the East Eighteenth Street city car line. Stops were made at Wesleyville, Power House at 6 Mile Creek in Harborcreek, and the steel bridge at 16 Mile Creek. The trolley arrived in North East at 1:55 p.m. Regular service began on November 28, 1901. As the Lake Erie Fast Line began trolley car service from North East to Ripley, New York, on Sunday, May 3, 1903, the Buffalo Dunkirk and Western was building westward from Fredonia along what is today U.S. Highway 20. Lake Erie Fast Line began through operation from Erie to Westfield on October 14, 1903. The Erie Electric Motor Company, Hamburg Railway, Buffalo, Dunkirk and Western, Dunkirk and Fredonia, and the Lake Erie Fast Line were merged into the Buffalo and Lake Erie Traction Company on December 24, 1906. On Friday, November 10, 1911, the Buffalo and Lake Erie Traction Company completed a new route through Lawrence Park just east of Erie. The new line went out to Harborcreek via Iroquois Avenue, eliminating congested Buffalo Road as an entranceway into Erie. On July 14, 1915, the Buffalo and Lake Erie Traction Company was in the hands of a receiver. A petition was filed to the New York State Public Service Commission on April 19, 1918, to abandon the line from Fredonia to the Pennsylvania state line by Buffalo and Lake Erie receiver George Bullock unless the company was granted a fare increase. Revenues continued to decline. On May 29, 1920, the company petitioned to abandon the entire Erie to Buffalo line. The company was sold and became the Buffalo and Erie Railway Company on September 5, 1924. Fourteen new one-man operated cars built by Cincinnati Car Company were placed in service on December 17, 1924. The new cars lowered operating costs, but the company went into receivership on June 8, 1928. On Thursday, December 1, 1932, the company discontinued trolley service from Buffalo to Angola and between Erie and the New York state line. Operator William S. Morgan of Fredonia operated the last trolley, No. 50, from Fredonia at 8:00 p.m. on Friday, January 27, 1933. The trolley arrived at Angola at 1:00 on Saturday morning, January 28, 1933, closing the final curtain on the Erie to Buffalo line.

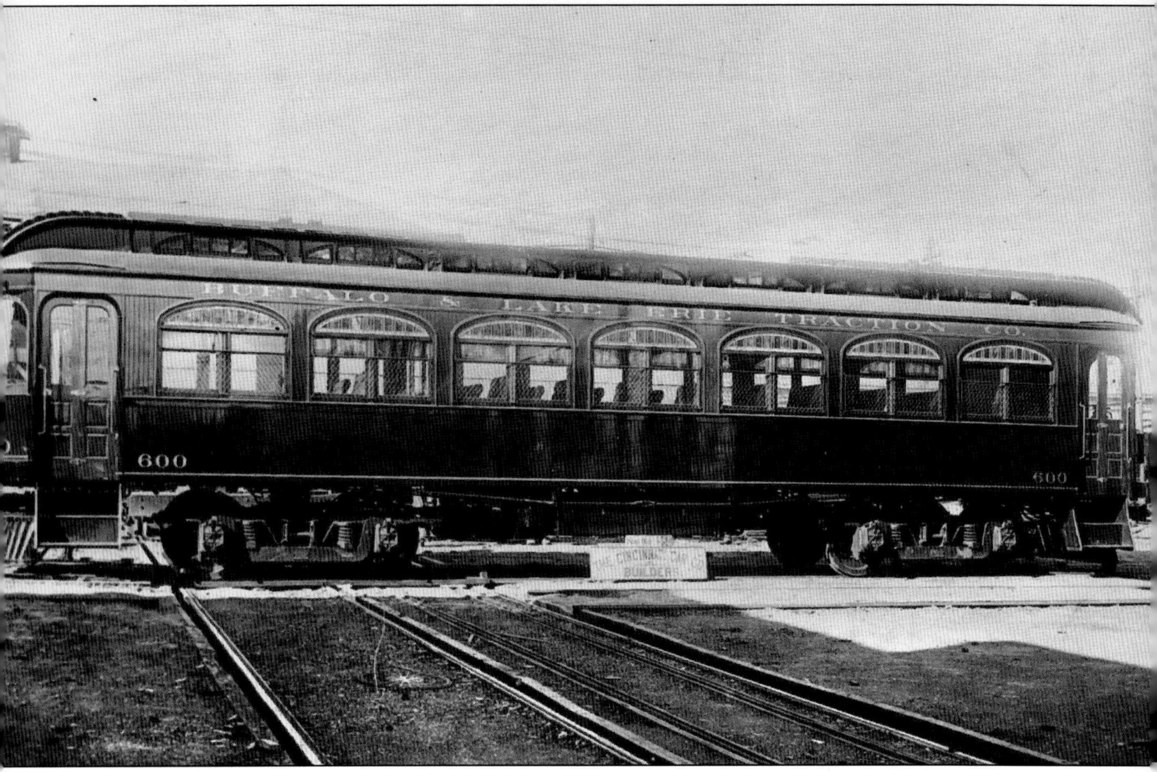

Buffalo and Lake Erie Traction Company car No. 600 is shown in this 1908 builder's photograph at Kuhlman Car Company. Each car had a top speed of 65 miles per hour and had four General Electric No. 204-A commutating pole motors with double type N control. The cars had Westinghouse air brakes and were mounted on Baldwin trucks with Symington journal boxes. Both the main passenger and smoking compartments were finished with Honduras mahogany. The cars featured art glass Gothic windows, a nickeline watercooler, reversible seats with mahogany armrests in the aisle, and smoking compartment seats with dark green leather. Cars Nos. 600, 601, 602, and 603 were passenger and smoker cars seating 54 passengers. Cars Nos. 604, 605, 606, and 607 were passenger, baggage, and smoker cars seating 54 passengers. (R. F. Corley photograph.)

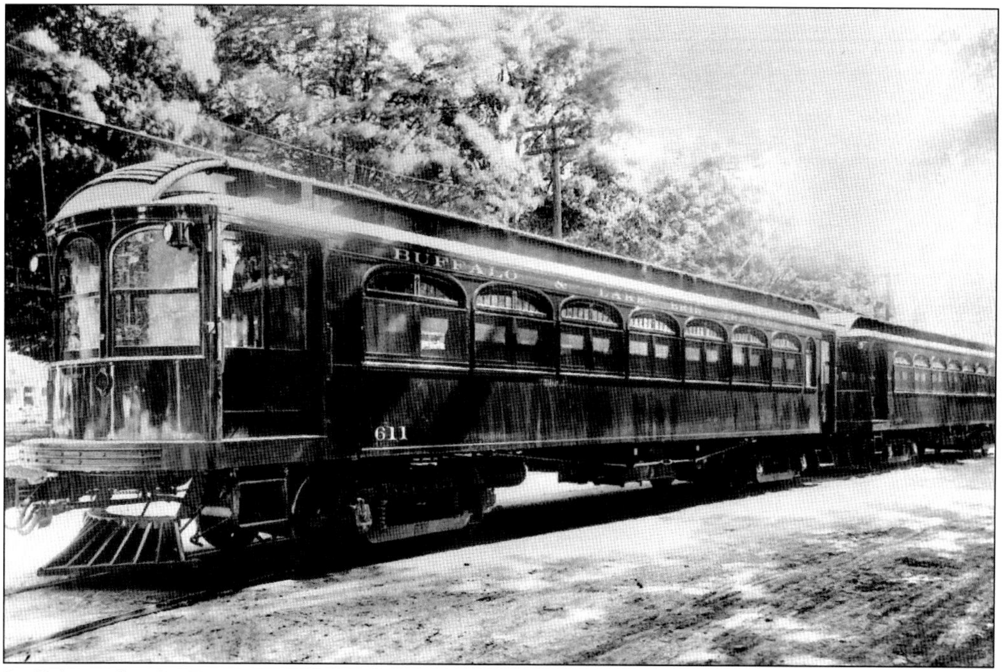

Buffalo and Lake Erie Traction Company car No. 611 in this builder's photograph was built by Cincinnati Car Company. This was a classic interurban trolley car with a metal frame and art glass Gothic windows, and the roof was the monitor deck type with a steam coach style of hood at each end.

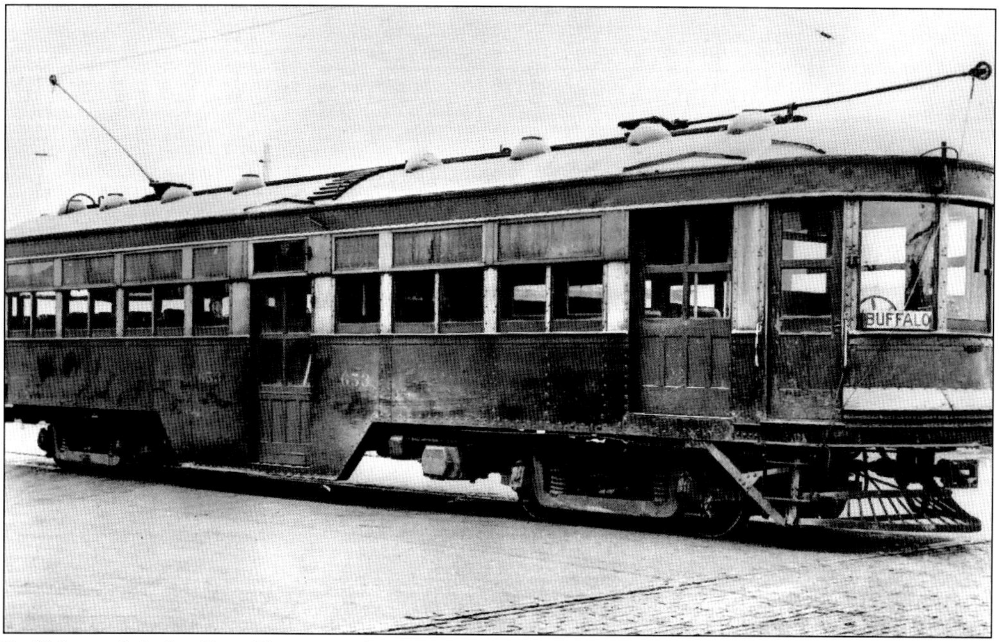

Buffalo and Lake Erie Traction Company car No. 653 is a center-entrance trolley with 4 GE-203-P motors in this 1923 scene in Erie. By December 31, 1924, all two-man cars were out of service having been replaced by one-man cars, which made a significant reduction in operating costs.

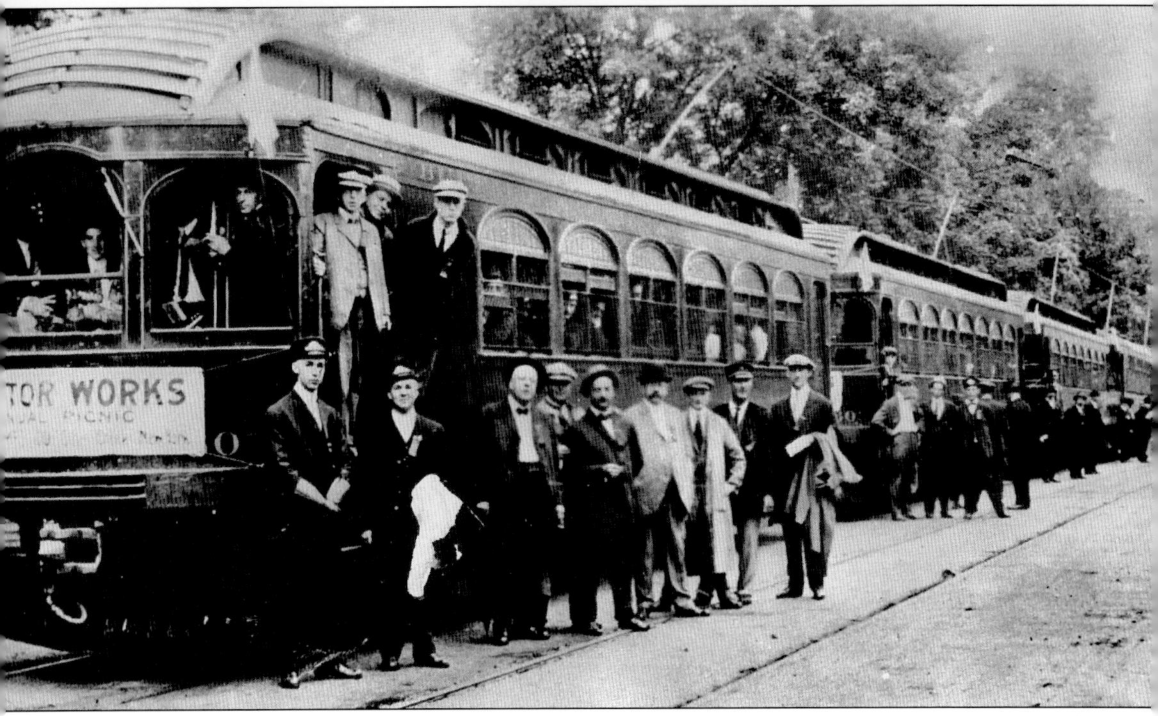

Buffalo and Lake Erie Traction Company trolley cars had lined up for the Monitor Works annual picnic on August 24, 1914. These trolleys below the sash rest are sheathed with five-eighths-inch by two-inch vertical poplar sheathing. The lower sash was arranged to rise into the roof. The upper sash of the side windows were semi-elliptic and were glazed with leaded art glass.

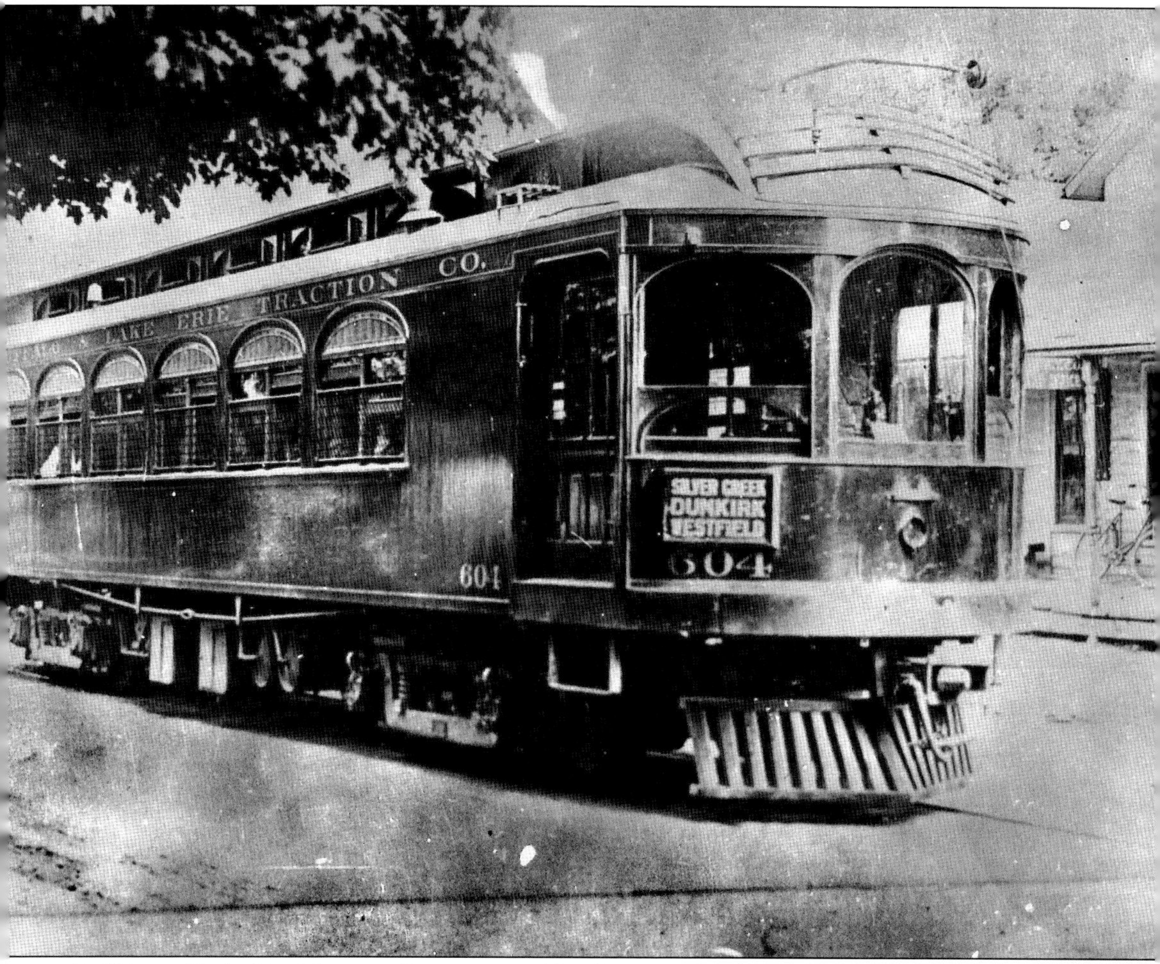

Buffalo and Lake Erie Traction Company car No. 604 was a combination passenger and baggage car. Interior illumination was by seven 12-inch hemisphere Holophone globes in the upper ceiling and some single lamps on the face of the doorsill. The car was used in through service from Erie to Buffalo, which began on January 1, 1909, with the completion of the 1,100-foot-long bridge over Chautauqua Creek at Westfield, New York. (R. Nash photograph.)

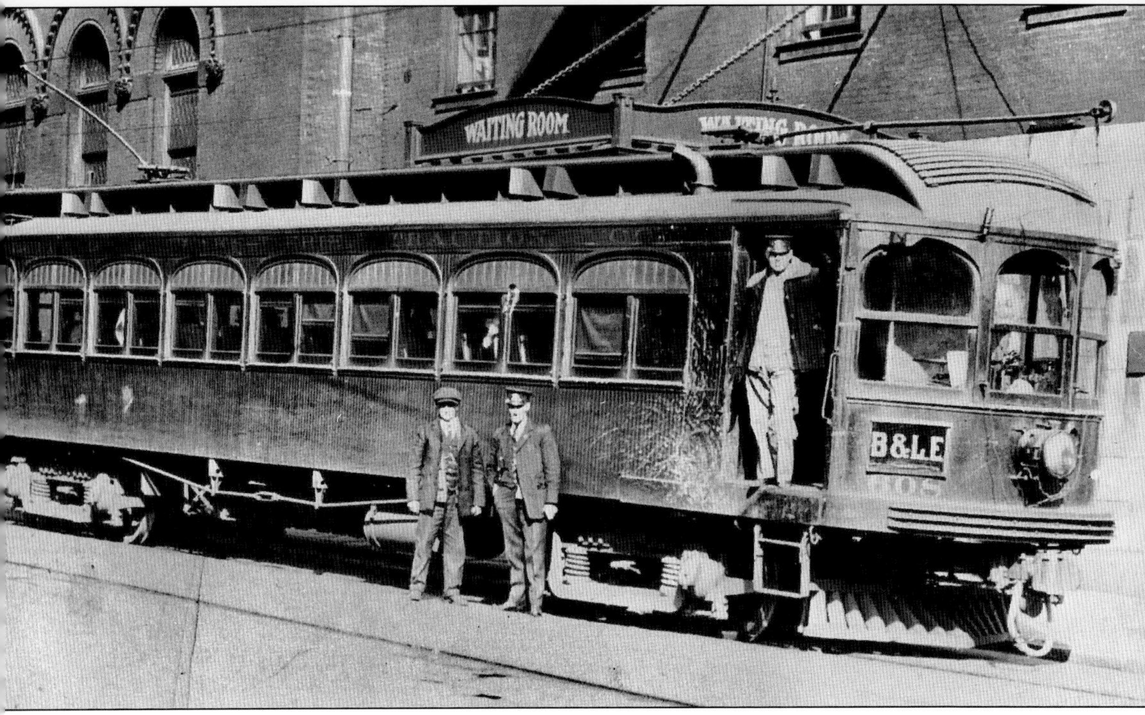

Buffalo and Lake Erie Traction Company car No. 608 is pictured at the trolley station near Lafayette Square in Buffalo. Beginning July 1, 1909, the Buffalo and Lake Erie Traction Company sold mileage books. Each book provided 300 miles of trolley riding for $5.25. Commutation books were also available and were sold at the rate of $1.25 per mile.

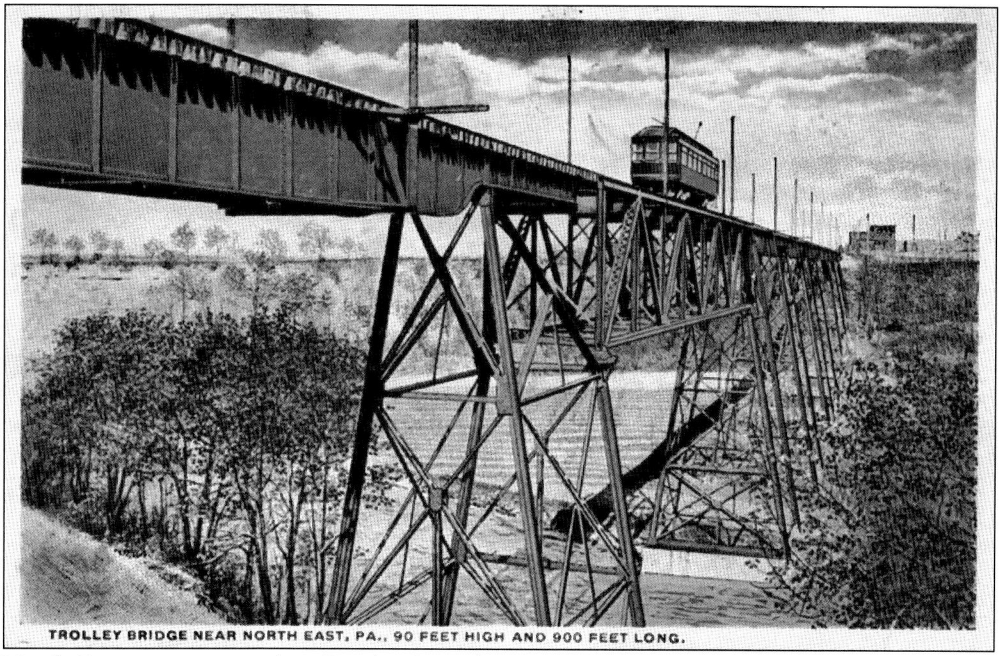

North East was connected to Erie by the Lake Erie Fast Line, which completed a trolley line from North East to Ripley, New York, on Sunday, May 3, 1903. To speed up service and eliminate heavy grades where the trolley line crossed 18 Mile Creek just east of North East, the Lake Erie Fast line built a 900-foot-long and 90-foot-high trestle.

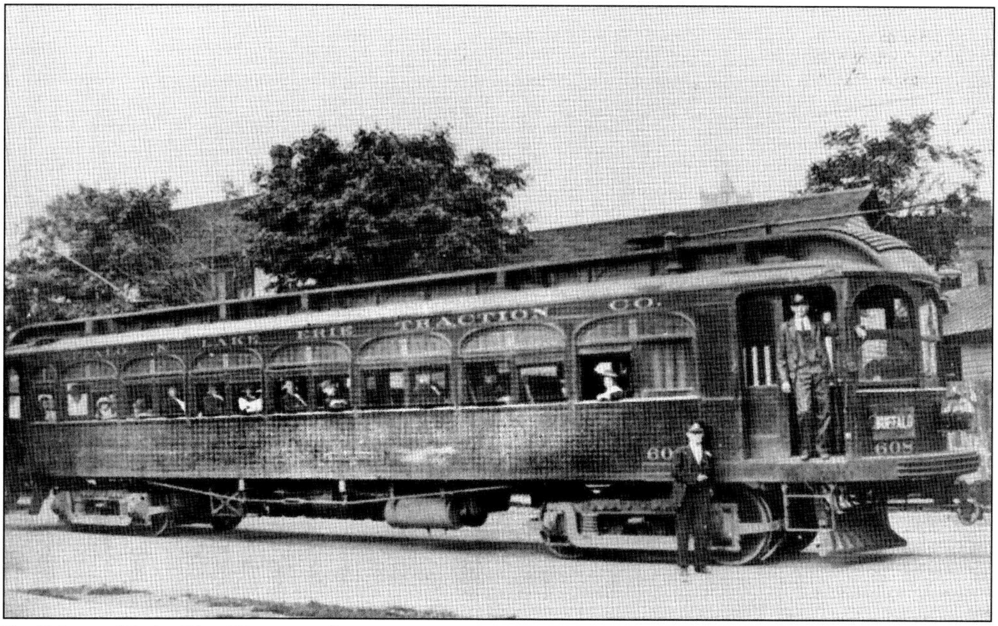

Buffalo and Lake Erie Traction Company car No. 608 is pictured in Erie in 1920 with motorman Mr. Rickman and conductor Bill Morgan. On June 1, 1922, a faster schedule was established between Erie and Buffalo with some trips covering the distance in three hours and 15 minutes. Schedules were also adjusted to make better connections with the Chautauqua Traction Company at Westfield, New York.

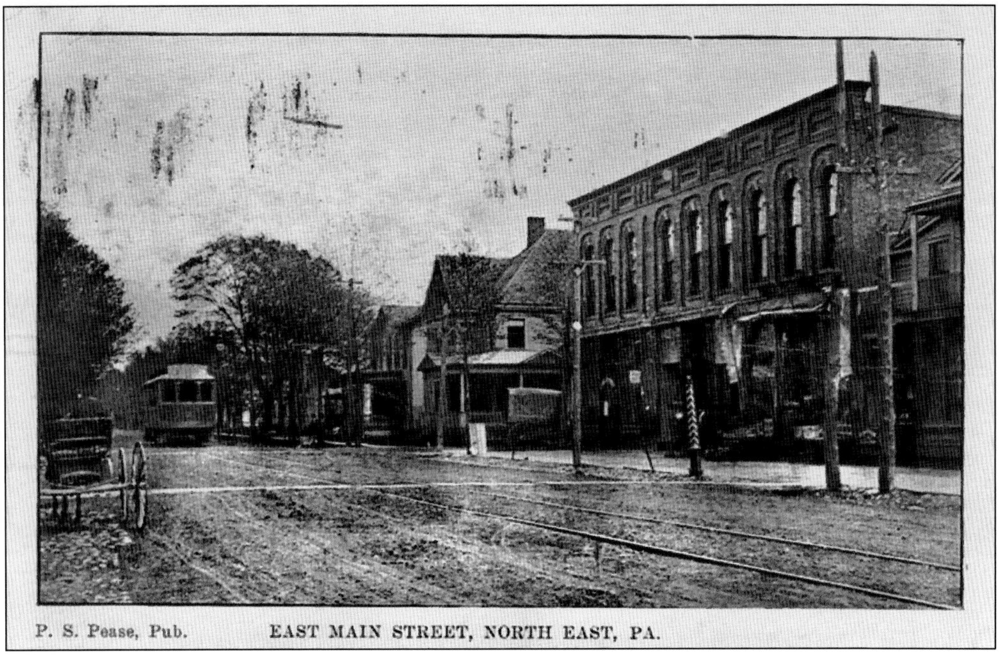

A Lake Erie Fast Line trolley passes through East Main Street in North East. The March 12, 1906, edition of the *Buffalo Express* headlined that a big trolley merger would result in one company operating trolley service between Erie and Buffalo. On August 8, 1906, the company was sold for $50,000 and was merged into the Buffalo and Lake Erie Traction Company.

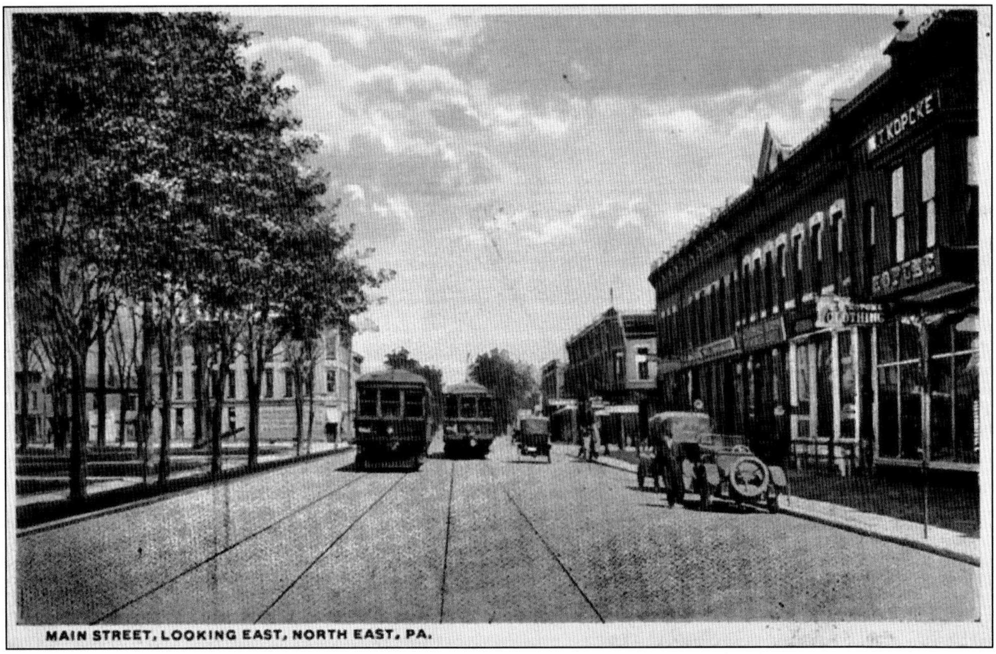

Two Buffalo and Lake Erie Traction Company cars pass on Main Street looking east to Lake Street in North East. The November 28, 1901, schedule from Erie to North East showed eastbound and westbound service was hourly from 6:00 a.m. to 6:00 p.m. The fare was 5¢ from Erie to Wesleyville and an additional 5¢ to Moorheadville. One-way fare to North East was 20¢.

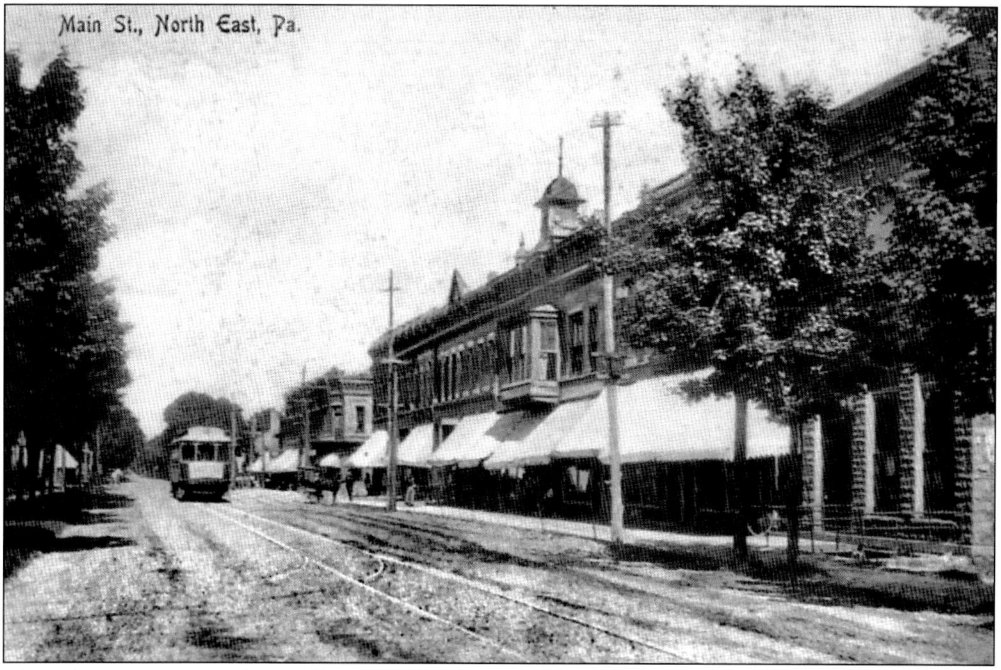

Main Street just west of Lake Street in North East provided the setting for a Lake Erie Fast Line trolley. The Buffalo and Lake Erie Traction Company was building westward from Fredonia, New York, along what is today U.S. Highway Route 20. Farmers were delighted with the prospect of shipping fruits and vegetables by trolley directly to the stores and hotels in Buffalo.

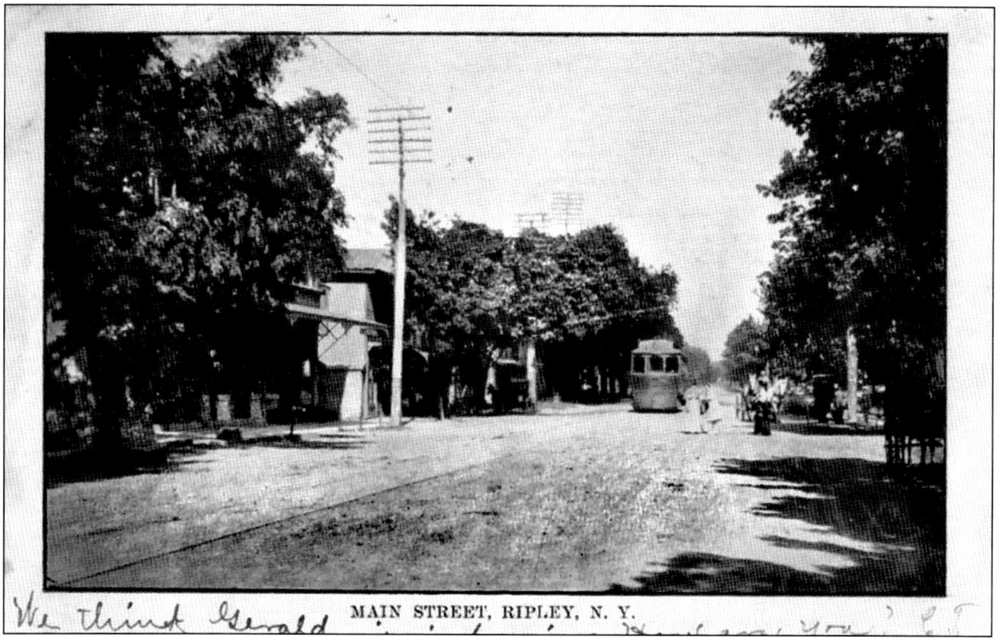

A Lake Erie Fast Line trolley car passes through Main Street in Ripley in this postcard scene. The company had financial problems, which resulted in the seizure of their trolleys and chaining them to telegraph poles on July 6, 1904. Fortunately agreement was reached to permit trolley service to resume.

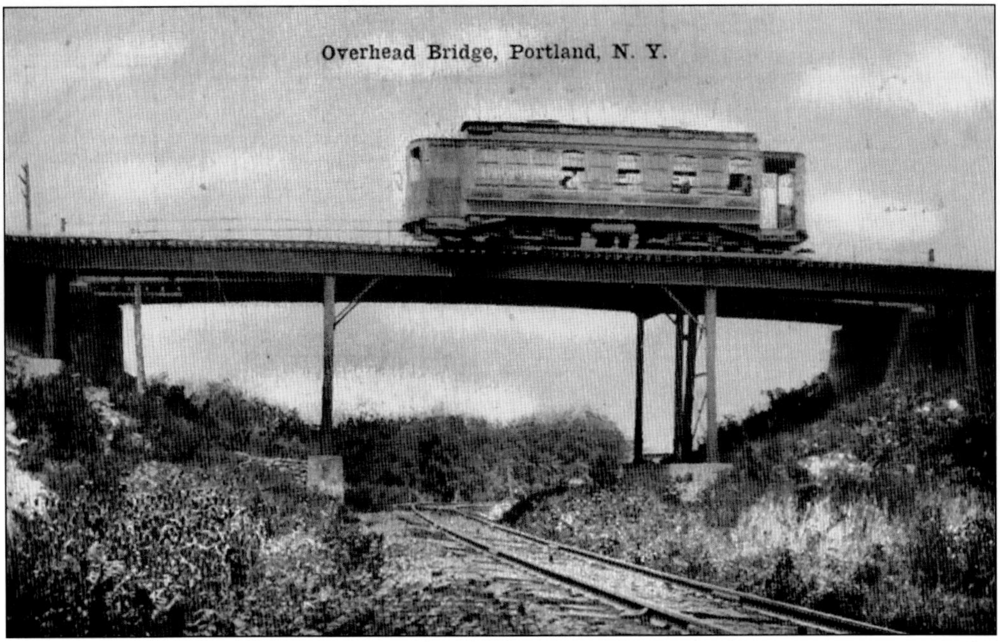

At Portland, New York, a Buffalo and Lake Erie Traction Company car crosses over the Pennsylvania Railroad line from East Brady, Pennsylvania, to Brocton, New York. Effective May 1, 1910, through service was operated hourly between Fredonia, New York, and Erie. Fredonia, which is east of Portland, was halfway between Erie and Buffalo, and it was a natural division point with a carbarn and offices.

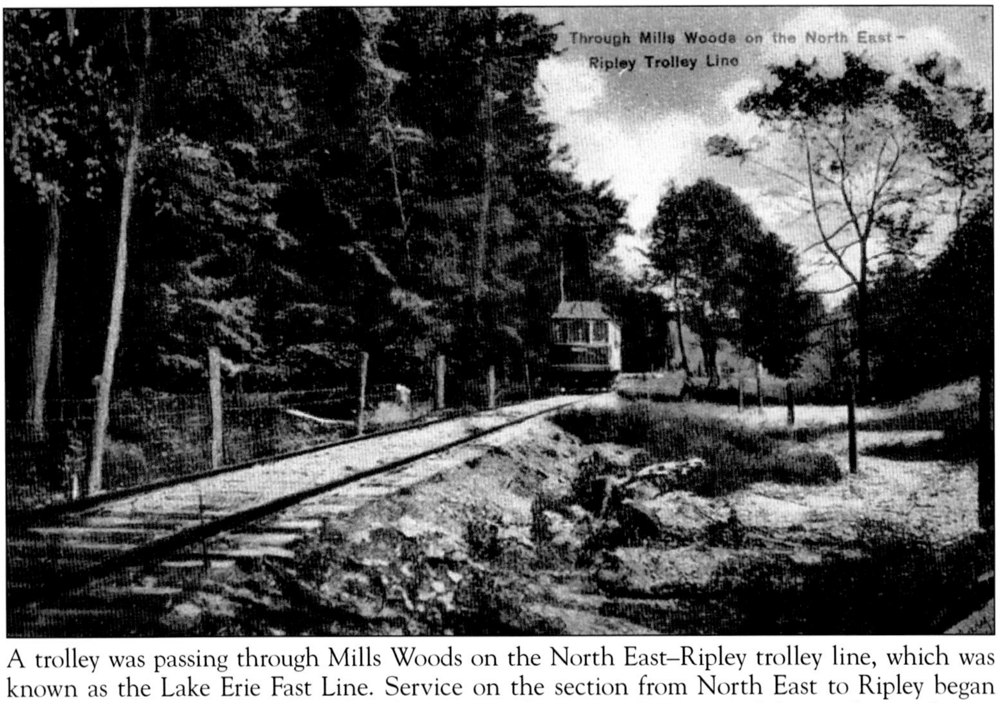

A trolley was passing through Mills Woods on the North East–Ripley trolley line, which was known as the Lake Erie Fast Line. Service on the section from North East to Ripley began Sunday, May 3, 1903. This line played a unique role in providing accessibility to the rural areas of northwestern Pennsylvania and southwestern New York.

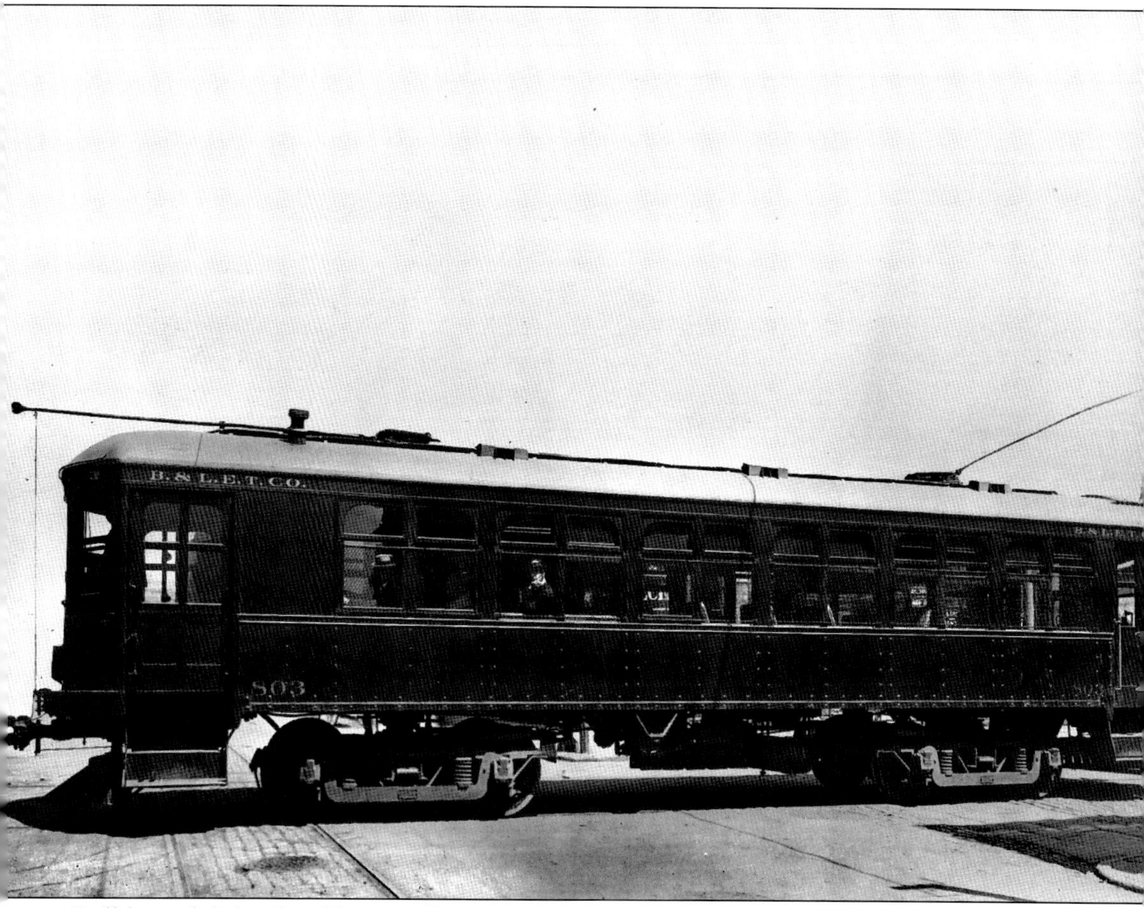

Buffalo and Lake Erie Traction Company car No. 803 was a heavy weight car. Effective December 26, 1909, cars for Buffalo left Fredonia at 5:45 a.m., 6:46 a.m., and every hour until 10:46 p.m. Cars from Buffalo to Fredonia were hourly on the hour. Cars for Westfield, New York, left Fredonia at 4:50 a.m., 6:00 a.m., and then every hour until 11:00 p.m. Cars from Westfield arrived at Fredonia at 6:50 a.m. and every hour until 10:50 p.m.

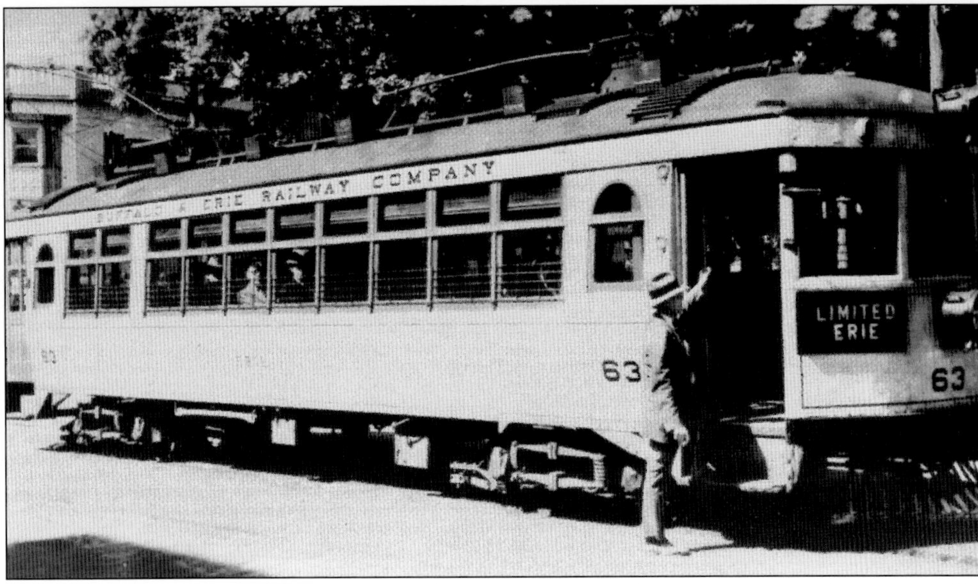

Buffalo and Erie Railway Company car No. 63 was one of 14 cars built by the Cincinnati Car Company and placed in service on the Erie to Buffalo run on December 17, 1924. The car featured curved side construction with steel side panels, wood window posts, and wood letter boards. The exterior was painted medium cadmium yellow.

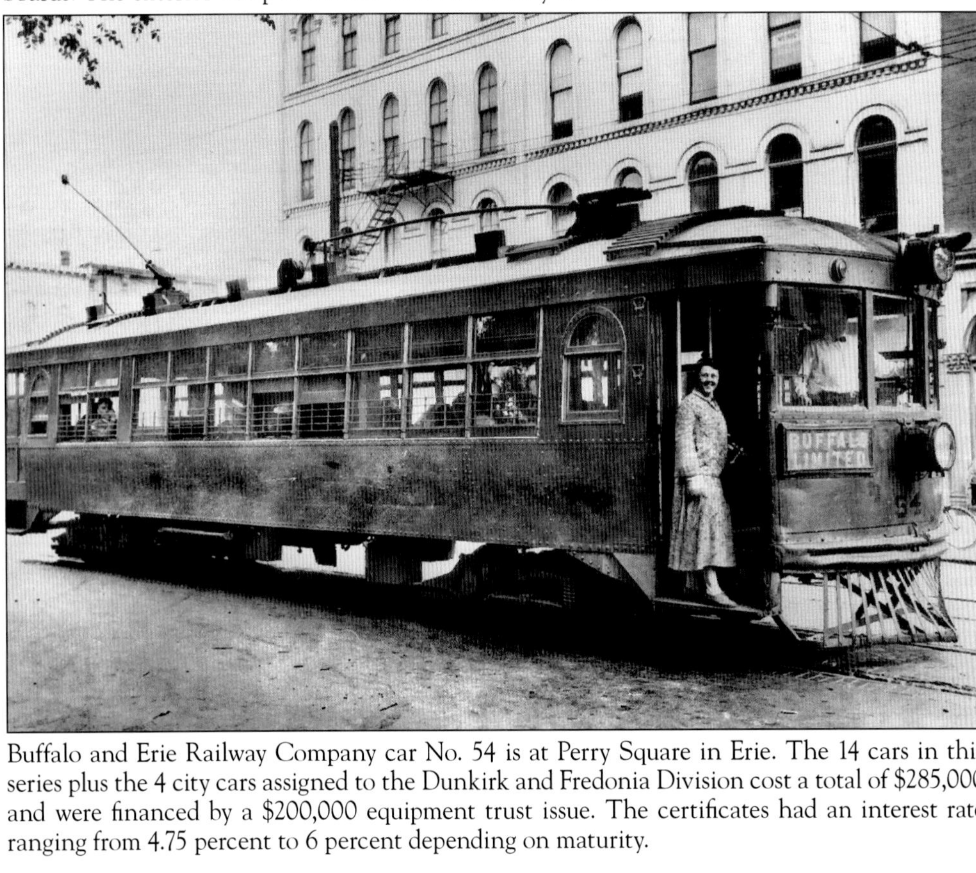

Buffalo and Erie Railway Company car No. 54 is at Perry Square in Erie. The 14 cars in this series plus the 4 city cars assigned to the Dunkirk and Fredonia Division cost a total of $285,000 and were financed by a $200,000 equipment trust issue. The certificates had an interest rate ranging from 4.75 percent to 6 percent depending on maturity.

FICIAL TIME RECORD — BUFFALO & ERIE RAILWAY COMPANY — EFFECTIVE OCT (Eastern Stand

WESTWARD	Daily Except Sunday	Daily Except Sunday	Daily	Daily	Daily Except Sunday	Daily	*Daily	Daily	Daily	Daily Limited	Daily	Daily	Daily Limited	Daily	Daily	Daily Limited	Daily	Daily	Daily Limited	Daily	Daily	Daily Limited	Daily	†Daily	Daily Except Sunday	Daily
	A.M.	A.M.	A.M.	A.M.	A.M.	A.M.	A.M.	A.M.	A.M.	A.M.	A.M.	P.M.	A.M.	Noon	P.M.	P.M.	P.M.	P.M.	P.M.	P.M.	P.M.	P.M.	P.M.	P.M.	P.M.	P.M.
ffalo							7 00	8 00		9 00	10 00		11 00	12 00		1 00	2 00		3 00	4 00		5 00	5 00	6 00	6 00	7 2
ckawanna				5 10	6 10	6 20	7 20	8 17		9 17	10 17		11 17	12 17		1 17	2 17		3 17	4 17		5 17	5 17	6 17	6 17	7 4
odlawn				5 15	6 15	6 25	7 25	8 23			10 23			12 23			2 23			4 22			5 23		6 23	7 4
nol Springs				5 20	6 20	6 30	7 31	8 32			10 32			12 32			2 32			4 32			5 32		6 38	7 5
nakah				5 25	6 25	6 35	7 38	8 38			10 38			12 38			2 38			4 38			5 38		6 48	8 0
ke View				5 28	6 28	6 38	7 43	8 41			10 41			12 41			2 41			4 43			5 41		6 52	8 0
rth Evans				5 30	6 30	6 40	7 44	8 45			10 45			12 45			2 45			4 45			5 45		6 54	8 0
rby				5 38	6 35	6 43	7 48	8 51			10 51			12 51			2 51			4 50			5 51		6 59	8 1
gola				5 48	6 43	6 48	7 55	8 57		9 51	10 57		11 51	12 57		1 51	2 57		3 51	5 00		5 51	5 57	6 51	7 08	8 1
ke Erie Beach				5 51		6 51	7 59	9 00			11 00			1 00			3 00			5 03			6 00	6 54		8 2
rnham				5 57		6 59	8 05	9 05		9 58	11 05		11 58	1 05		1 58	3 05		3 58	5 10		5 58	6 05	7 00		8 2
ing				6 02		7 02	8 09	9 09			11 09			1 09			3 09			5 14			6 09	7 05		8 3
nford's Bay				6 07		7 06	8 12	9 12			11 12			1 12			3 12			5 24			6 12	7 09		8 3
ver Creek				6 15		7 12	8 18	9 17		10 10	11 17		12 10	1 17		2 10	3 17		4 10	5 30		6 10	6 17	7 17		8 4
eridan				6 29		7 25	8 29	9 31			11 31			1 31			3 31			5 42			6 31	7 28		8 5
nkirk 4th & Main				6 47		7 39	8 46	9 46		10 34	11 46		12 34	1 46		2 34	3 46		4 34	6 00		6 34	6 46	7 46		9 1
nkirk 4th & Central				6 48		7 40	8 47			10 35			12 35			2 35			4 35			6 35	6 47	7 47		9 1
donia		5 15	5 55	7 03		7 55	9 00		10 05	10 49		12 05	12 49		2 05	2 49		4 05	4 49		6 05	6 49	7 00	8 00		9 2
cton		5 27	6 07	7 16		8 10	9 11		10 19	11 00		12 19	1 00		2 19	3 00		4 26	5 00		6 19	7 00		8 12		9 3
tland		5 32	6 11	7 20		8 15	9 14		10 23	11 03		12 23	1 03		2 23	3 03		4 31	5 03		6 23	7 03		8 16		9 4
stfield		5 43	6 24	7 35		8 30	9 23		10 35	11 12		12 35	1 12		2 35	3 12		4 46	5 12		6 35	7 12		8 28		9 5
ley		6 04	6 38	7 56		8 55	9 38		10 55	11 30		12 55	1 30		2 55	3 30		5 07	5 30		6 55	7 30		8 45		10 10
te Line		6 15	6 49	8 06		9 05			11 05			1 05			3 05			5 16			7 05			8 53		10 19
rth East	5 55	6 24	6 58	8 20		9 13	9 53		11 14	11 45		1 14	1 45		3 14	3 45		5 25	5 45		7 14	7 45		9 02		10 27
orheadville	6 05	6 35	7 07	8 34		9 30			11 30			1 30			3 30			5 35			7 30			9 12		10 38
rbor Creek	6 12	6 39	7 13	8 38		9 34	10 04		11 35	11 57		1 35	1 57		3 35	3 57		5 42	5 57		7 35	7 59		9 17		10 43
e	6 35	7 05	7 40	9 03		9 57	10 30		11 57	12 20		1 57	2 20		3 57	4 20		6 05	6 20		7 57	8 20		9 40		11 05
	A.M.	A.M.	A.M.	A.M.	A.M.	A.M.	A.M.	A.M.	A.M.	P.M.	A.M.	P.M.	P.M.	P.M.	P.M.	P.M.	P.M.	P.M.	P.M.	P.M.	P.M.	P.M.	P.M.	P.M.	P.M.	P.M.

EASTWARD	Daily Except Sunday	Daily Except Sunday	Daily Except Sunday	Daily	Daily Except Sunday	Daily	Daily	Daily Limited	Daily	Daily	Daily Limited	Daily	Daily	Daily Limited	Daily	Daily	Daily Limited	Daily	Daily	Daily Limited	Daily	Daily	Daily	Daily Limited	Daily	Daily
	A.M.	A.M.	A.M.	A.M.	A.M.	A.M.	A.M.	A.M.	A.M.	A.M.	A.M.	A.M.	A.M.	A.M.	P.M.	P.M.	P.M.	P.M.	P.M.	P.M.	P.M.	P.M.	P.M.	P.M.	P.M.	P.M.
e	5 10		4 45				5 50	7 05	8 05		9 05	10 05		11 05	12 05		1 05	2 05		3 05	4 05		4 30	5 05	6 00	7 25
rbor Creek	5 31		5 07				6 11	7 25	8 28		9 25	10 28		11 25	12 28		1 25	2 28		3 25	4 28		4 53	5 25	6 23	7 46
orheadville	5 35		5 12				6 17		8 33			10 33			12 33			2 33			4 33		5 00		6 28	7 54
th East	5 45		5 21				6 26	7 36	8 43		9 36	10 43		11 36	12 43		1 36	2 43		3 36	4 43		5 14	5 36	6 36	8 03
e Line			5 32				6 36		8 55			10 55			12 55			2 55			4 55		5 26		6 45	8 14
ley			5 37				6 43	7 51	9 01		9 51	11 01		11 51	101		1 51	3 01		3 51	5 01		5 35	5 51	6 50	8 20
tfield			5 53				6 58	8 07	9 22		10 07	11 22		12 07	1 22		2 07	3 22		4 07	5 22		5 53	6 07	7 12	8 39
tland			6 11				7 12	8 22	9 37		10 22	11 37		12 22	1 37		2 22	3 37		4 22	5 37		6 11	6 22	7 26	8 52
cton			6 15				7 17	8 27	9 42		10 27	11 42		12 27	1 42		2 27	3 42		4 27	5 42		6 19	6 27	7 31	8 56
lonia		4 45	6 30	5 50		6 55	7 35	8 42	9 56		10 42	11 56		12 42	1 56		2 42	3 56		4 42	5 56		6 33	6 42	7 47	9 10
kirk 4th & Central		4 54	6 44	6 00		7 09	7 44	8 51			10 51			12 51			2 51			4 51				6 51	7 56	9 19
kirk 4th & Main		4 55	6 45	6 01		7 10	7 45	8 52		9 54	10 52		11 54	12 52		1 54	2 52		3 54	4 52		6 04		6 52	7 57	9 20
ridan		5 16		6 16		7 24	7 59			10 08			12 08			2 08			4 08			6 20			8 15	9 37
er Creek		5 26		6 27		7 35	8 09	9 17		10 21	11 17		12 21	1 17		2 21	3 17		4 21	5 17		6 31		7 17	8 29	9 47
ford's Bay		5 29		6 30		7 38	8 13			10 25			12 25			2 25			4 25			6 35			8 33	9 51
ng		5 35		6 36		7 43	8 18			10 30			12 ;0			2 30			4 30			6 39			8 36	9 56
nham		5 40		6 41		7 48	8 23	9 27		10 25	11 27		12 35	1 27		2 35	3 27		4 35	5 27		6 43		7 27	8 40	10 00
e Erie Beach		5 43		6 43		7 52	8 28			10 40			12 40			2 40			4 40			6 48			8 44	10 05
ola		5 50		6 48	7 06	7 56	8 31	9 35		10 43	11 35		12 43	1 35		2 43	3 35		4 43	5 35		6 51		7 35	8 46	10 08
by		5 56		6 54	7 11	8 04	8 41			10 50			12 50			2 50			4 50			6 59			8 53	10 16
h Evans		5 58		6 58	7 14	8 07	8 45			10 54			12 54			2 54			4 54			7 02			8 55	10 18
e View		6 00		7 00	7 16	8 09	8 47			10 56			12 56			2 56			4 56			7 04			8 57	10 20
akah		6 04		7 04	7 20	8 13	8 50			11 00			1 00			3 00			5 00			7 08			9 00	10 24
ol Springs		6 11		7 11	7 29	8 17	8 56			11 05			1 05			3 05			5 05			7 15			9 05	10 29
dlawn		6 16		7 15	7 32	8 22	9 01			11 09			1 09			3 09			5 09			7 19			9 09	10 34
kawanna		6 20		7 20	7 36	8 27	9 05	10 02		11 15	12 02		1 15	2 02		3 15	4 02		5 19	6 05		7 23		8 01	9 14	10 37
falo		6 47		7 47	8 00	8 50	9 40	10 25		11 40	12 25		1 40	2 25		3 40	4 25		5 40	6 30		7 47		8 25	9 35	11 00
	A.M.	A.M.	A.M.	A.M.	A.M.	A.M.	A.M.	A.M.	A.M.	A.M.	P.M.	A.M.	P.M.	P.M.	P.M.	P.M.	P.M.	P.M.	P.M.	P.M.	P.M.	P.M.	P.M.	P.M.	P.M.	P.M.

Limited trains stop where time is shown only. *Local Buffalo to Fredonia, limited Fredonia to Erie. †Limited Buffalo to Angola, loc

The October 1, 1925, timetable of the Buffalo and Erie Railway Company showed 11 daily westbound trips from Buffalo to Erie and 10 eastbound trips from Erie to Buffalo. In addition, there were trips that operated over portions of the line from Fredonia to Erie and from Buffalo to Dunkirk.

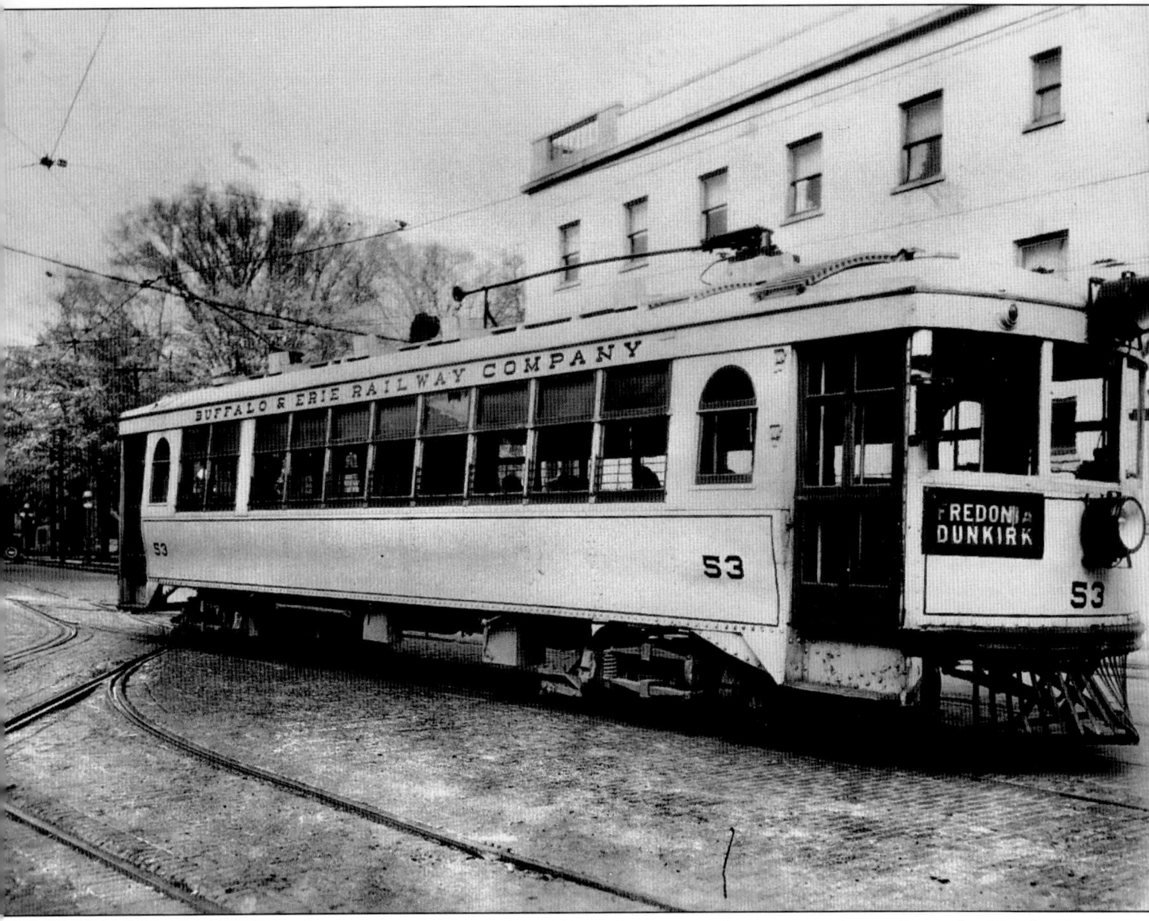

Buffalo and Erie Railway Company car No. 53 is shown on the approach track to the Fredonia carbarn. The company established a weekly pass effective Monday, February 18, 1929, for unlimited rides between Fredonia and various locations. The rate from Fredonia was as follows: Buffalo, $6.50; Silver Creek, $2.30; Sheridan, $1.75; Dunkirk, $1.25; Brocton, $2.30; Portland, $2.30; and Westfield, $4.00. A system weekly pass could be obtained for $8.00. During 1930, the company sponsored a series of radio programs designed to make the audience more familiar with the communities served by the trolley line. The company made every effort to encourage ridership but was not successful. The last run was made into the early hours of Saturday morning, January 28, 1933. (R. Nash photograph.)

Four

Northwestern Pennsylvania Railway

On Sunday, September 23, 1900, the first trolley car arrived in Edinboro from Erie, and the line was completed to Cambridge Springs on October 19, 1900. The line from Meadville to Cambridge Springs opened in 1903. During 1907, the Meadville and Conneaut Lake Traction Company completed a line from Meadville to Conneaut Lake Park, and by 1908, it reached Linesville with an extension to the Pennsylvania Railroad station in Linesville. On July 23, 1910, it was announced that the Erie Traction Company (Erie, Edinboro and Cambridge Springs line) would be merged with the Meadville and Cambridge Springs Street Railway line. The only time a United States president rode a trolley car in northwestern Pennsylvania was when Pres. William Howard Taft arrived by Erie Railroad to Cambridge Springs on October 26, 1912. After he visited the mineral springs at Cambridge Springs, he traveled by trolley car to Edinboro. The Meadville and Cambridge Springs Street Railway and the Erie Traction Company were taken over by the Northwestern Pennsylvania Railway on November 6, 1912. Much of the area between Erie and Meadville was rural, and there were occasional encounters between the trolley and livestock. On December 8, 1912, a trolley car smashed into a flock of 80 sheep, and 17 were instantly killed. A cow wandered on the track and derailed the trolley at Nicholson Hill on May 31, 1913. None of the passengers were injured, but the cow was killed. Trolleys provided cheap transportation, and the farmer could get produce to the marketplace by trolley in all kinds of weather. When a farmer sold land that was on the trolley line, it would be mentioned in the real estate advertisement. The Northwestern Pennsylvania Railway was ordered to be sold on December 27, 1919, for failure to pay $493,937.50 that was due September 1, 1912. Felix F. Curtz of the Erie Trust Company bought the company for $115,000 at the receiver's sale held on December 27, 1919. The Meadville city lines and the Meadville to Linesville branch were sold for only $2,500. On October 1, 1922, the Northwestern Pennsylvania Railway and the Peoples' Incandescent Light Company were merged into the Northwestern Electric Service Company of Pennsylvania. The new company was involved with transportation, light, heat, and power for Erie and Crawford Counties. On September 1, 1925, the Penn Public Service Company established a bus line from Erie to Meadville. Labor Day 1927 was the last day for local streetcar service in Meadville. Service to Linesville ended during 1927, and the Meadville to Conneaut Lake Park line was abandoned August 1, 1928. The last trolley operated on the Erie to Meadville line on September 28, 1928.

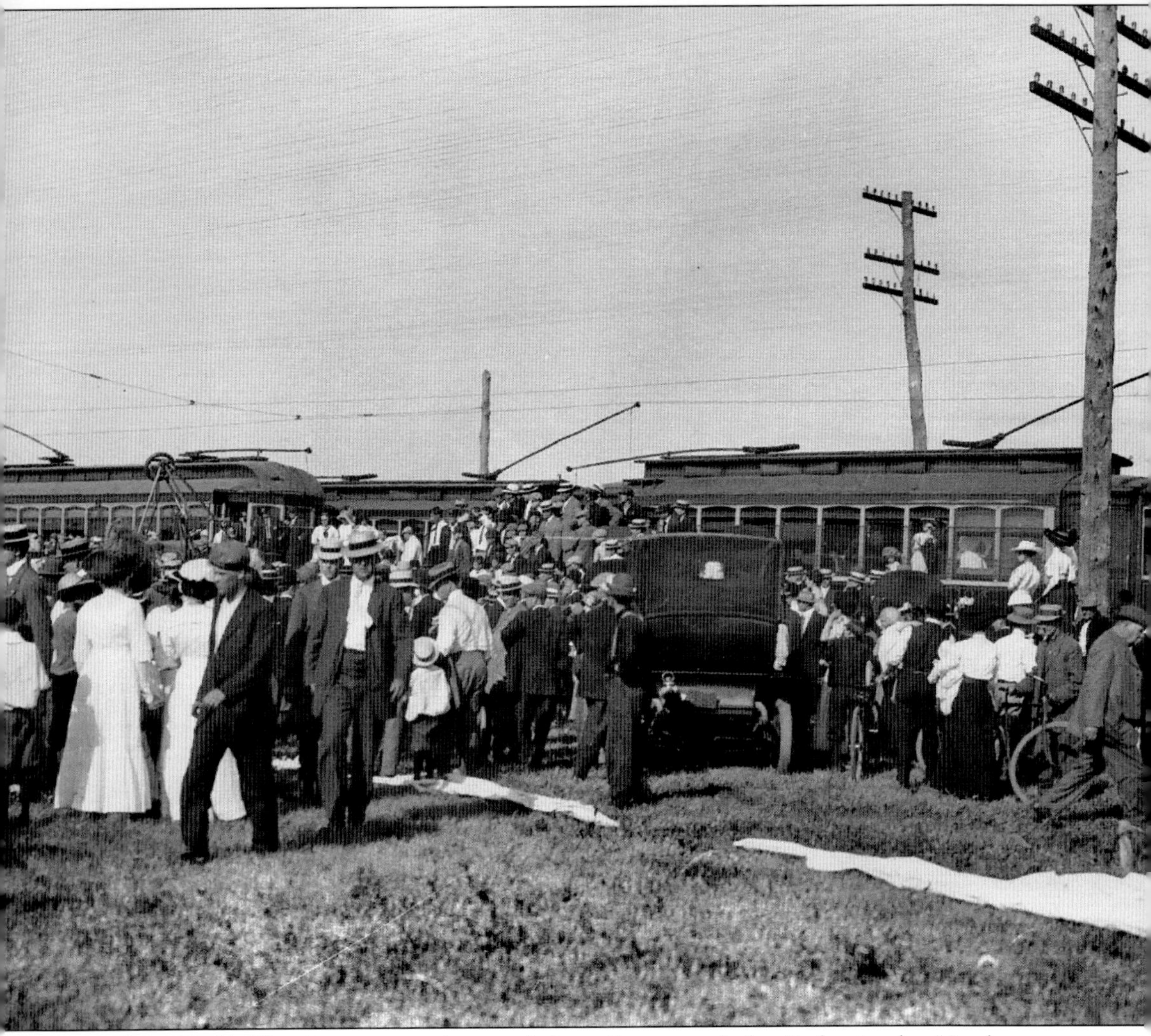

Before World War I, most people traveled to Conneaut Lake Park via the Northwestern Pennsylvania Railway trolley line to Meadville. During the peak summer season, there was trolley car service every 20 minutes from Meadville to Conneaut Lake Park. Trains from Pittsburgh unloaded crowds of people at Linesville who would crowd the trolleys to Conneaut Lake Park. (M. V. Grimler photograph.)

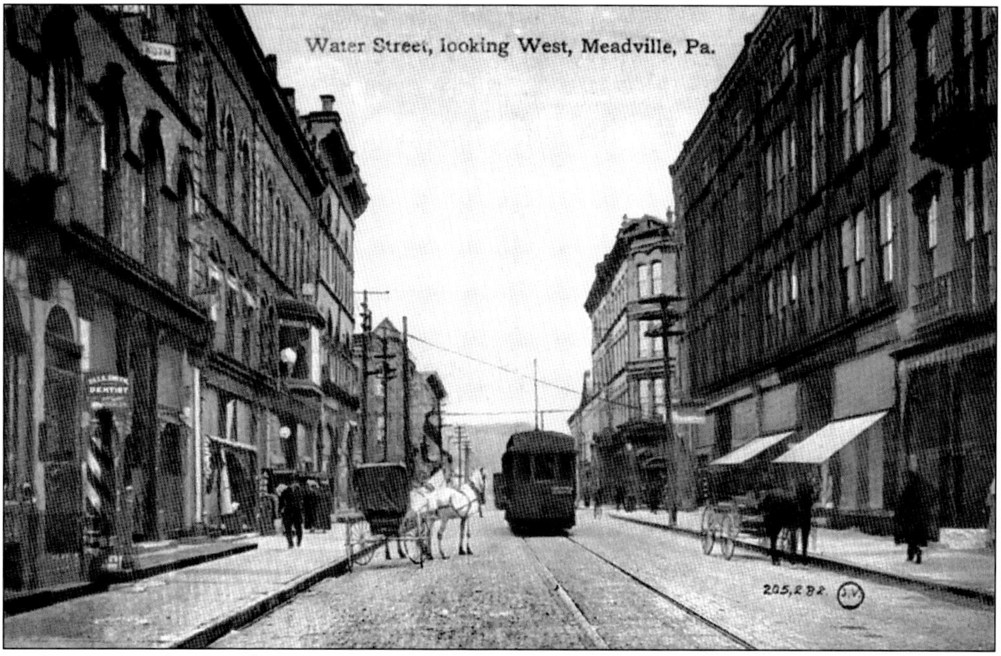

In this postcard view of Water Street in downtown Meadville, a Meadville Traction Company car passes by the horse-drawn vehicle before the advent of the automobile. The fare was 5¢, and transfers could be obtained at intersecting points. There were five trolley routes in Meadville: Vallonia, Greendale, Kerrtown, Ponce de Leon Springs, and Fredericksburg.

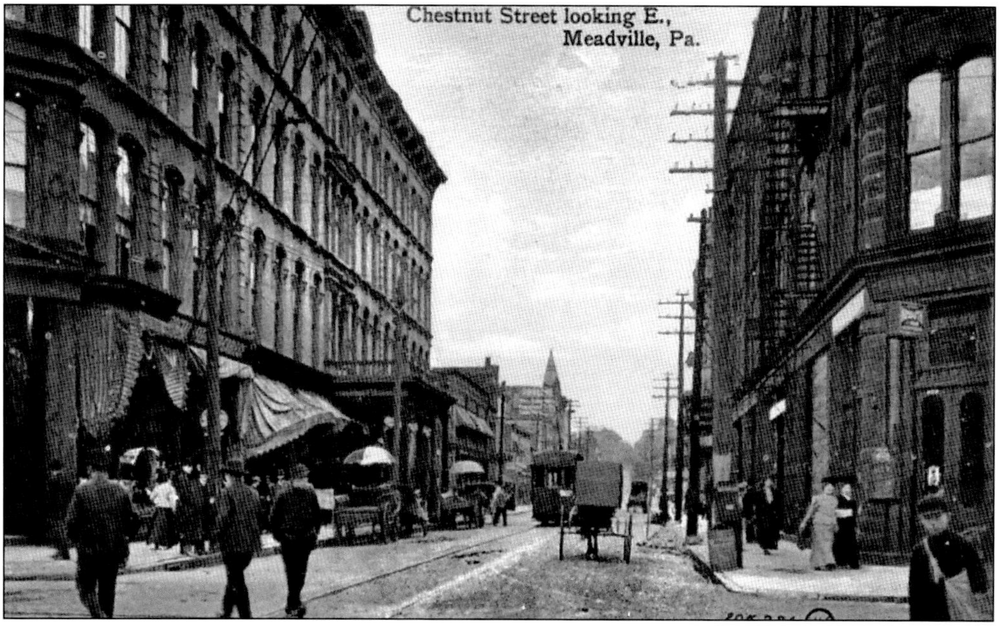

A Meadville Traction Company trolley passes along Chestnut Street. The trolley lines to Ponce de Leon Springs, Vallonia, and Greendale used Chestnut Street from Water Street to South Main Street. During 1900, the Ponce de Leon line was extended to Oakwood Park, which became a popular resort. As Conneaut Lake Park grew, Oakwood Park gradually ceased to exist.

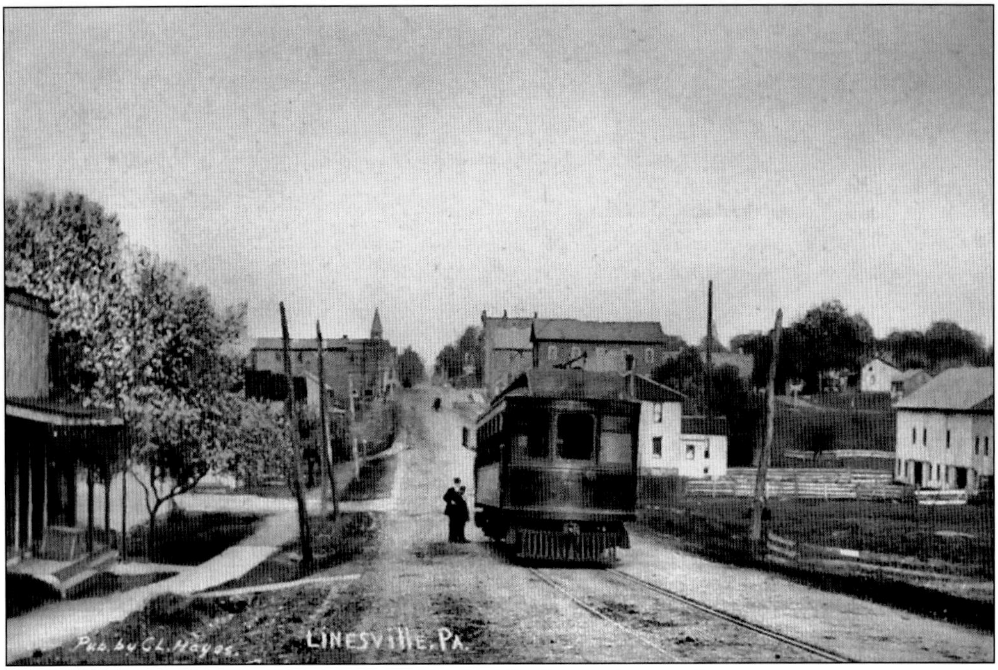

This postcard view shows the terminus at Linesville, Pennsylvania. Summertime passenger traffic was heavy from the Pennsylvania Railroad line at Linesville traveling to Conneaut Lake Park. When the park was closed, ridership was low. By 1924, the Harmonsburg trestle needed to be rebuilt, about 4,500 ties needed replacement, and the Linesville Bridge needed to be rehabilitated.

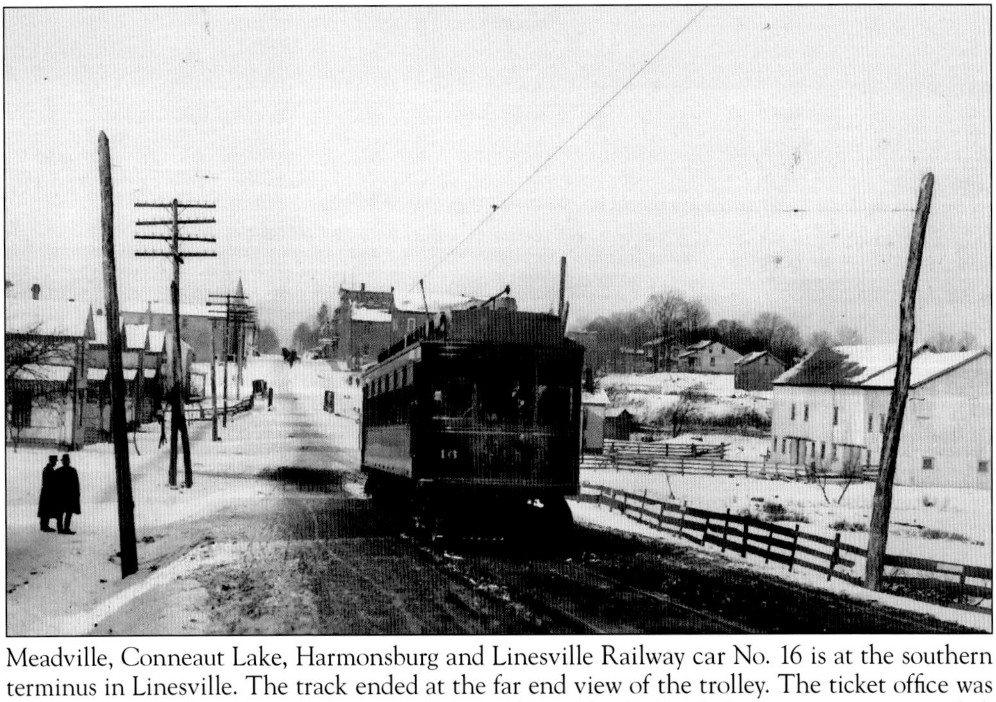

Meadville, Conneaut Lake, Harmonsburg and Linesville Railway car No. 16 is at the southern terminus in Linesville. The track ended at the far end view of the trolley. The ticket office was to the left of the picture in a shoe repair shop where Charles Reid the station agent presided. (Richard W. Farley photograph.)

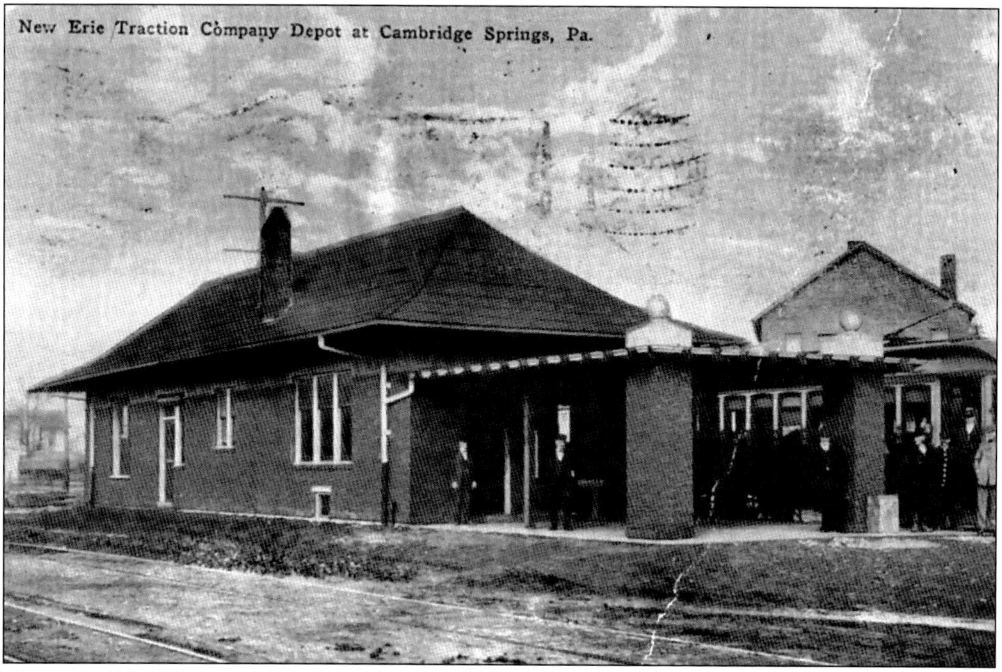

The new Erie Traction Company depot at Cambridge Springs was an important destination on the trolley line, plus it served as a transfer point to the Erie Railroad for connections east to New York City and west to Chicago. In 1916, the fare from Erie to Edinboro was 60¢, 90¢ to Saegertown, 75¢ to Cambridge Springs, and $1.25 to Conneaut Lake Park.

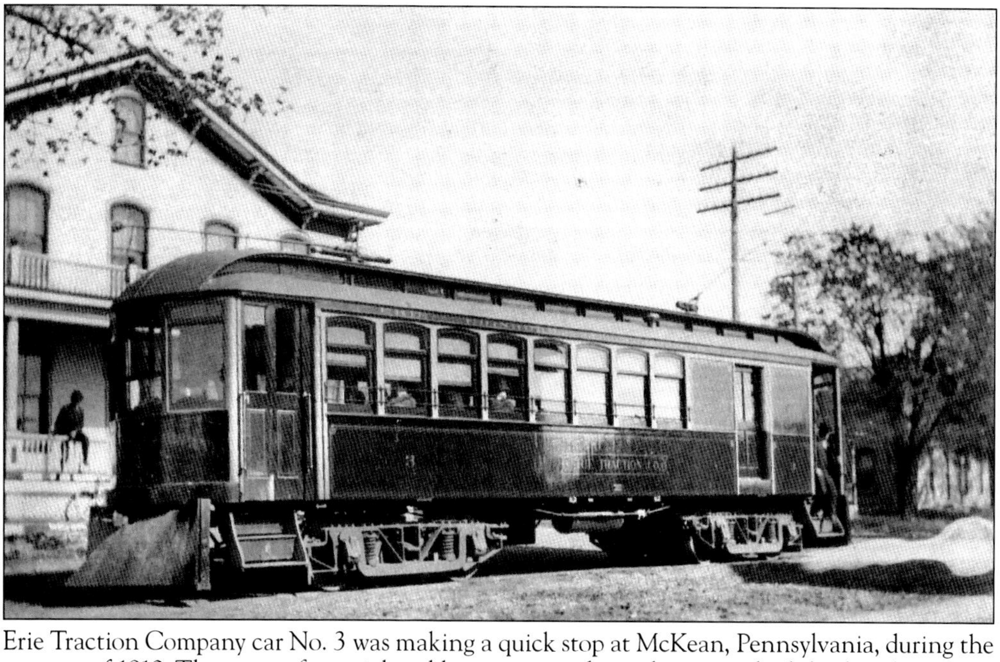

Erie Traction Company car No. 3 was making a quick stop at McKean, Pennsylvania, during the summer of 1910. There were financial problems even in the early years, which lead to the merger of the Erie Traction Company (Erie to Cambridge Springs) with the Meadville and Cambridge Springs Street Railway line in 1910.

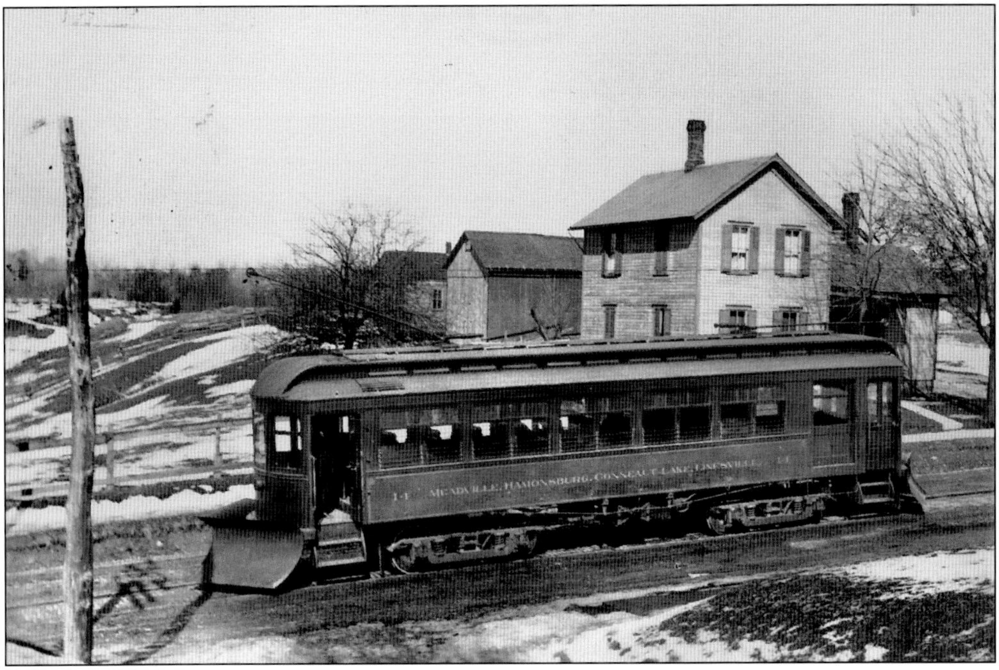

Meadville and Conneaut Lake Traction Company car No. 14 is on Erie Street in Linesville, Pennsylvania, around 1908. The line from Meadville to Linesville opened in 1907, but within a short time, the company went into receivership. Population density of the area served by the trolley line was light. (Richard W. Farley photograph.)

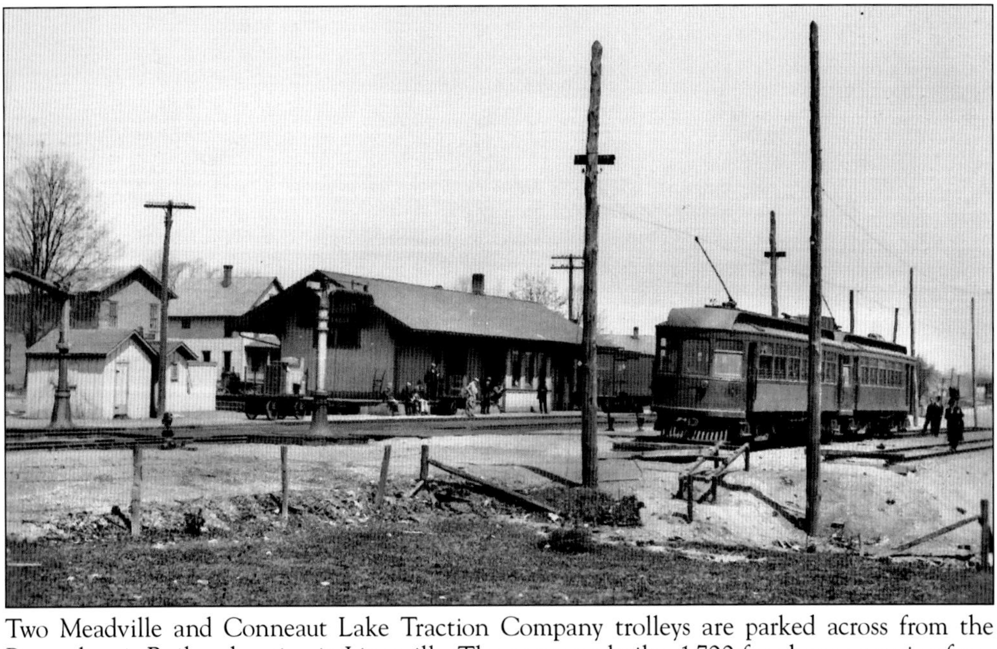

Two Meadville and Conneaut Lake Traction Company trolleys are parked across from the Pennsylvania Railroad station in Linesville. The company built a 1,700-foot-long extension from the Linesville terminus to reach the railroad station. In the summertime, there was heavy train ridership from the Pittsburgh area transferring to the trolley at Linesville to reach Conneaut Lake Park. (Richard W. Farley photograph.)

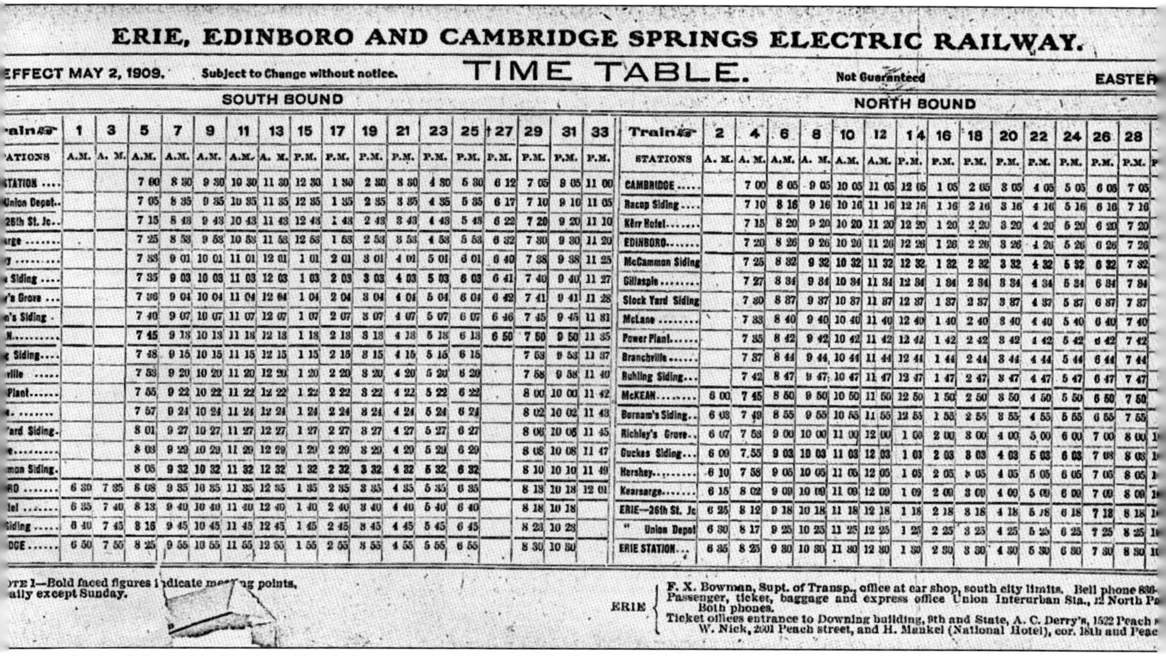

ERIE, EDINBORO AND CAMBRIDGE SPRINGS ELECTRIC RAILWAY.

EFFECT MAY 2, 1909. Subject to Change without notice. TIME TABLE. Not Guaranteed EASTER

SOUTH BOUND

Trains	1	3	5	7	9	11	13	15	17	19	21	23	25	†27	29	31	33
STATIONS	A.M.	A. M.	A.M.	A.M.	A.M.	A.M.	A. M.	P.M.	P.M.	P.M.	P.M.	P.M.	P.M.	P.M.	P.M.	P.M.	P.M.
STATION			7 00	8 30	9 30	10 30	11 30	12 30	1 30	2 30	3 30	4 30	5 30	6 12	7 05	9 05	11 00
Union Depot..			7 05	8 35	9 35	10 35	11 35	12 35	1 35	2 35	3 35	4 35	5 35	6 17	7 10	9 10	11 05
26th St. Jc..			7 15	8 43	9 43	10 43	11 43	12 43	1 43	2 43	3 43	4 43	5 43	6 22	7 20	9 20	11 10
arge			7 25	8 53	9 53	10 53	11 53	12 53	1 53	2 53	3 53	4 53	5 53	6 32	7 30	9 30	11 20
y			7 33	9 01	10 01	11 01	12 01	1 01	2 01	3 01	4 01	5 01	6 01	6 40	7 38	9 38	11 25
Siding			7 35	9 03	10 03	11 03	12 03	1 03	2 03	3 03	4 03	5 03	6 03	6 41	7 40	9 40	11 27
's Grove ...			7 36	9 04	10 04	11 04	12 04	1 04	2 04	3 04	4 04	5 04	6 04	6 42	7 41	9 41	11 28
n's Siding .			7 40	9 07	10 07	11 07	12 07	1 07	2 07	3 07	4 07	5 07	6 07	6 46	7 45	9 45	11 31
N.........			7 45	9 13	10 13	11 13	12 13	1 13	2 13	3 13	4 13	5 13	6 13	6 50	7 50	9 50	11 35
Siding....			7 48	9 15	10 15	11 15	12 15	1 15	2 15	3 15	4 15	5 15	6 15		7 53	9 53	11 37
ville			7 53	9 20	10 20	11 20	12 20	1 20	2 20	3 20	4 20	5 20	6 20		7 58	9 58	11 40
Plant......			7 55	9 22	10 22	11 22	12 22	1 22	2 22	3 22	4 22	5 22	6 22		8 00	10 00	11 42
. ...			7 57	9 24	10 24	11 24	12 24	1 24	2 24	3 24	4 24	5 24	6 24		8 02	10 02	11 43
ard Siding.			8 01	9 27	10 27	11 27	12 27	1 27	2 27	3 27	4 27	5 27	6 27		8 06	10 06	11 45
e.........			8 03	9 29	10 29	11 29	12 29	1 29	2 29	3 29	4 29	5 29	6 29		8 08	10 08	11 47
mon Siding.			8 05	9 32	10 32	11 32	12 32	1 32	2 32	3 32	4 32	5 32	6 32		8 10	10 10	11 49
RO	6 30	7 35	8 08	9 35	10 35	11 35	12 35	1 35	2 35	3 35	4 35	5 35	6 35		8 13	10 13	12 01
tel	6 35	7 40	8 13	9 40	10 40	11 40	12 40	1 40	2 40	3 40	4 40	5 40	6 40		8 18	10 18	
Siding	6 40	7 45	8 16	9 45	10 45	11 45	12 45	1 45	2 45	3 45	4 45	5 45	6 45		8 23	10 23	
DGE......	6 50	7 55	8 25	9 55	10 55	11 55	12 55	1 55	2 55	3 55	4 55	5 55	6 55		8 30	10 30	

NORTH BOUND

Trains	2	4	6	8	10	12	14	16	18	20	22	24	26	28	
STATIONS	A. M.	A. M.	A.M.	A. M.	A.M.	A.M.	P.M.	P.M.	P.M.	P.M.	P.M.	P.M.	P.M.	P.M.	P
CAMBRIDGE		7 00	8 05	9 05	10 05	11 05	12 05	1 05	2 05	3 05	4 05	5 05	6 05	7 05	
Racop Siding		7 10	8 16	9 16	10 16	11 16	12 16	1 16	2 16	3 16	4 16	5 16	6 16	7 16	
Kerr Hotel........		7 15	8 20	9 20	10 20	11 20	12 20	1 20	2 20	3 20	4 20	5 20	6 20	7 20	
EDINBORO.......		7 20	8 26	9 26	10 26	11 26	12 26	1 26	2 26	3 26	4 26	5 26	6 26	7 26	
McCammon Siding		7 25	8 32	9 32	10 32	11 32	12 32	1 32	2 32	3 32	4 32	5 32	6 32	7 32	
Gillaspie		7 27	8 34	9 34	10 34	11 34	12 34	1 34	2 34	3 34	4 34	5 34	6 34	7 34	
Stock Yard Siding		7 30	8 37	9 37	10 37	11 37	12 37	1 37	2 37	3 37	4 37	5 37	6 37	7 37	
McLane		7 33	8 40	9 40	10 40	11 40	12 40	1 40	2 40	3 40	4 40	5 40	6 40	7 40	
Power Plant......		7 35	8 42	9 42	10 42	11 42	12 42	1 42	2 42	3 42	4 42	5 42	6 42	7 42	
Branchville		7 37	8 44	9 44	10 44	11 44	12 44	1 44	2 44	3 44	4 44	5 44	6 44	7 44	
Ruhling Siding...		7 42	8 47	9 47	10 47	11 47	12 47	1 47	2 47	3 47	4 47	5 47	6 47	7 47	
McKEAN........	6 00	7 45	8 50	9 50	10 50	11 50	12 50	1 50	2 50	3 50	4 50	5 50	6 50	7 50	
Burnam's Siding..	6 03	7 49	8 55	9 55	10 55	11 55	12 55	1 55	2 55	3 55	4 55	5 55	6 55	7 55	
Richley's Grove..	6 07	7 53	9 00	10 00	11 00	12 00	1 00	2 00	3 00	4 00	5 00	6 00	7 00	8 00	1
Guckes Siding...	6 09	7 55	9 03	10 03	11 03	12 03	1 03	2 03	3 03	4 03	5 03	6 03	7 03	8 03	1
Hershey.........	6 10	7 58	9 05	10 05	11 05	12 05	1 05	2 05	3 05	4 05	5 05	6 05	7 05	8 05	1
Kearsarge.......	6 15	8 02	9 09	10 09	11 09	12 09	1 09	2 09	3 09	4 09	5 09	6 09	7 09	8 09	1
ERIE—26th St. Jc	6 25	8 12	9 18	10 18	11 18	12 18	1 18	2 18	3 18	4 18	5 18	6 18	7 18	8 18	1
" Union Depot	6 30	8 17	9 25	10 25	11 25	12 25	1 25	2 25	3 25	4 25	5 25	6 25	7 25	8 25	1
ERIE STATION...	6 35	8 25	9 30	10 30	11 30	12 30	1 30	2 30	3 30	4 30	5 30	6 30	7 30	8 30	10

OTE 1—Bold faced figures indicate meeting points,
aily except Sunday.

ERIE { F. X. Bowman, Supt. of Transp., office at car shop, south city limits. Bell phone 886-
Passenger, ticket, baggage and express office Union Interurban Sta., 12 North Pa
Both phones.
Ticket offices entrance to Downing building, 9th and State, A. C. Derry's, 1522 Peach
W. Nick, 2001 Peach street, and H. Munkel (National Hotel), cor. 18th and Peac

The May 2, 1909, schedule for the Erie, Edinboro and Cambridge Springs Electric Railway showed 13 southbound trips from Erie to Cambridge Springs and 14 northbound trips from Cambridge Springs to Erie. Travel time from Erie to Cambridge Springs was one hour and 25 minutes. At Cambridge Springs, connections were made with the Meadville and Cambridge Springs Street Railway line. The two companies merged into the Northwestern Pennsylvania Railway Company on November 6, 1912, and through service was soon established between Erie and Meadville.

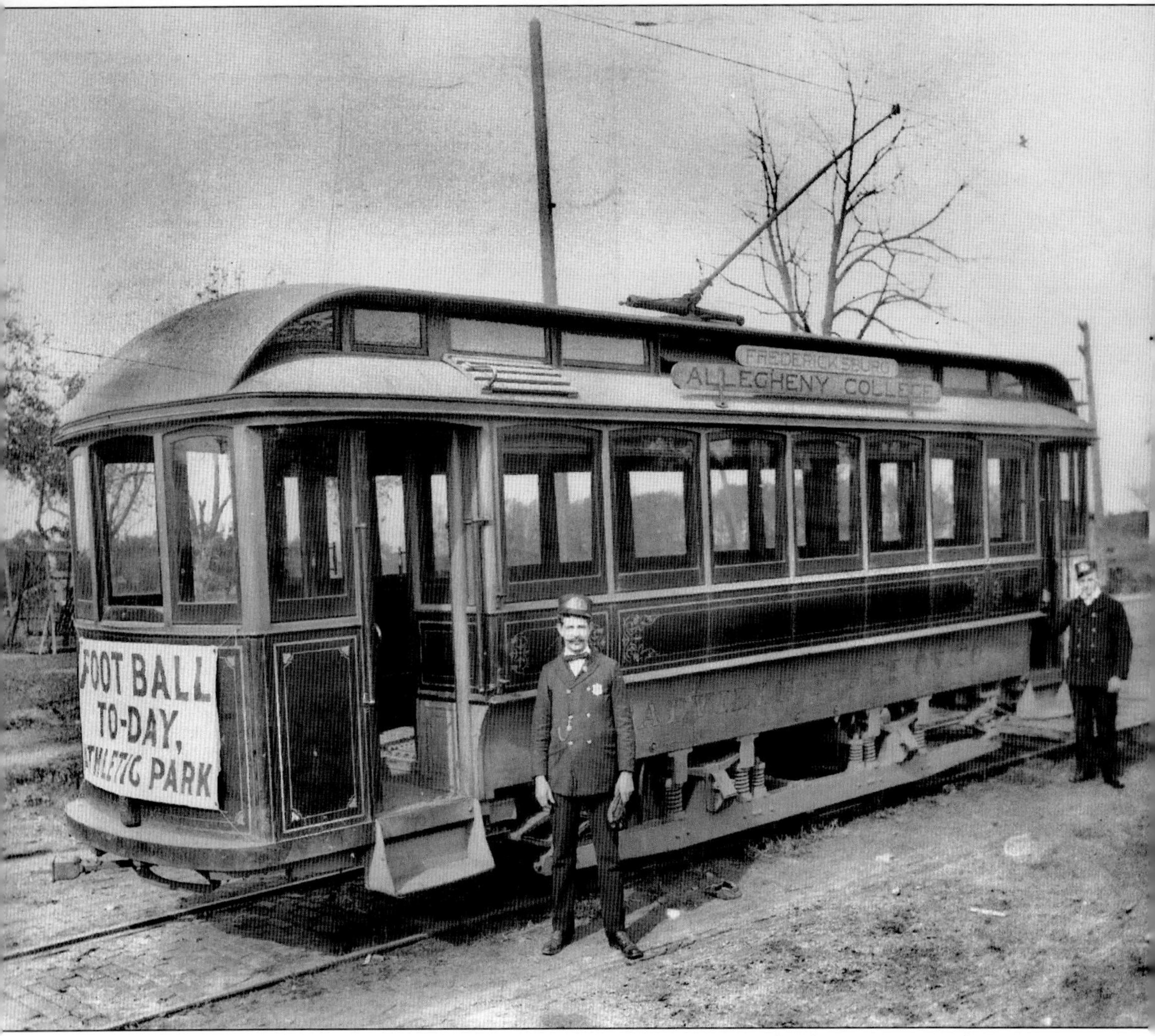

Meadville Traction Company car No. 4, with its crew, waits to make the next run. This was one of eight cars built by St. Louis Car Company at a cost of $2,000 each and was painted cream and Harvard crimson with black and silver trimming plus gold leaf numbers and the company name in silver. The car seated 35 passengers and was mounted on a Dupont four-wheeled truck powered by two Westinghouse motors. (Mrs. L. S. Welling photograph.)

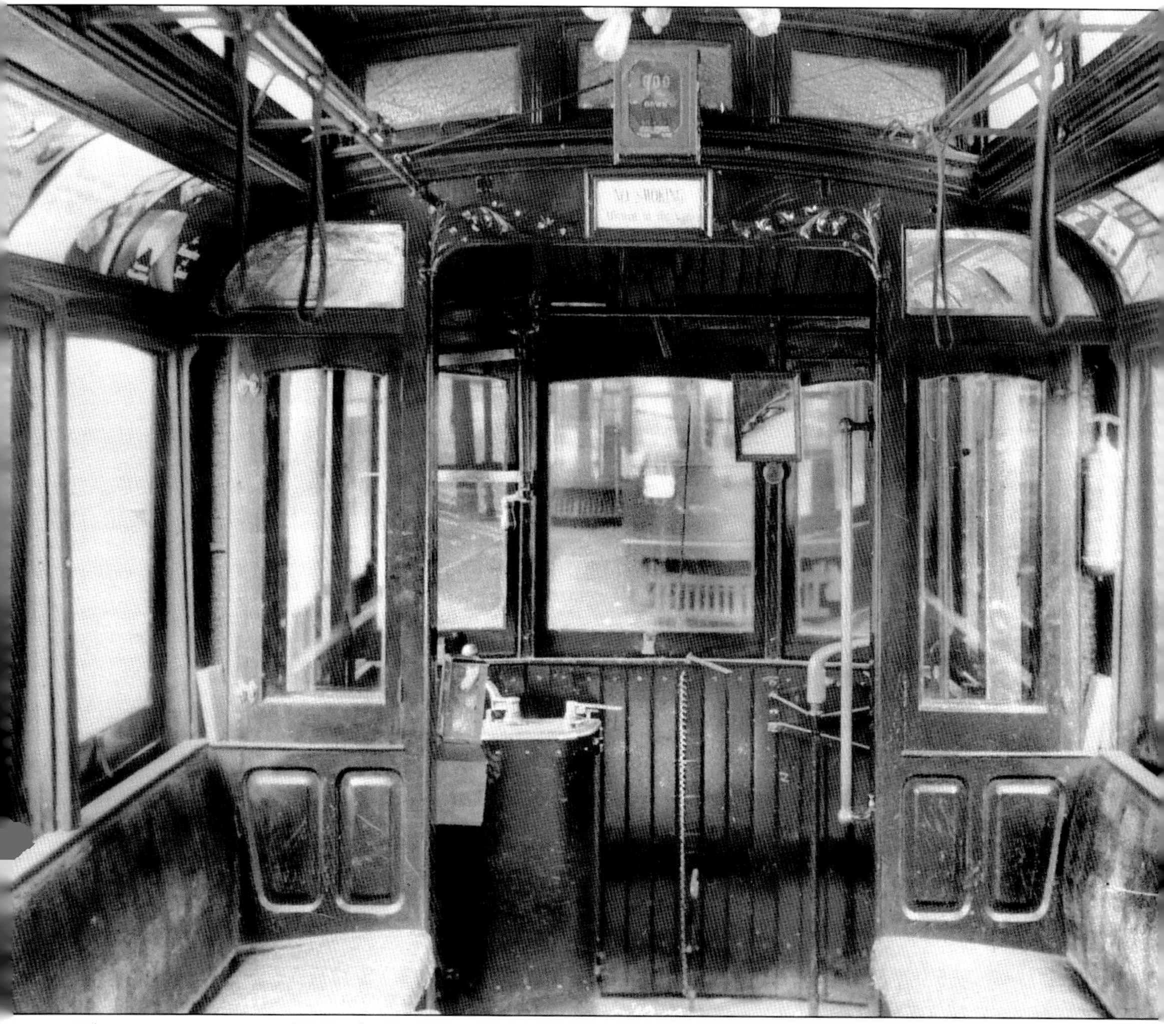

The interior view of Meadville Traction Company car No. 4 shows the operator's controls. Construction of the first trolley line in Meadville began on June 15, 1897. Car No. 7 made the first run on April 14, 1898. In 1922, the cash fare was 10¢, and a weekly pass was established for $1. (Mrs. L. S. Welling photograph.)

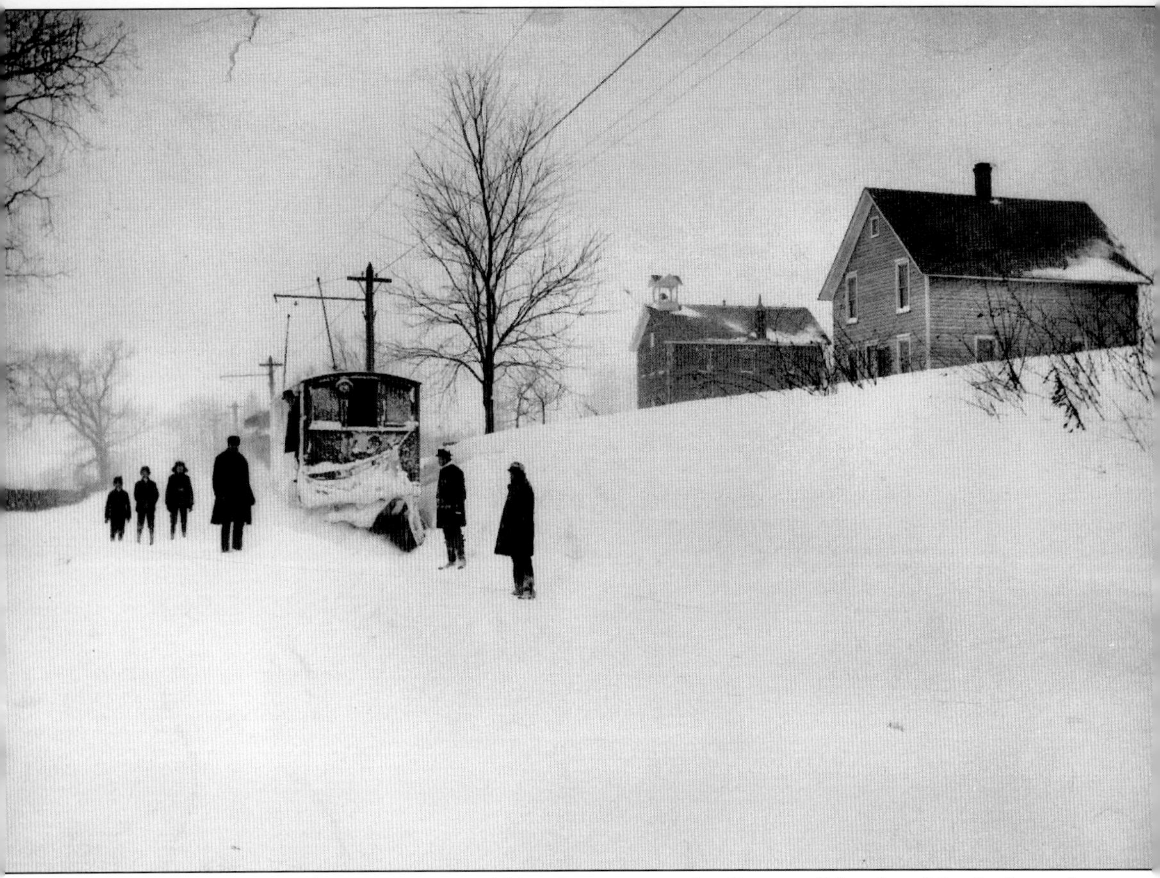

The snowplow was plowing snow on Alden Street near the Pierson School in Meadville with Frank Shryock, Lawrence Kressling, and Virgil Gillen near the plow in this February 9, 1902, scene. Heavy winter snows in Meadville presented a challenge to keep the system running. The McGraw Electric Railway List for August 1918 showed the system had 71.5 miles of track and 28 trolley cars. (Mrs. L. S. Welling photograph.)

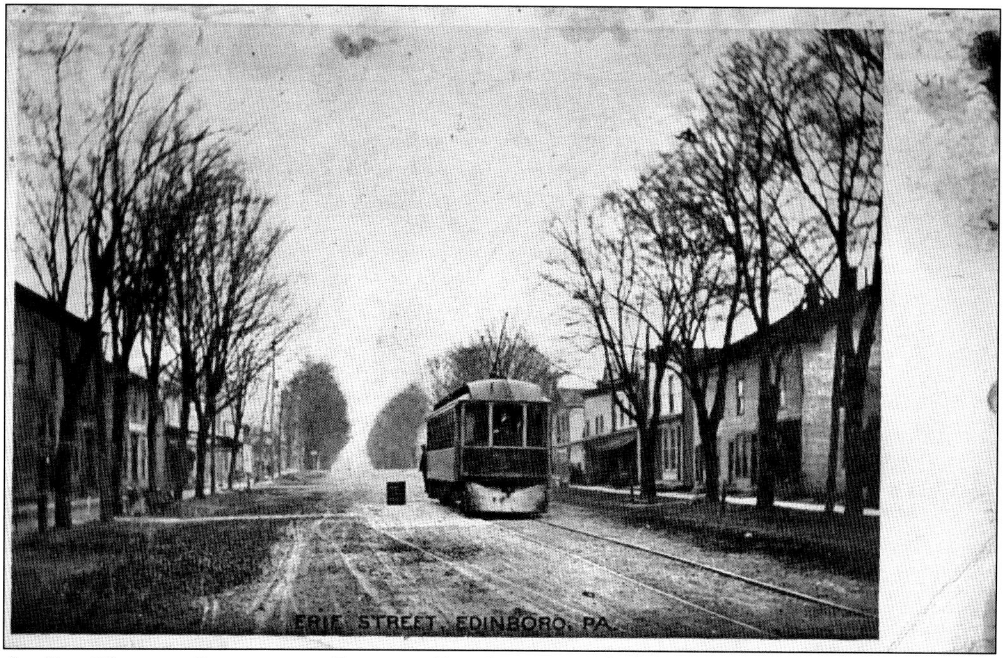

An Erie Traction Company trolley is on Erie Street in Edinboro. Trolley riding was so popular that in the summer of 1904, there was service every 30 minutes from Erie to the Edinboro Fair. Thirty couples of young people chartered two trolleys for a hayride during September 1904. The party traveled from Erie to Cambridge Springs and after an evening of dancing returned to Erie via their special trolleys.

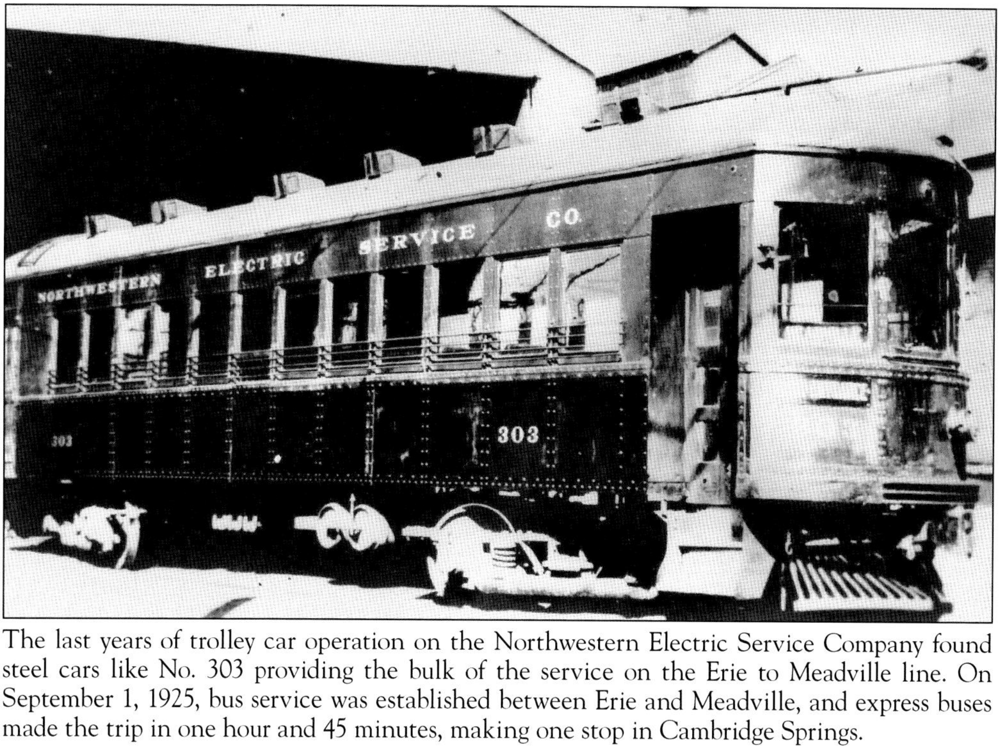

The last years of trolley car operation on the Northwestern Electric Service Company found steel cars like No. 303 providing the bulk of the service on the Erie to Meadville line. On September 1, 1925, bus service was established between Erie and Meadville, and express buses made the trip in one hour and 45 minutes, making one stop in Cambridge Springs.

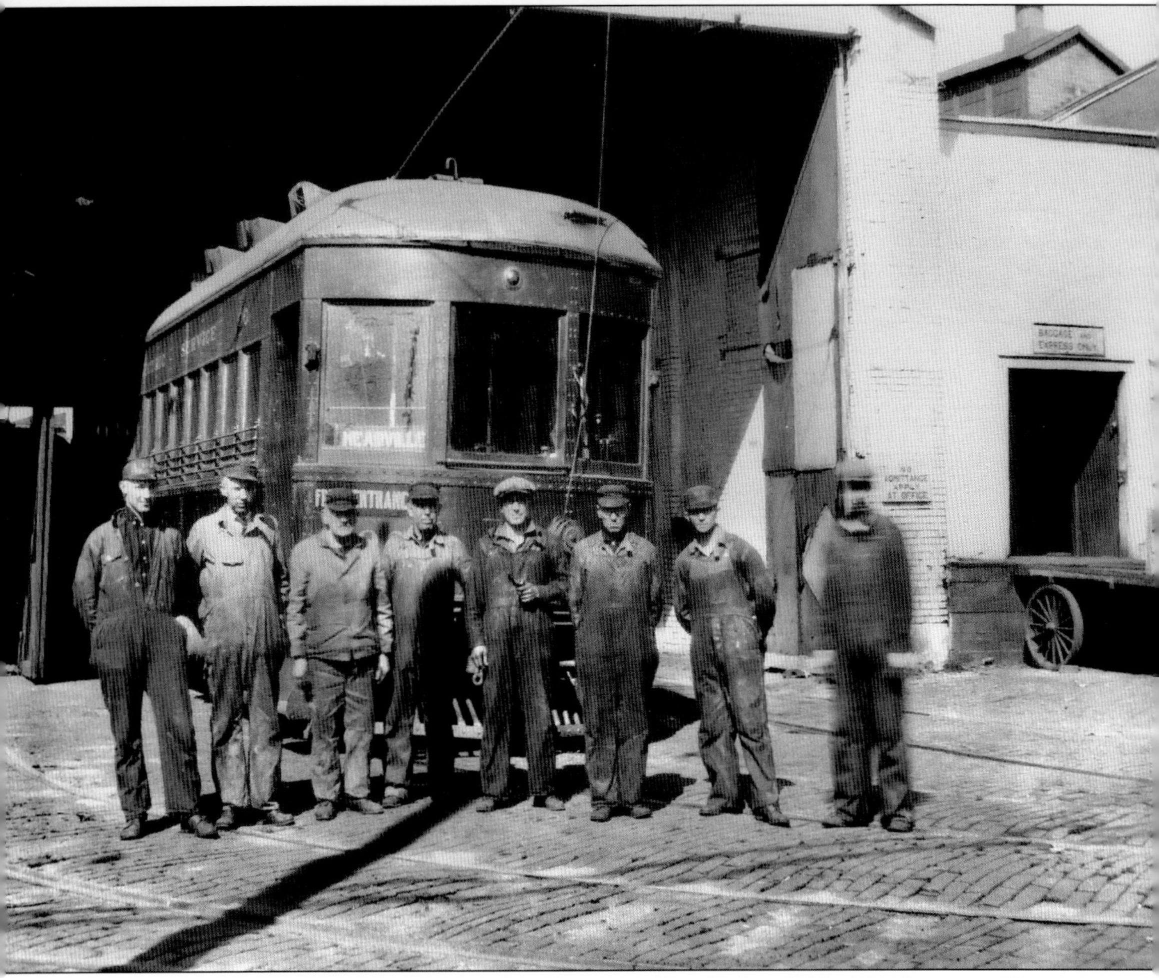

As the number of automobiles increased, trolley car riding declined. The Northwestern Electric Service Company shop crew did their best to maintain equipment. The 11-mile Meadville to Conneaut Lake Park line for the year ending May 31, 1928, had revenues of $18,140 and expenses of $26,488. It was abandoned August 1, 1928. The Erie to Meadville line closed September 28, 1928. (A. Rust photograph.)

Five

Westfield to Jamestown by Trolley

The Broadhead family of Jamestown owned the Jamestown Street Railway system and decided to build the Chautauqua Traction Company line on the western side of Lake Chautauqua. The line was completed from Jamestown to Chautauqua on April 27, 1904. On September 24, 1906, four elegant trolley cars arrived in Westfield, New York, from Jamestown over the new Chautauqua Traction Company line. During 1910, the company constructed an extension from Westfield to Barcelona Harbor, New York. Unfortunately the extension was poorly patronized and was abandoned in 1920. The section from Westfield to Mayville, New York, was abandoned in 1925. It was revealed that the Chautauqua Traction Company suffered substantial losses every year since 1909, and since 1918, it had not even earned operating expenses. For 1925, revenues were $115,076, expenses were $147,064, and taxes were $17,395, leaving a loss of $49,383. On March 20, 1926, the last trolley operated from Mayville to Ashville. West Ridge Transportation Company began bus service the next day from Westfield to Jamestown. The Jamestown Street Railway extended service from Ashville via its Celeron line and took over 2.6 miles of track between Lakewood and Ashville.

A steam railroad had been built from Jamestown to Mayville. After several organizational changes by 1901, it became known as the Jamestown, Chautauqua, and Lake Erie Railway and was extended from Mayville to Westfield during 1901. In 1907, the Buffalo and Lake Erie Traction Company became the owner. On October 15, 1913, the *Fredonia Censor* reported that S. B. and A. N. Broadhead bought the line for $475,000. The line was renamed Jamestown, Westfield and Northwestern Railroad, and electrification of the line was completed on August 20, 1914. Four new interurban trolley cars built by St. Louis Car Company were placed in service during 1917. G. L. Maltby, superintendent of the company, designed the cars with centrally located entrances to separate the smoking and main passenger compartments. One car, No. 312, was provided with an observation platform. During 1922, the company inaugurated through freight rates with the Pennsylvania Railroad at Mayville. During 1923, new 90-pound rail was laid from Jamestown to Mayville to handle heavier freight cars. There were two daily freight trains from Jamestown to Westfield handling between 15 and 30 freight cars. Passenger ridership declined, and the emergence of trucking companies hurt the freight business. Following the end of World War II, passenger business dwindled rapidly and the decision was made to end service. Car No. 302 made the last run Sunday night, November 30, 1947, operated by veteran motorman Arthur L. Seldon. This was the last interurban trolley line operated in New York State. Freight service was dieselized and operated until 1950.

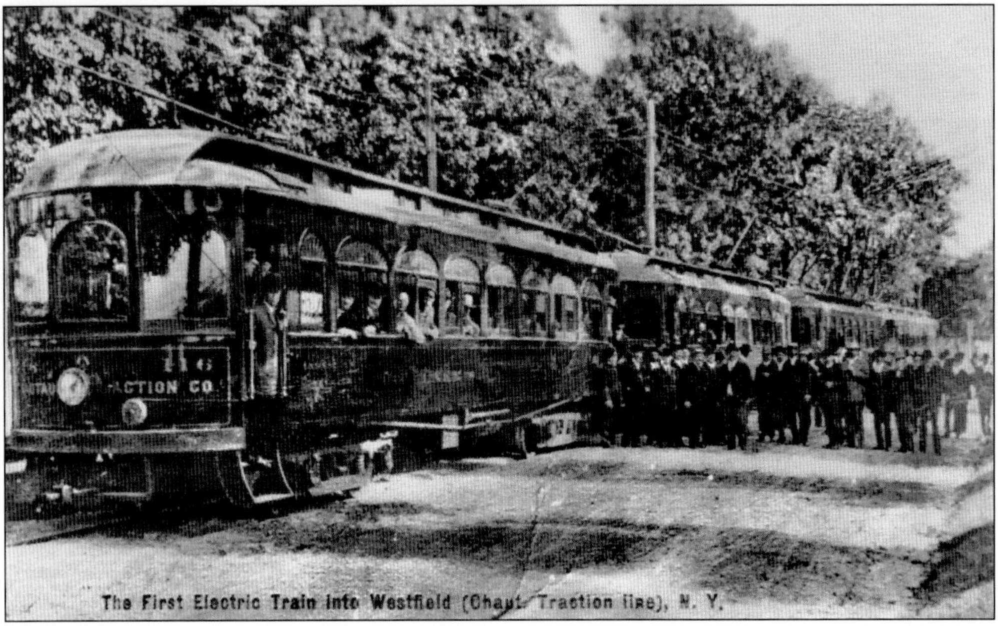

Four elegant trolley cars arrived in Westfield from Jamestown on Monday, September 24, 1906, over the new Chautauqua Traction Company line. On board were the Broadhead family, the mayor and city council members from Jamestown, supervisors, county officers, and many prominent citizens to celebrate the opening of the new line.

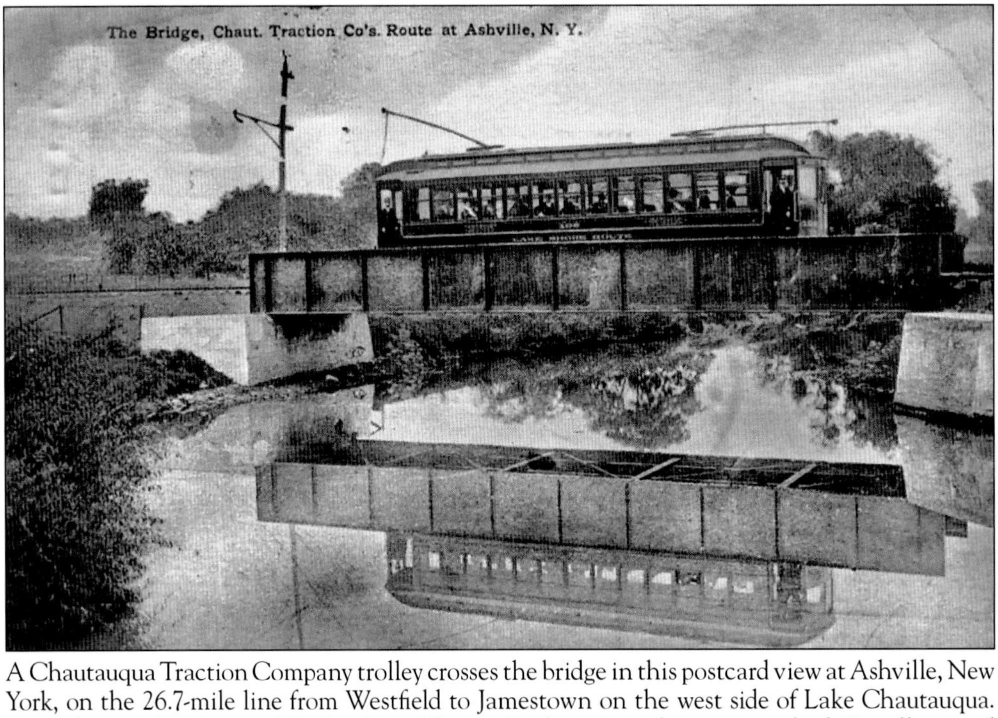

A Chautauqua Traction Company trolley crosses the bridge in this postcard view at Ashville, New York, on the 26.7-mile line from Westfield to Jamestown on the west side of Lake Chautauqua. According to the August 1918 McGraw Electric Railway List, the company had 19 trolleys, and repair shops were located at Jamestown.

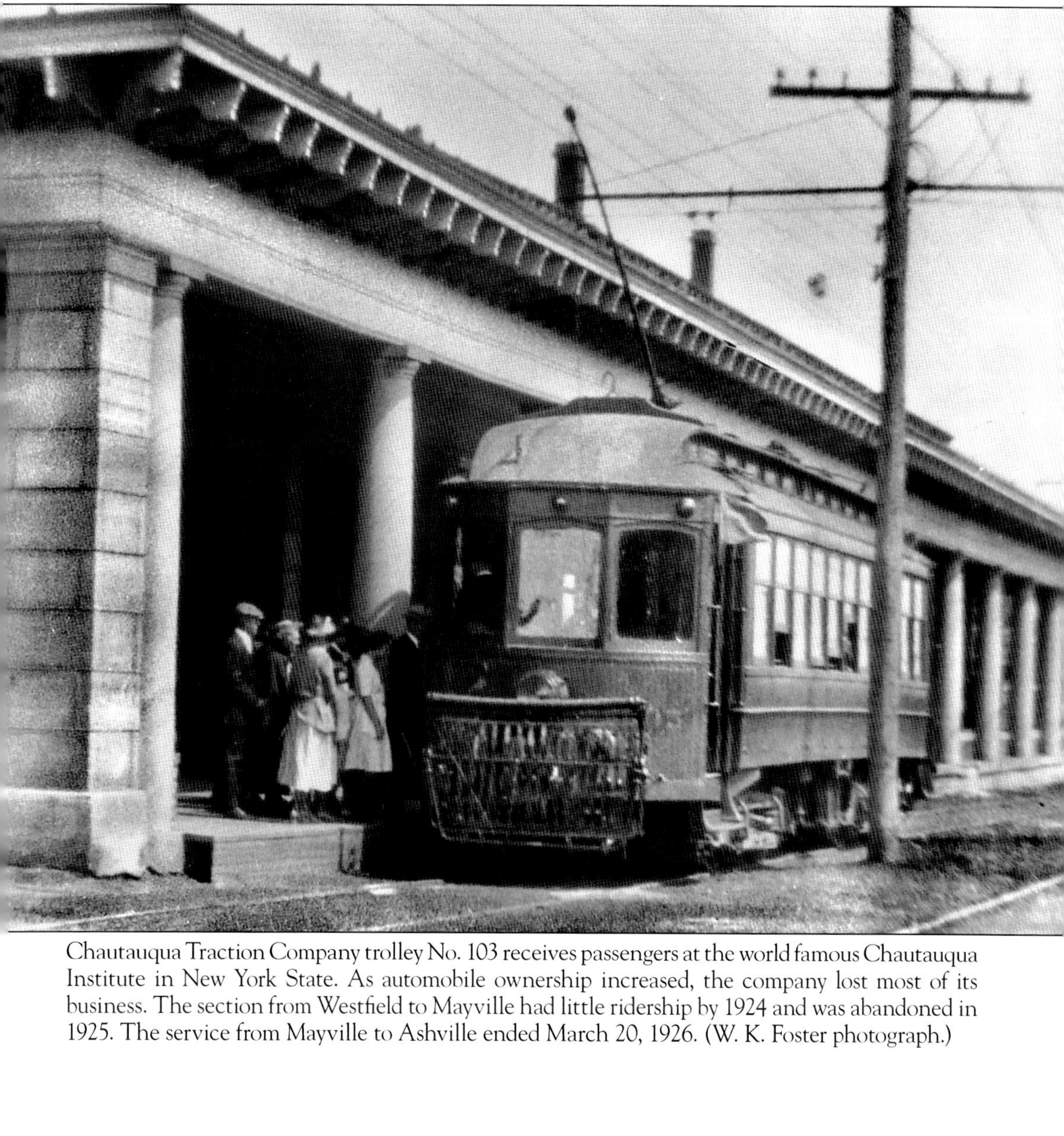

Chautauqua Traction Company trolley No. 103 receives passengers at the world famous Chautauqua Institute in New York State. As automobile ownership increased, the company lost most of its business. The section from Westfield to Mayville had little ridership by 1924 and was abandoned in 1925. The service from Mayville to Ashville ended March 20, 1926. (W. K. Foster photograph.)

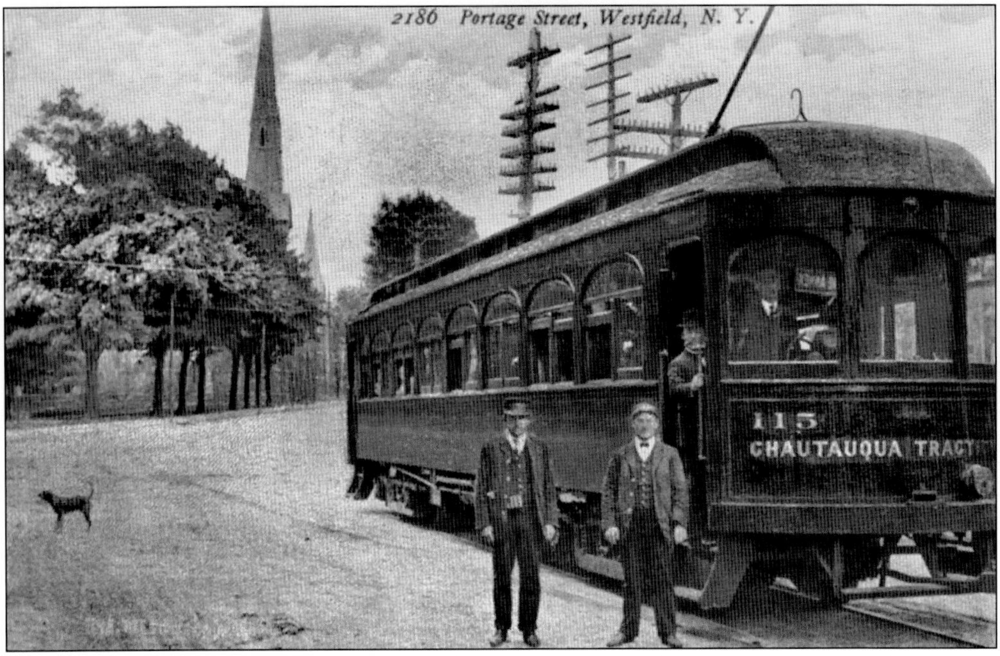

Chautauqua Traction Company car No. 115 is on Portage Street in this postcard scene in Westfield. The line from Westfield to Jamestown had a one-and-a-half hour running time. The Jamestown, Westfield and Northwestern had faster service, making the Westfield to Jamestown run in one hour and three minutes, and attracted most of the remaining riders.

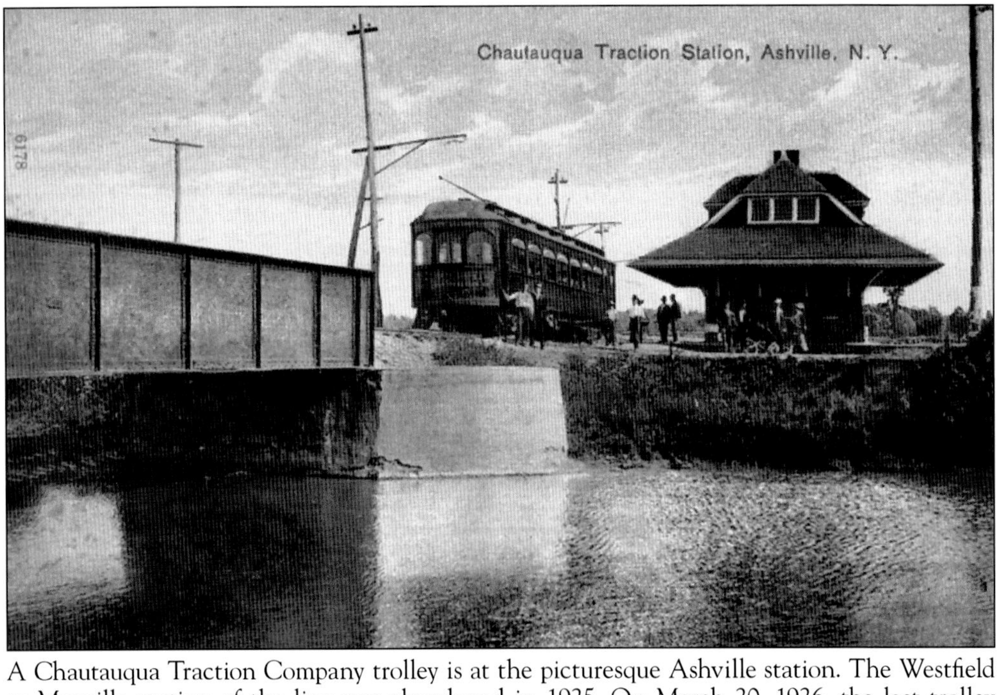

A Chautauqua Traction Company trolley is at the picturesque Ashville station. The Westfield to Mayville section of the line was abandoned in 1925. On March 20, 1926, the last trolley operated from Mayville to Ashville. The Jamestown, Westfield and Northwestern continued service on its Jamestown to Westfield line.

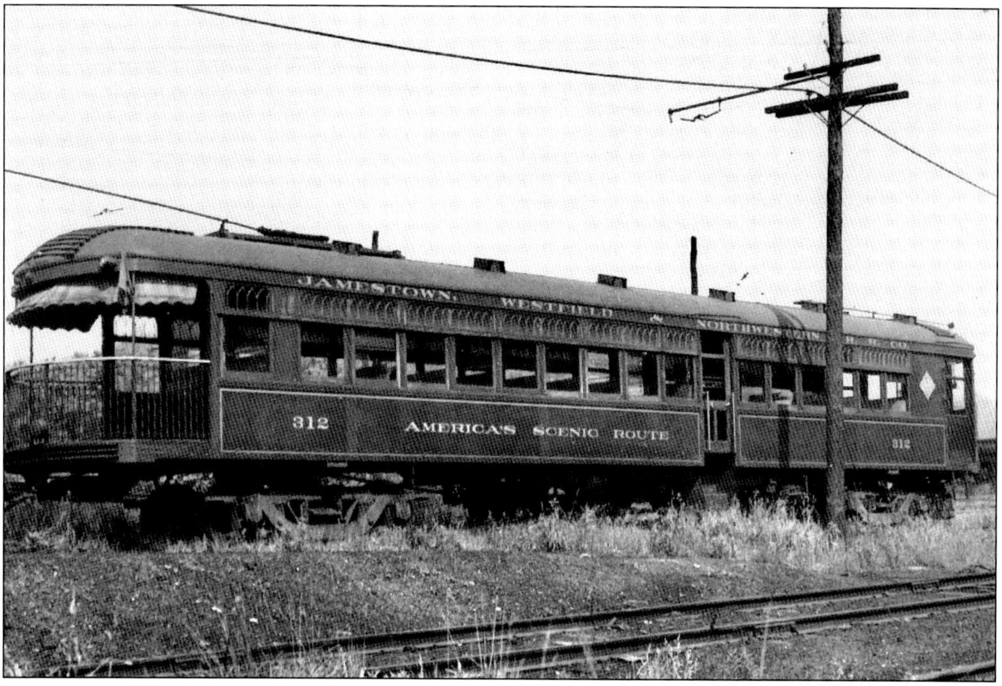

Jamestown, Westfield and Northwestern Railroad trolley No. 312 was built by the St. Louis Car Company and placed in service during 1917. Pictured at Jamestown, the car was equipped with Westinghouse No. 547-A 600 volt field control motors and Westinghouse type HL control and had a maximum speed of 50 miles per hour.

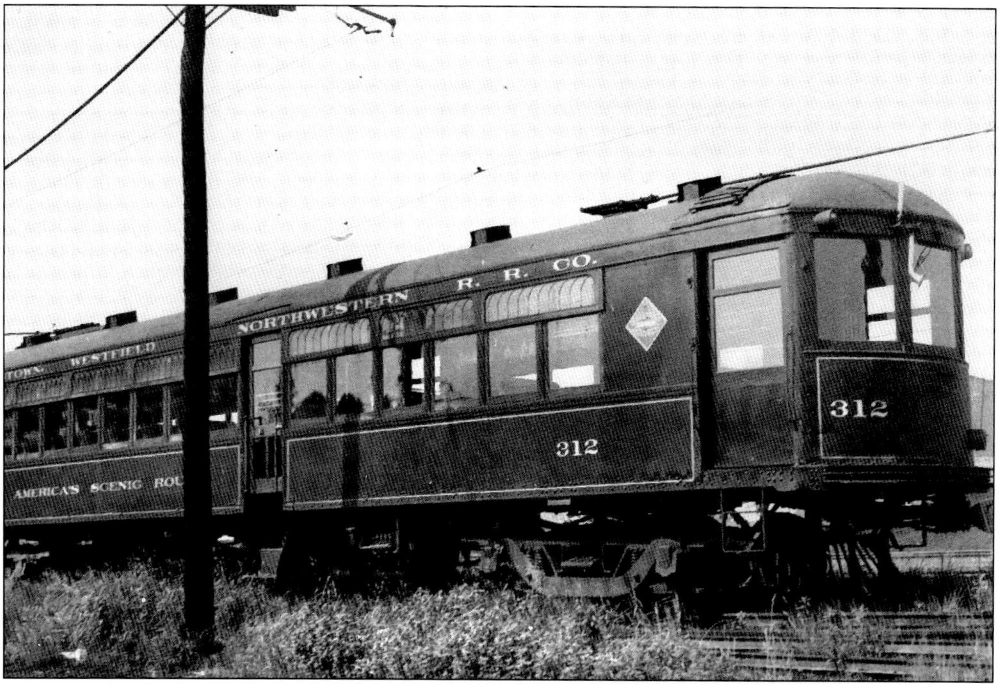

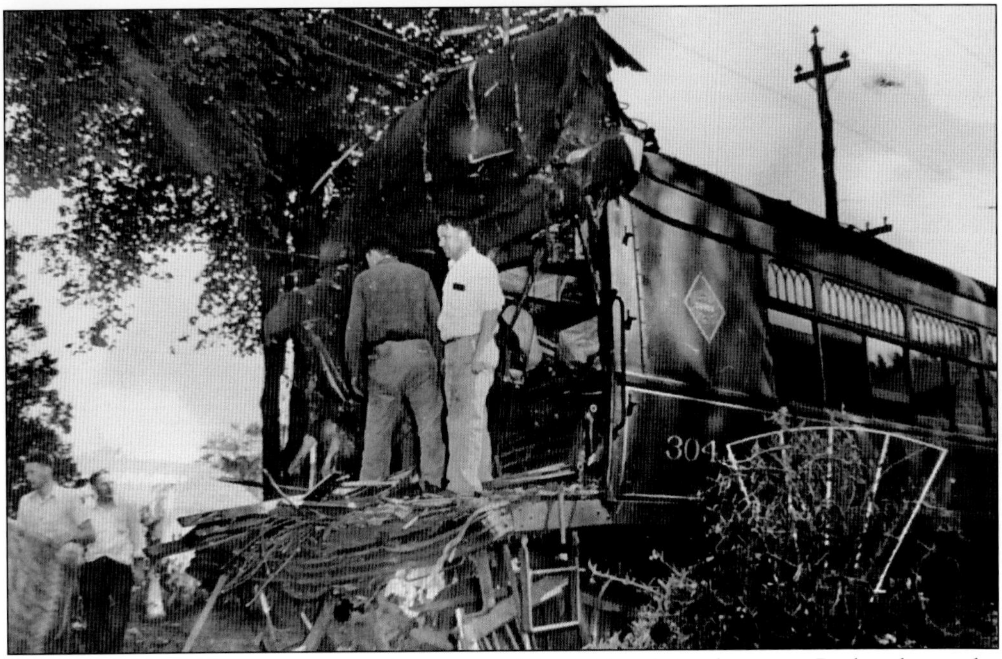

A head-on collision occurred on the Jamestown, Westfield and Northwestern Railroad near the Pennsylvania Railroad Junction between Mayville and Hartfield, New York. The northbound car had orders to pass at the Mayville Junction switch. However, the southbound car reportedly left Mayville without receiving orders. Both cars met south of the junction, and the end result is shown in these pictures. (W. K. Foster photographs.)

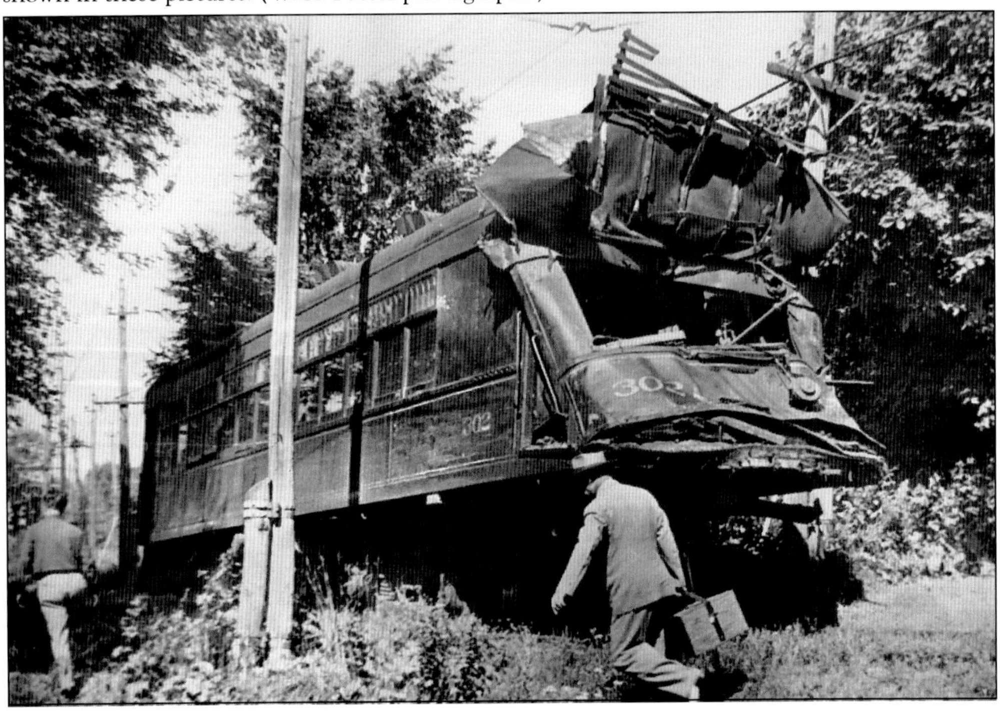

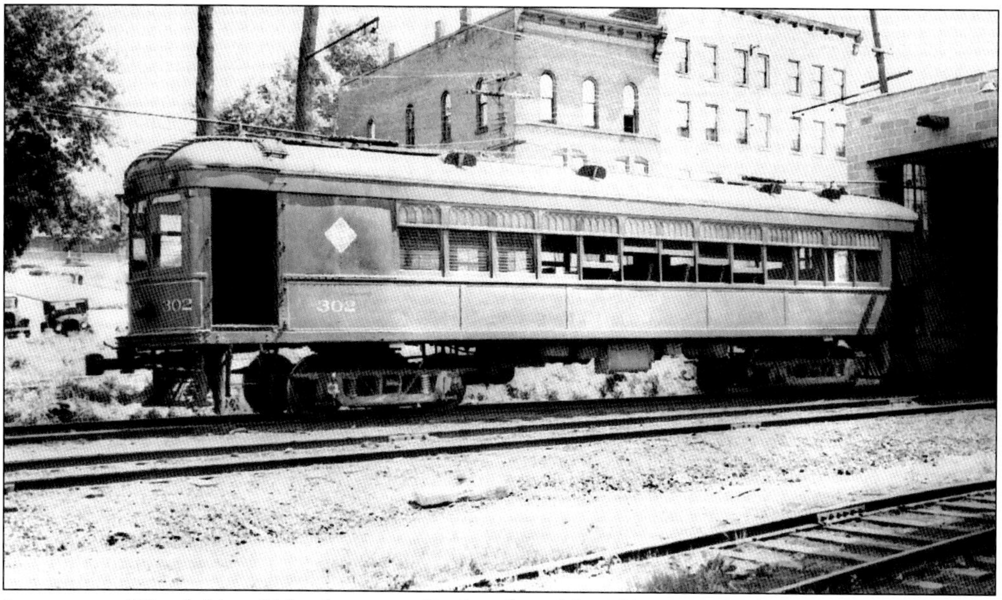

Jamestown, Westfield and Northwestern Railroad car No. 302 was parked outside the Jamestown carbarn on July 20, 1940. Built by St. Louis Car Company in 1917, the car sides were made from 36-inch by 1/8-inch thick steel sheets with a 3-inch by 3/8-inch belt rail at the top. The bumpers were eight-inch channels with the flanges turned inward. (B. H. Nichols photograph.)

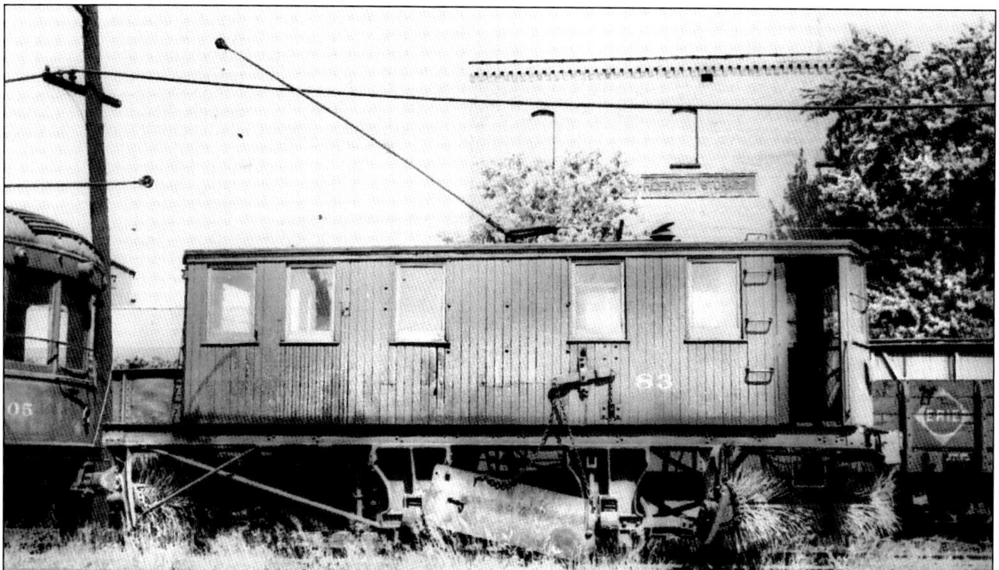

Snow sweeper No. 83 was stationed at the Jamestown carbarn in this July 20, 1940, scene. The 1924 McGraw Electric Railway Directory noted that the 40-mile Jamestown, Westfield and Northwestern Railroad line had 13 trolley cars and one snow sweeper. With the heavy winter snowfalls in this region, it was not an easy task to keep the line open. (B. H. Nichols photograph.)

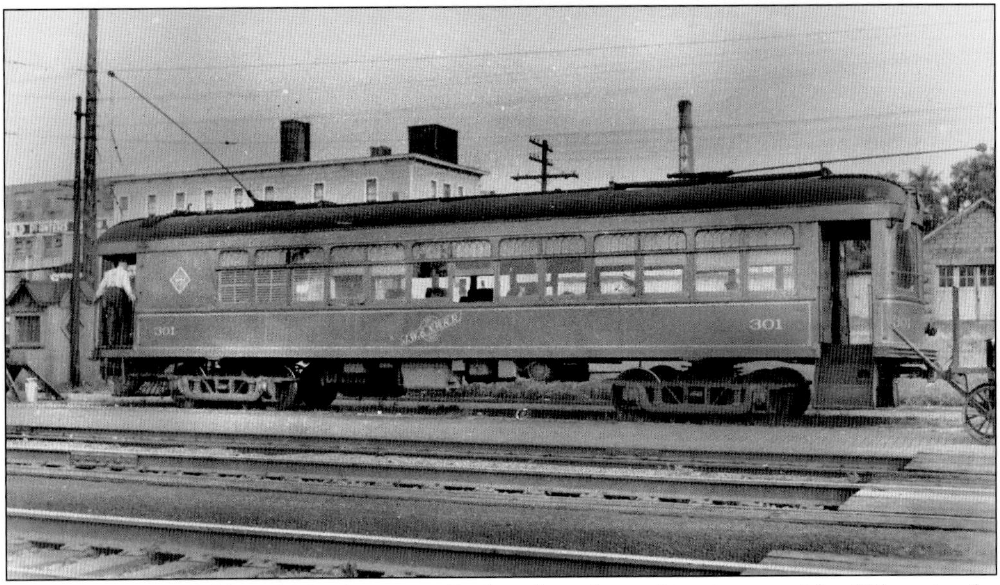

Jamestown, Westfield and Northwestern Railroad steel combination car No. 301 waits for passengers at the Westfield passenger station of the New York Central Railroad on August 19, 1942. This was an excellent example of a trolley line acting as a feeder to a main line railroad. The company coordinated its schedules to meet the passenger trains that stopped at Westfield. (B. H. Nichols photograph.)

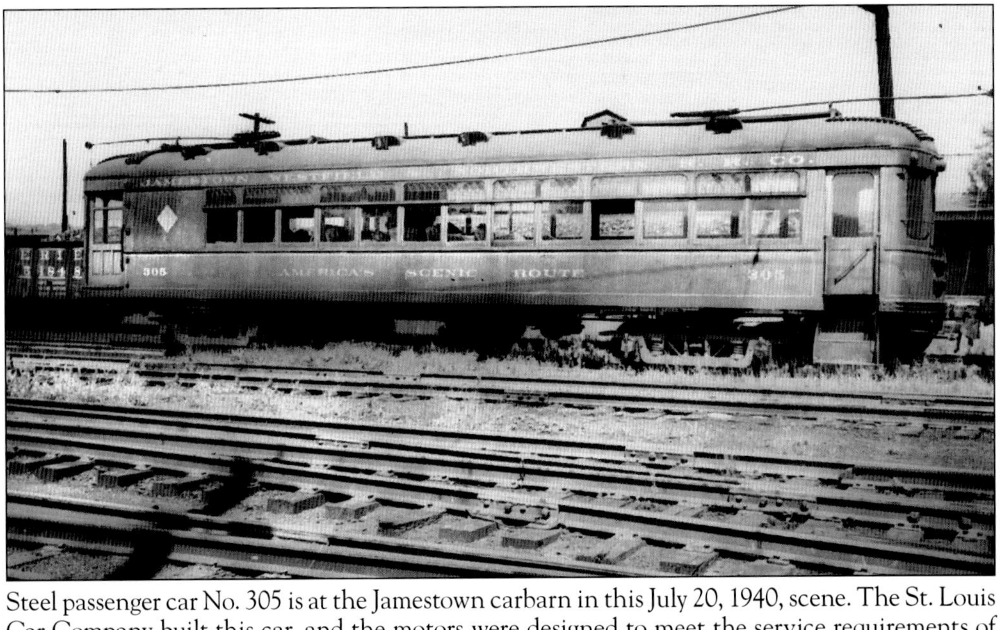

Steel passenger car No. 305 is at the Jamestown carbarn in this July 20, 1940, scene. The St. Louis Car Company built this car, and the motors were designed to meet the service requirements of sustained speed over rolling country with relatively few stops, which characterized the Jamestown, Westfield and Northwestern Railroad line. (B. H. Nichols photograph.)

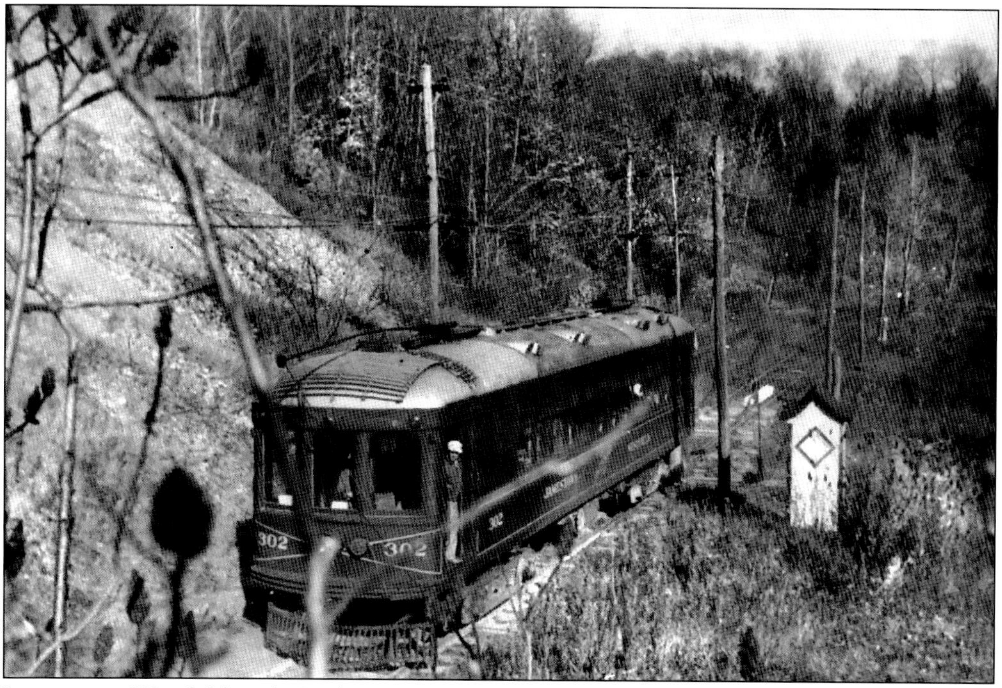

Jamestown, Westfield and Northwestern Railroad car No. 302 is at Glenewen siding on the single-track line. Much of the line went through a sparsely populated rural area. Ridership from the communities of Mayville, Dewittville, Maple Springs, Bemus Point, and Colburns between Jamestown and Westfield declined as the automobile became commonplace.

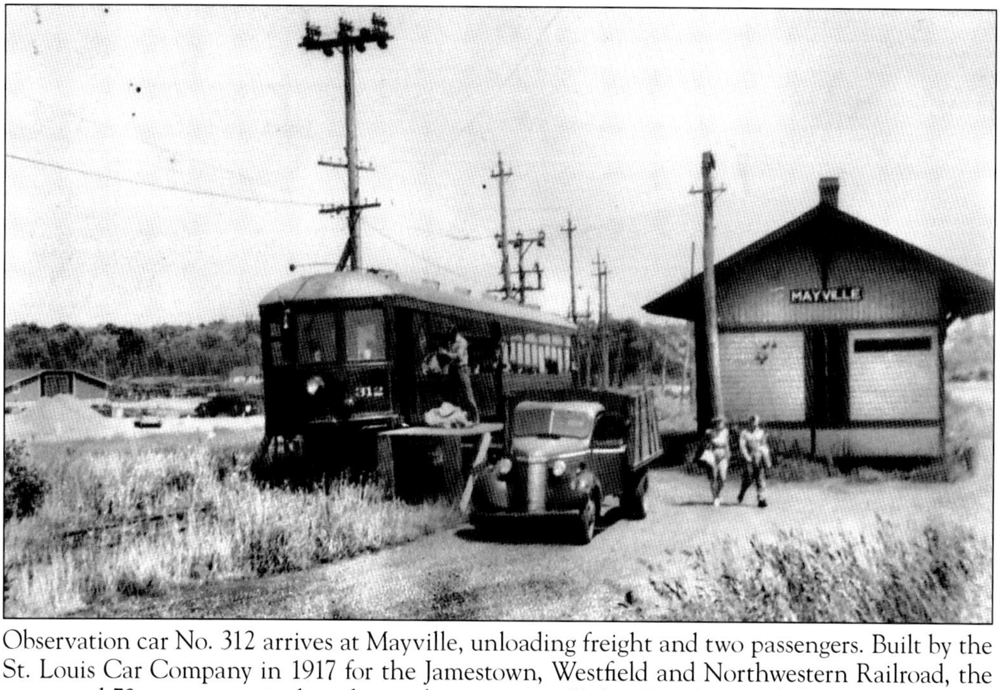

Observation car No. 312 arrives at Mayville, unloading freight and two passengers. Built by the St. Louis Car Company in 1917 for the Jamestown, Westfield and Northwestern Railroad, the car seated 72 passengers, its length over bumpers was 62 feet 2 inches, and the total car weight was 88,400 pounds.

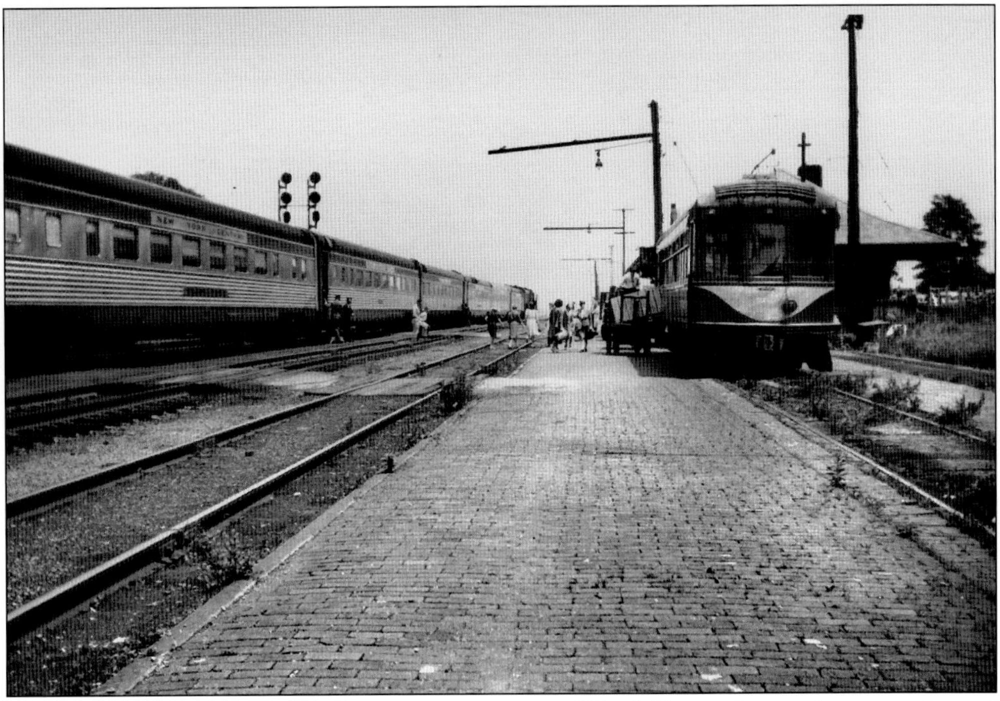

The New York Central Railroad passenger station at Westfield was the northern terminus of the Jamestown, Westfield and Northwestern Railroad. Car No. 302 has met the New York Central Railroad passenger train, and this station served as an important transfer point for riders heading to Jamestown, plus the communities served by the trolley line had access to east and west railroad passenger service. (W. K. Foster photograph.)

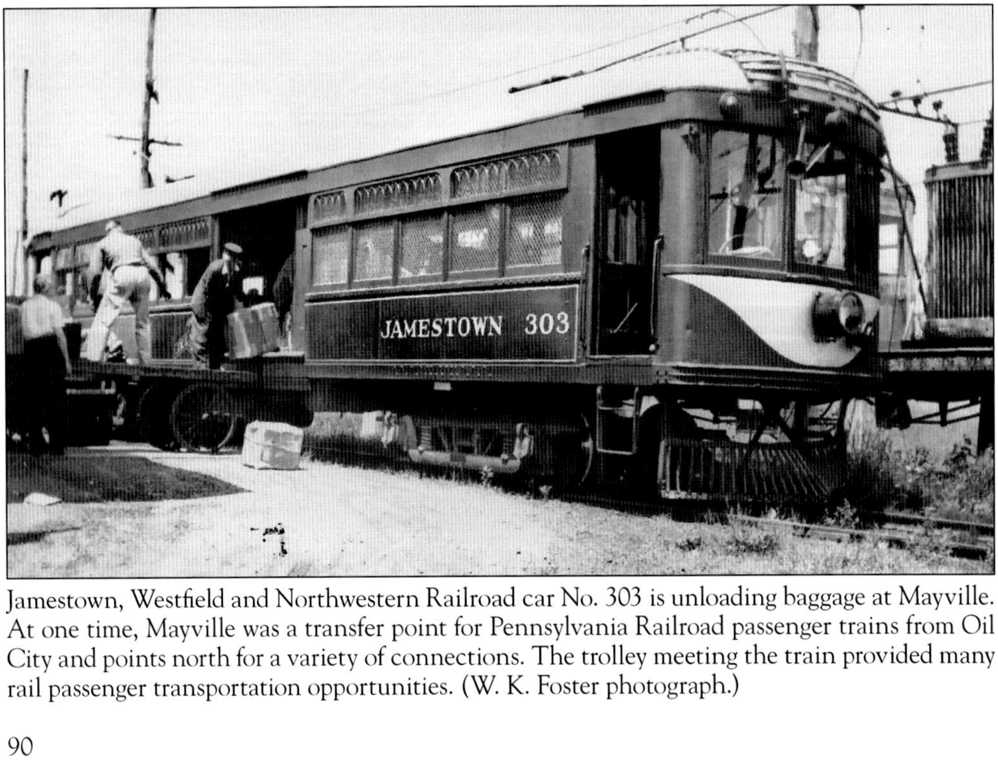

Jamestown, Westfield and Northwestern Railroad car No. 303 is unloading baggage at Mayville. At one time, Mayville was a transfer point for Pennsylvania Railroad passenger trains from Oil City and points north for a variety of connections. The trolley meeting the train provided many rail passenger transportation opportunities. (W. K. Foster photograph.)

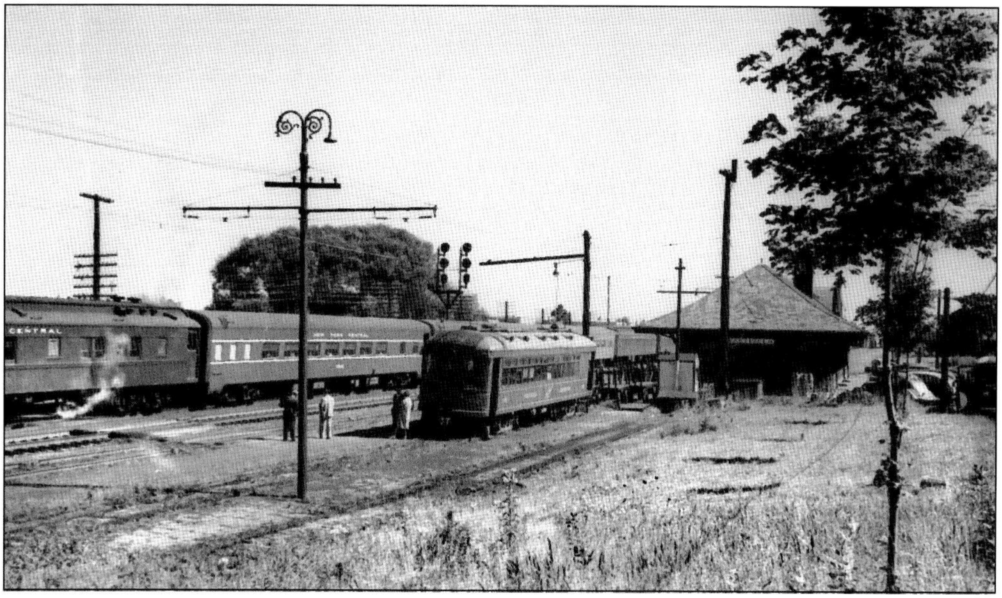

In this Westfield scene on September 2, 1946, passengers are getting scarce transferring from the New York Central Railroad passenger train to the trolley. The Jamestown, Westfield and Northwestern Railroad struggled during the Depression years, and business increased during World War II. Following the end of the war, there was a rapid decline in the number of passengers. (B. H. Nichols photograph.)

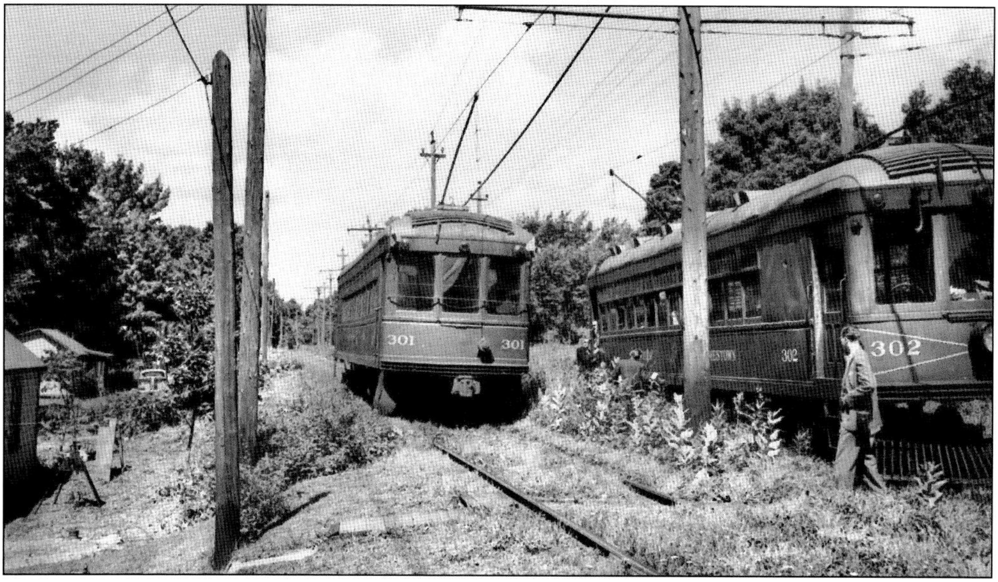

In this September 2, 1946, meeting at Coburn siding, Jamestown, Westfield and Northwestern Railroad car No. 301 is northbound and car No. 302 is southbound. Vegetation covers the right-of-way as maintenance was trimmed to reduce expenses because of the serious decline in passenger revenues as more automobiles captured the business. (B. H. Nichols photograph.)

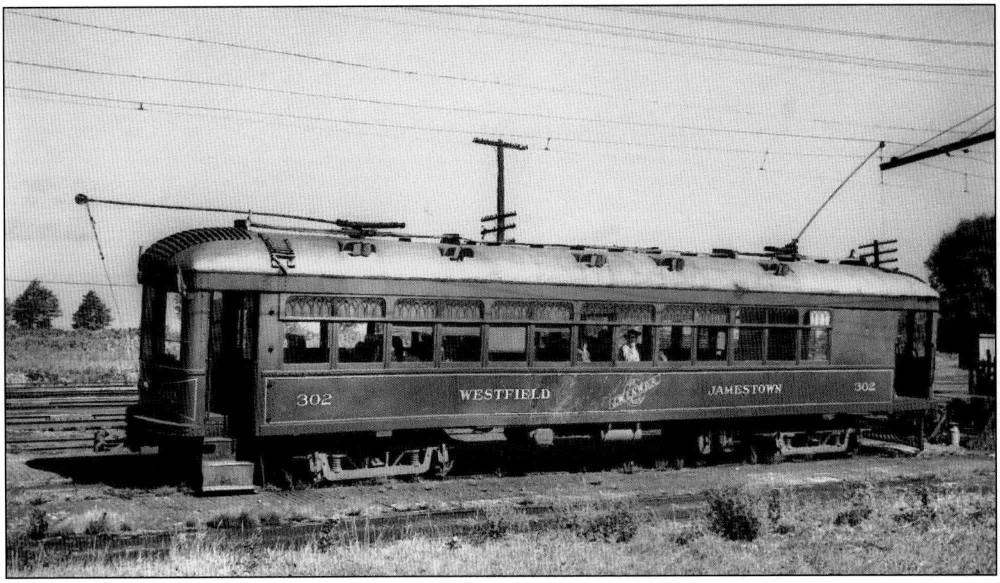

Jamestown, Westfield and Northwestern Railroad steel combination passenger and baggage car No. 302 waits for the next train at the New York Central Railroad passenger station at Westfield on September 2, 1946. The car had a mahogany interior finish with black leather seat coverings. In the baggage compartment, the finish was natural ash. (B. H. Nichols photograph.)

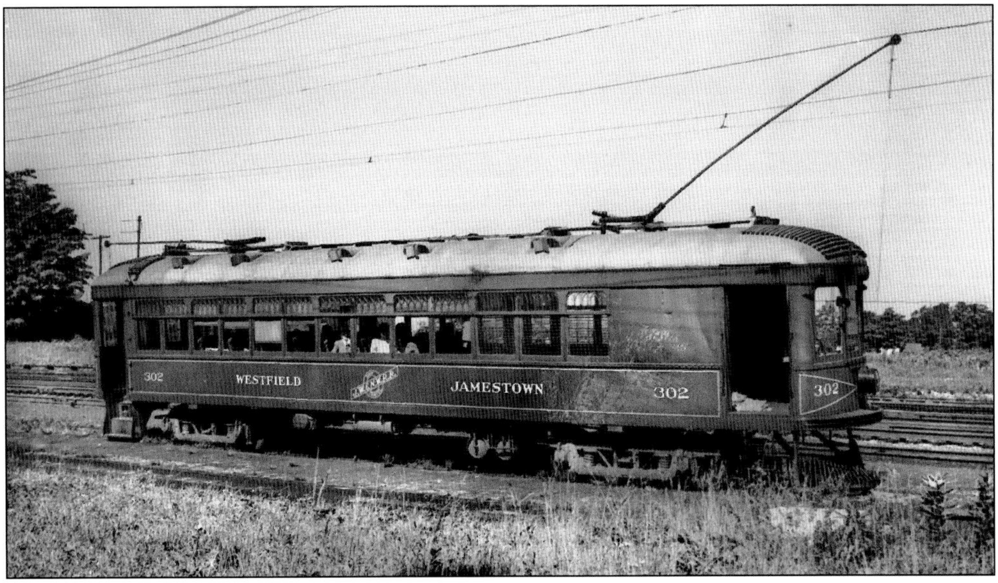

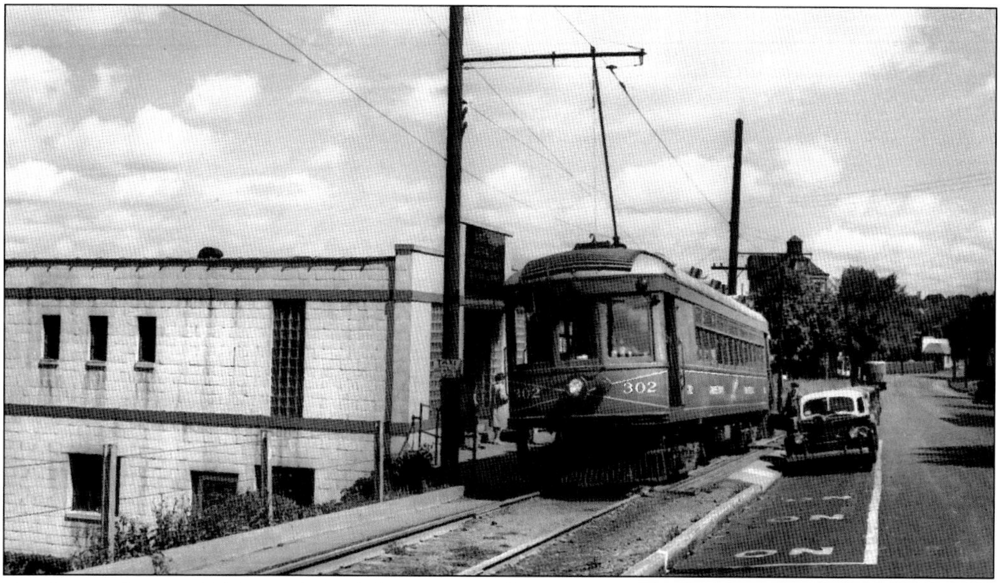

On September 2, 1946, car No. 302 arrives at Jamestown, which was the southern terminus of the Jamestown, Westfield and Northwestern Railroad. Jamestown was a key transfer point for the Erie Railroad passenger service east to New York City and west to Chicago. Although rapidly declining, travel by rail was still a viable option. (B. H. Nichols photograph.)

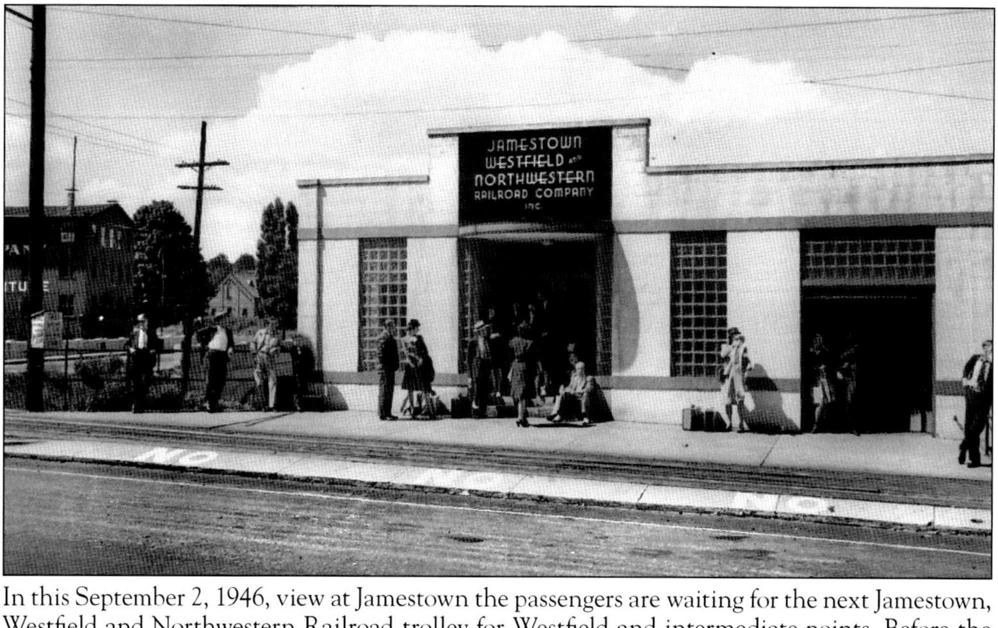

In this September 2, 1946, view at Jamestown the passengers are waiting for the next Jamestown, Westfield and Northwestern Railroad trolley for Westfield and intermediate points. Before the advent of the interstate highway, travel by train was still commonplace, but this was the last interurban trolley line in southwestern New York State. (B. H. Nichols photograph.)

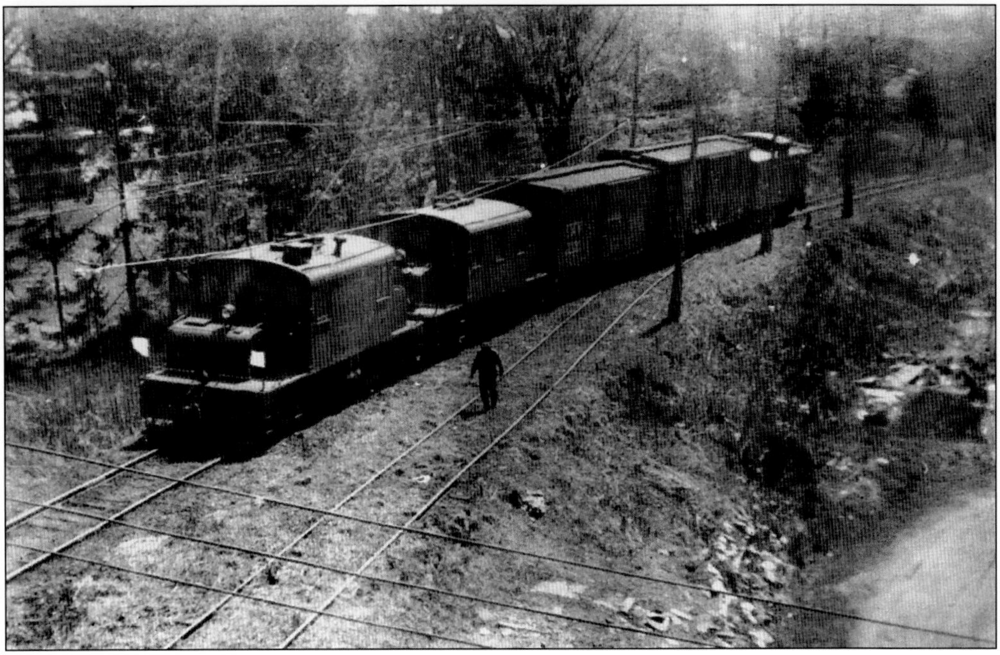

Two Jamestown, Westfield and Northwestern Railroad electric freight motors pulling two boxcars and a caboose approach Westfield. In earlier years, a typical freight train on this line would have had 15 to 30 freight cars. Not only was the company faced with declining passenger ridership, it was also losing freight business with the emergence of trucking companies.

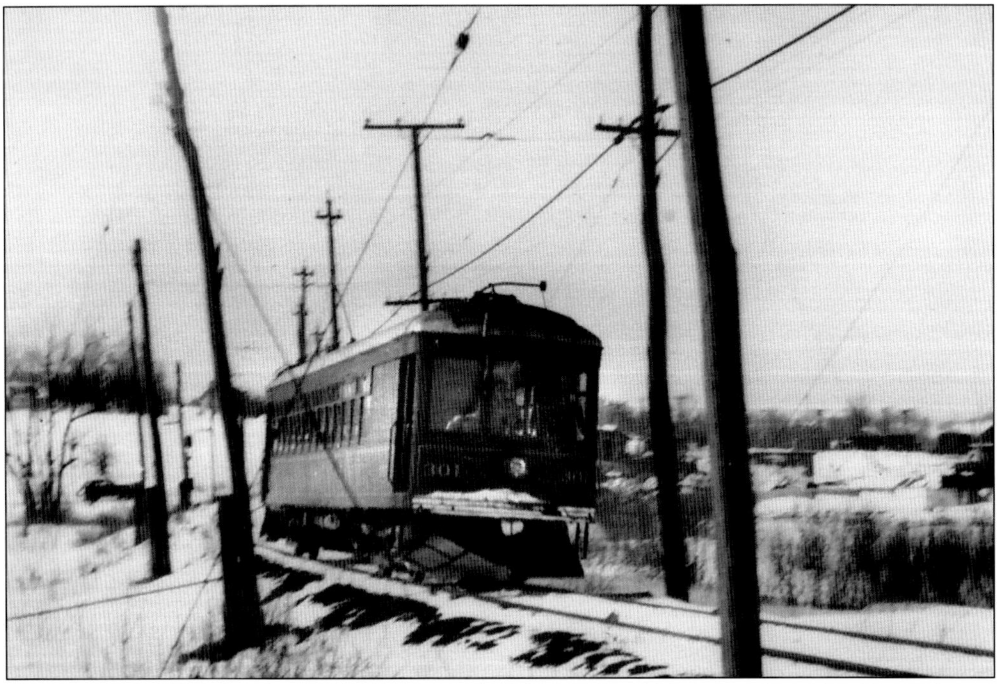

Jamestown, Westfield and Northwestern Railroad car No. 301 approaches the Pennsylvania Railroad Junction at Mayville in this winter scene. In addition to this transfer point, the line provided a connection to the New York Central at Westfield and the Erie Railroad at Jamestown.

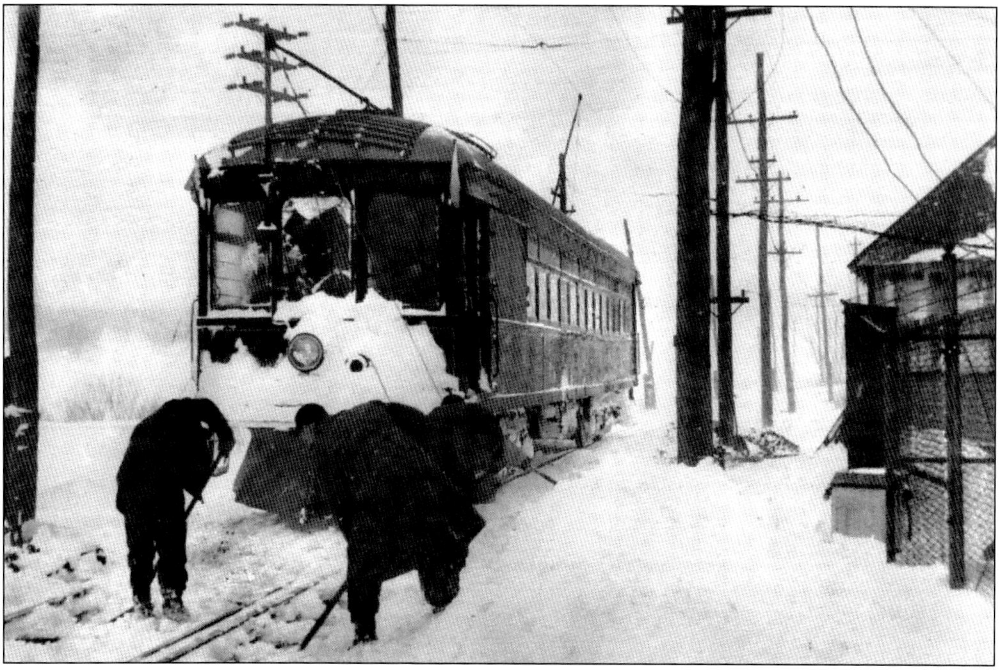

Jamestown, Westfield and Northwestern Railroad car No. 301 is in a snowstorm in February 1947 at the Pennsylvania Railroad Junction at Mayville. The company had one snow sweeper, but with the massive snowstorms that blanketed the area and not having the benefit of modern snow-removal equipment available today, it was necessary to hand dig out the switches to keep the line in service.

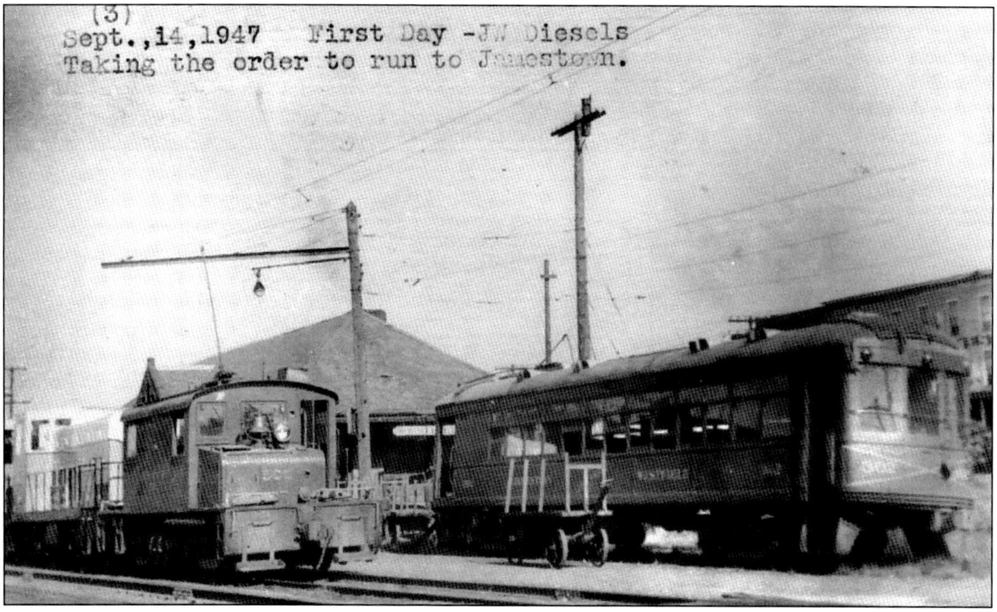

On September 14, 1947, Jamestown, Westfield and Northwestern Railroad electric freight motor No. 500 pauses with the new diesels that had just arrived for the first run to Jamestown. Trolley No. 302 is parked at the Westfield Station of the New York Central Railroad. Trolley service ended November 30, 1947. Freight service was dieselized, but by 1950, the line was abandoned.

JAMESTOWN WESTFIELD & NORTH WESTERN R. R. (ELECTRIFIED)

TRACK CONNECTIONS WITH THE NEW YORK CENTRAL R. R. AT WESTFIELD, N. Y.
PENNSYLVANIA R. R. AT MAYVILLE, N. Y.
ERIE R. R. AT JAMESTOWN, N. Y.
HANDLES ALL FOREIGN EQUIPMENT

General Offices, Jamestown, New York — **William H. Pickard, Traffic Manager**

THROUGH TICKETS AND PULLMAN RESERVATIONS TO ALL POINTS IN UNITED STATES AND CANADA

READ DOWN / READ UP

12 Daily	10 Daily	8 Daily	6 Daily	4 Daily	2 Daily	Eastern Standard Time Toledo and East, Central Time West Thereof	1 Daily	3 Daily	5 Daily	7 Daily	9 Daily	11 Daily
P.M.	P.M.	P.M.	P.M.	A.M.	A.M.	Leave] [Arrive	A.M.	A.M.	P.M.	P.M.	P.M.	P.M.
*8 15	*7 10	*4 05	*1 10	*10 55	*7 30	Jamestown	7 28	10 23	1 19	4 32	7 03	10 43
8 34	7 29	4 24	1 29	11 14	7 50	Bemus Point	7 09	10 04	12 59	4 13	6 44	10 24
8 41	7 36	4 31	1 36	11 21	7 57	Maple Springs	7 01	9 56	12 51	4 05	6 36	10 16
8 50	7 45	4 40	1 45	11 30	8 06	Point Chautauqua	6 53	9 48	12 43	3 57	6 28	10 08
8 57	7 52	4 47	1 52	11 37	8 13	Mayville	6 46	9 41	12 36	3 50	6 21	10 01
9 18	8 13	5 08	2 13	11 58	8 33	Westfield	*6 25	* 9 20	*12 15	*3 25	*6 00	*9 40
P.M.	P.M.	P.M.	P.M.	A.M.	A.M.	Arrive] (N.Y.C. Station) [Leave	A.M.	A.M.	P.M.	P.M.	P.M.	P.M.
P.M.	P.M.	P.M.	P.M.	P.M.	A.M.	Leave] (N.Y.C. East) [Arrive	A.M.	A.M.	P.M.	P.M.	P.M.	P.M.
9 33	8 26	7 46	3 24	12 08	8 40	Westfield	6 13	9 17	......	2 25	5 17	9 38
P.M.	P.M.	P.M.	P.M.	P.M.	A.M.	Arrive] [Leave	A.M.	A.M.	......	P.M.	P.M.	P.M.
10 50	9 40	9 25	5 00	1 10	9 45	Buffalo	5 10	8 10	......	1 14	4 15	8 20
......	......	......	......	3 41	......	Niagara Falls	......	†6 10	......	12 01	2 55	5 50
12 05	11 09	......	6 57	2 37	11 13	Rochester	3 29	6 38	......	11 23	2 52	6 50
1 26	12 39	......	8 40	4 00	12 46	Syracuse	2 05	5 05	......	9 35	1 28	5 00
2 25	1 40	......	9 56	4 53	1 49	Utica	1 04	3 33	......	8 00	12 34	3 29
4 00	3 27	......	12 15	6 42	3 44	Albany	11 15	1 40	......	5 20	10 42	12 46
7 00	......	......	4 40	9 45	7 00	New York	8 10	11 30	......	1 35	8 00	9 15
7 09	6 35	......	3 40	......	6 40	Springfield	7 15	9 25	......	1 37	†6 24	9 30
8 16	8 02	......	5 03	......	8 04	Worcester	5 59	8 09	......	11 26	†4 32	8 08
9 20	9 10	......	6 25	......	9 15	Boston	4 50	7 00	......	10 00	†2 50	7 00
A.M.	A.M.	P.M.	A.M.	P.M.	P.M.	Arrive] [Leave	P.M.	P.M.	......	P.M.	A.M.	A.M.
P.M.	......	P.M.	P.M.	EMPIRE STATE EXPRESS ALL SEATS RESERVED	A.M.	Leave] (N.Y.C. West) [Arrive	A.M.	A.M.	P.M.	P.M.	EMPIRE STATE EXPRESS ALL SEATS RESERVED	P.M.
9 38	......	5 17	2 25		9 17	Westfield	5 43	8 40	12 08	3 24		9 33
P.M.	......	P.M.	P.M.		A.M.	Arrive] [Leave	A.M.	A.M.	P.M.	P.M.		P.M.
10 21	......	5 48	3 00		9 56	Erie	5 10	8 10	11 40	2 45		9 05
12 30	......	7 40	5 20		12 10	Cleveland	2 25	6 20	9 55	12 30		6 55
......	......	9 05	......		12 40	Youngstown	12 10	......	......	12 05		6 28
......	......	10 40	......		2 15	Pittsburgh	10 20	......	......	10 30		5 00
3 05	......	12 45	7 57		2 58	Toledo	9 25	4 00	......	9 45		4 30
5 10	......	5 10	9 50		......	Detroit	......	11 05	......	8 00		1 00
11 45	......	11 45	5 30		......	Grand Rapids	......	......	......	11 50		......
7 00	......	6 50	12 30		7 30	Chicago	4 15	11 00	......	1 00		11 30
3 45	......	......	8 55		3 20	Columbus	8 20	1 10	......	8 10		3 15
7 05	......	......	5 15		6 20	Cincinnati	5 45	9 00	......	......		12 30
6 40	......	2 20	12 05		......	Indianapolis	5 30	10 40	......	4 35		......
11 30	......	7 25	7 10		......	St. Louis	11 40	6 00	......	11 32		......
A.M.	......	A.M.	A.M.		P.M.	Arrive] [Leave	A.M.	P.M.	A.M.	P.M.		P.M.

*Daily; †Daily, except Sunday. — Printed in U. S. A. — Effective April 27, 1947

SHIP—TRAVEL VIA "THE SCENIC ROUTE"

The April 27, 1947, schedule of the Jamestown, Westfield and Northwestern Railroad showed six round-trips in each direction. Eastbound and westbound connections with New York Central Railroad passenger trains at Westfield were conveniently chosen to minimize waiting time. Local riders benefited because it was easy to make one-day trips from either Jamestown or Westfield.

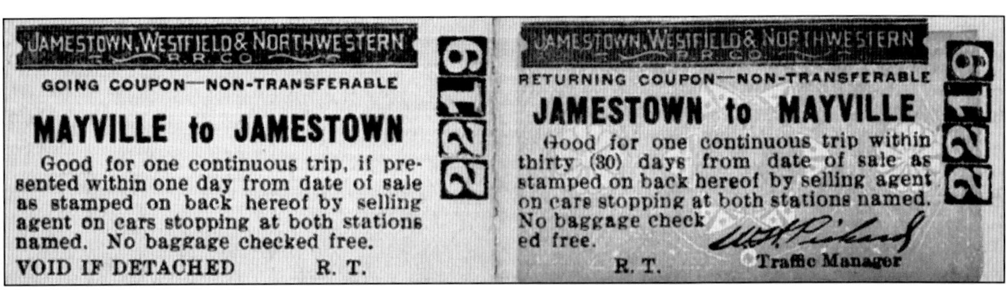

Jamestown, Westfield and Northwestern Railroad used tickets like the one shown above, and passengers had connections with the New York Central and Nickel Plate Railroads at Westfield, the Pennsylvania Railroad at Mayville, and the Erie Railroad at Jamestown. Passenger revenues had been declining as early as 1925, but freight business of coal, furniture, and general merchandise shipped to any part of the United States and Canada kept the line going until 1950.

Six

Warren County Trolleys

The first trolley car in Warren, Pennsylvania, operated on July 1, 1893, on Water Street from the Pennsylvania Railroad to the Conewango Creek Bridge. In 1897, a two-mile line was built from Liberty and Water Street to North Warren, and by 1898, a line was constructed on Conewango Avenue to New Street. In 1903, the Warren Street Railway Company built a 12-mile line to Sheffield. In 1904, the Warren and Jamestown Street Railway Company began constructing a line from Warren to Jamestown. The first trolley car was operated on this line on September 2, 1905, with W. J. Kribrill as motorman and Stewart Jenkins as conductor. Officials of the trolley company, newspaper personnel, and other invited guests made the run from North Warren to the Humphrey House in Jamestown. Because the line operated on single-phase alternating current in the early years, it was necessary to transfer to a Warren Street Railway car at North Warren for the trip to downtown Warren. When the line was converted to direct current, through service was operated to Warren.

Starting pay was 17¢ per hour, and in later years, it reached 35¢ per hour. An employee worked 11 to 12 hours per day, seven days a week, and there were no vacations. During the April 1913 flood when the Conewango Creek overflowed its banks, all operating cars were taken from the carbarn on Pennsylvania Avenue to higher ground. East-side cars were parked on Conewango Avenue. West-side cars were parked on Pennsylvania Avenue West. With Pennsylvania Avenue flooded, passengers would transfer to a horse-drawn carriage, which operated through the high water to Conewango Avenue where riders could transfer to the trolley for east-side points. The Warren-Sheffield line was flooded at Rogertown, and passengers had to walk almost a mile to reach the Glade Bridge, which was the terminus for Sheffield cars.

On April 10, 1924, the Warren Street Railway, Warren and Jamestown Street Railway, and the Warren-Sheffield line were sold to the Penn Public Service Corporation. About $12,000 was spent on refurbishing tracks and rolling stock during 1924 for the Warren Street Railway. Over 8,000 new ties were installed. The Warren trolley terminal at Liberty Street and Pennsylvania Avenue was completely remodeled. During the county fair, trolley riding was heavy. When the automobile became common, trolley riding declined. During 1928, the West Ridge Transportation Company purchased the Warren Street Railway Company. The Warren-Sheffield line was abandoned March 31, 1928. The Warren-Jamestown line was abandoned December 2, 1929. Warren Street Railway lines operating on Pennsylvania Avenue, Conewango Avenue, and the line to North Warren were abandoned October 18, 1930.

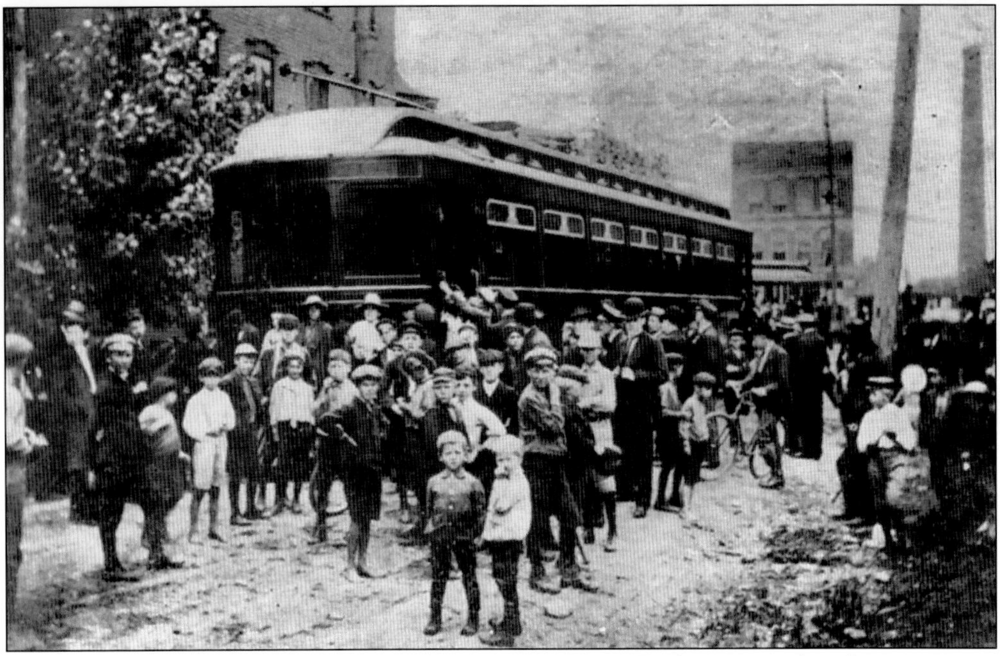

The first trolley car on the Warren and Jamestown Street Railway arrived in Jamestown on September 2, 1905. This was an important event as Warren was now linked by trolley to Buffalo and Cleveland. Initially the southern terminus of the line was at North Warren, because the line was operated on single-phase alternating current, but was later converted to direct current and service operated to downtown Warren.

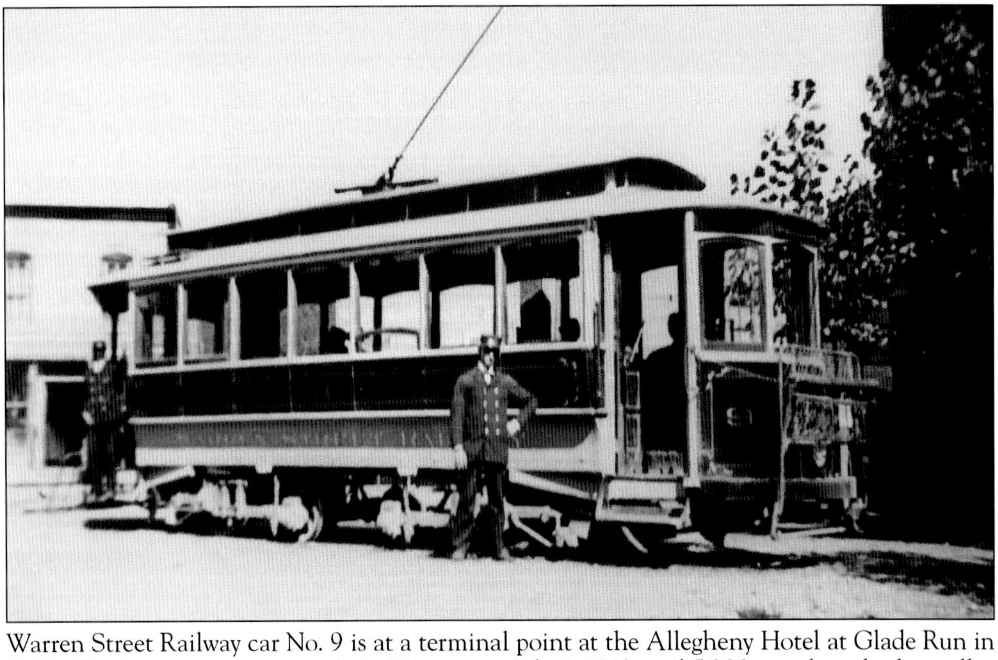

Warren Street Railway car No. 9 is at a terminal point at the Allegheny Hotel at Glade Run in 1898. The first test run was made in Warren on July 1, 1893, and 5,000 people rode the trolley system on July 4, 1893. The fare was 5¢ or six tickets for 25¢ and 25 tickets for $1. (Harold C. Putnam photograph.)

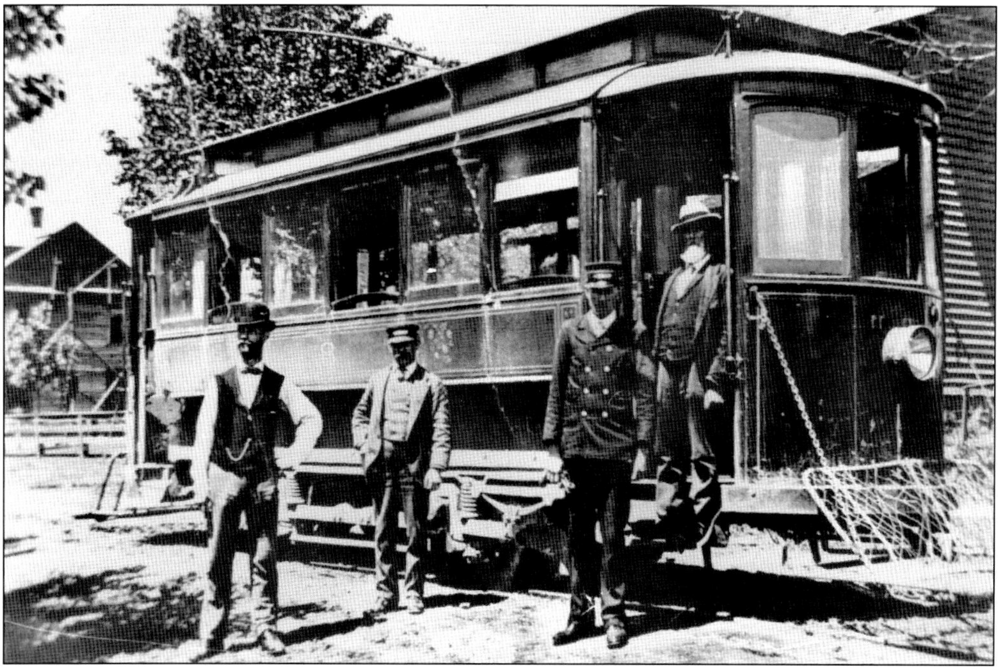

The Siggins family was prominent in the operation of the Warren trolleys with president D. H. Siggins and secretary-treasurer and general manager H. A. Siggins. Ben Siggins and Bill Siggins pose at the doorway of a Warren Street Railway trolley at New Street, which was the terminus of the Conewango line in 1898. (Harold C. Putnam photograph.)

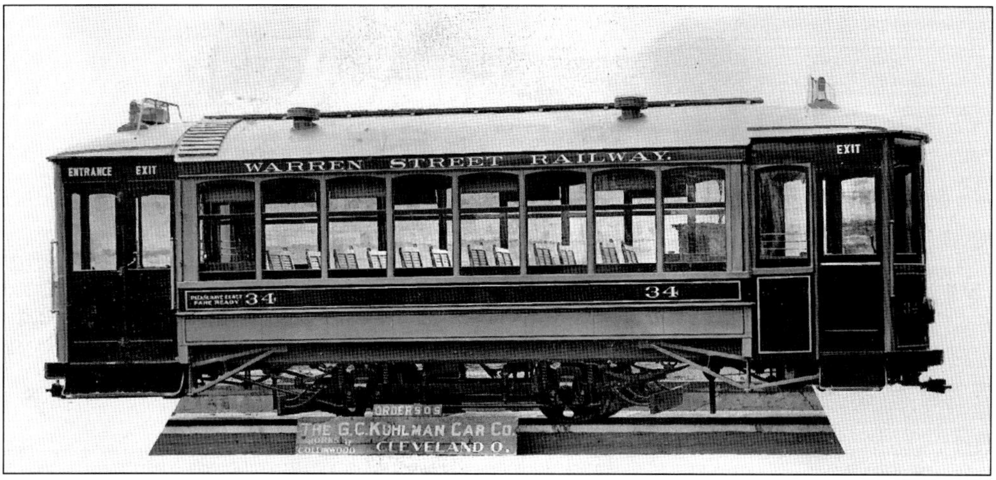

Warren Street Railway car No. 34 was built by G. C. Kuhlman Car Company of Cleveland. Residents in Warren literally loved their trolley car service, which operated from 6:00 a.m. to 11:00 p.m. The Pennsylvania Avenue line served both the Pennsylvania Railroad and New York Central Railroad passenger stations. Crowds of people would get off the train and pack awaiting trolley cars.

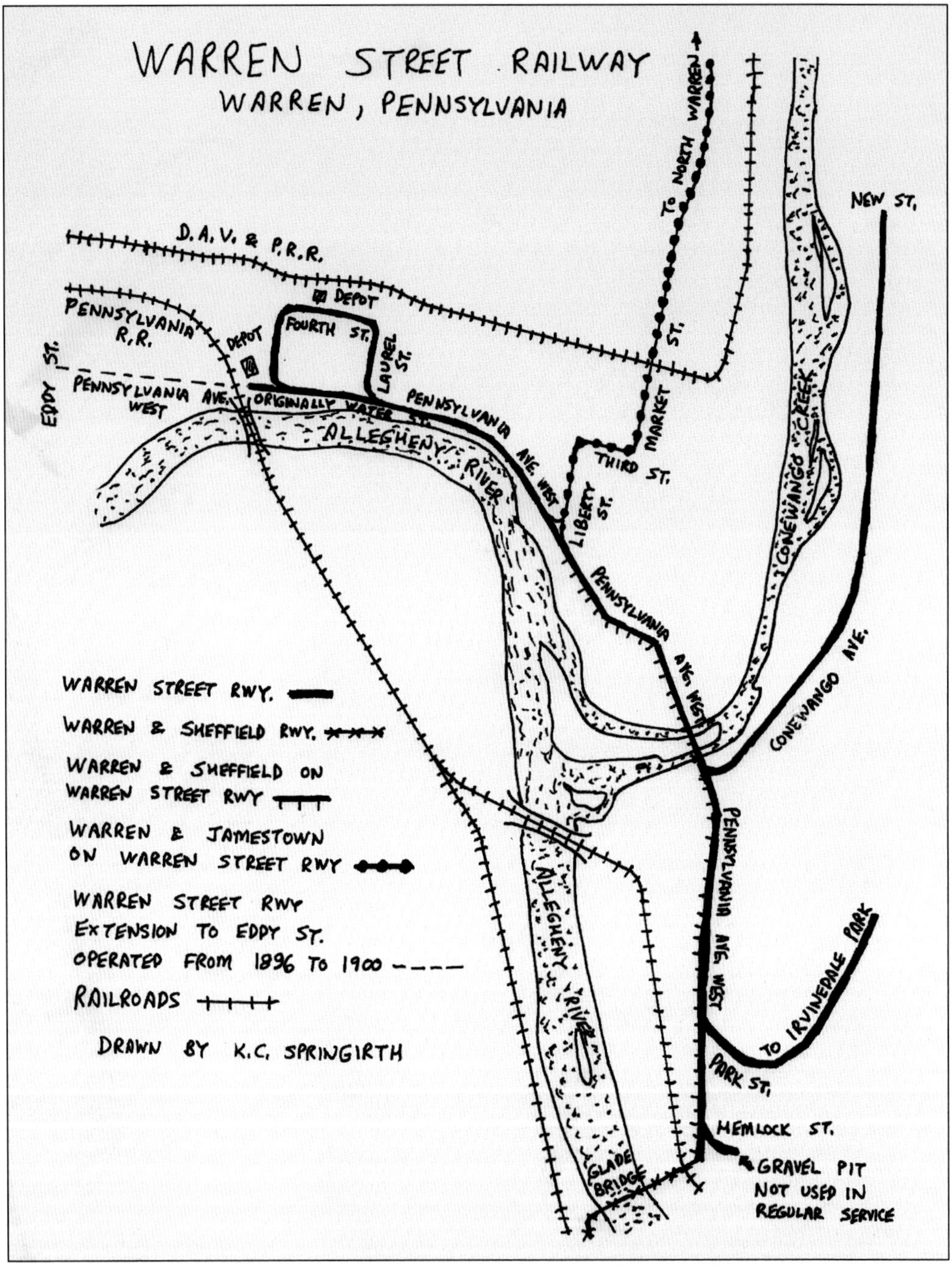

The Warren Street Railway operated 20.25 miles of track of which 7 miles were in paved street. Warren and Jamestown Street Railway operated 21.93 miles of track of which 1.5 miles were in paved street. Four cars provided a 10-minute headway on the Pennsylvania Avenue line. In addition, Warren and Sheffield cars used Pennsylvania Avenue to reach their terminus at Liberty Street. One car serviced the Conewango line, and one car operated from downtown Warren to North Warren.

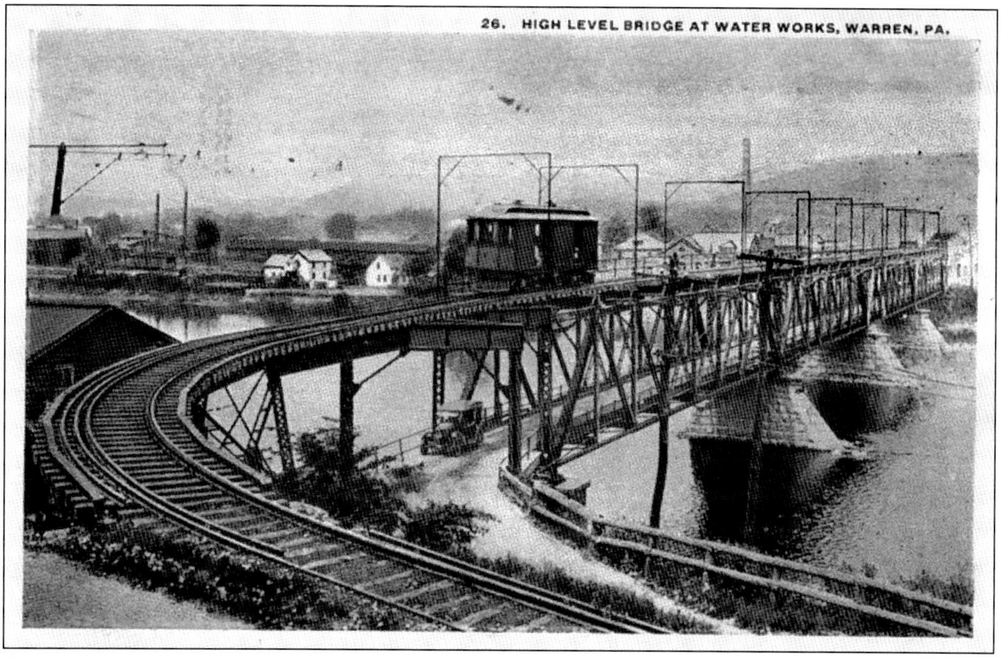

A Warren Street Railway trolley freight car makes its way across the High Level Bridge over the Allegheny River. Motor vehicle traffic was on the lower level of the bridge. Wells Fargo Express was handled on the Warren and Jamestown line. All of the trolley lines in Warren County were controlled by H. A. Siggins and were sold to the Penn Public Service Corporation on April 10, 1924.

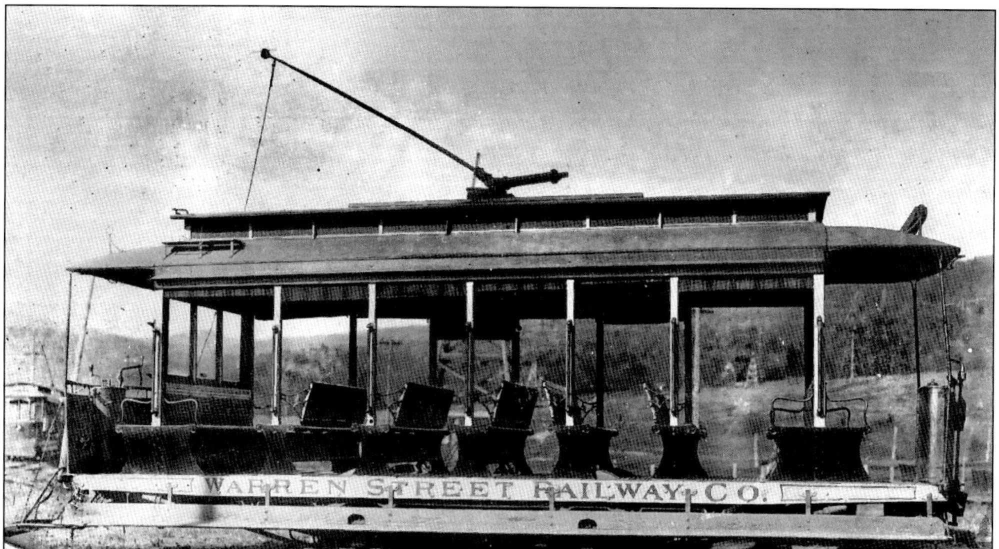

This was one of six open summer cars operated by the Warren Street Railway Company. They were originally used on the line to Irvinedale Park until both the park and trolley line closed. They were next assigned to handle the crowds to the Warren County Fair. When the fair folded in 1928, the cars were scrapped.

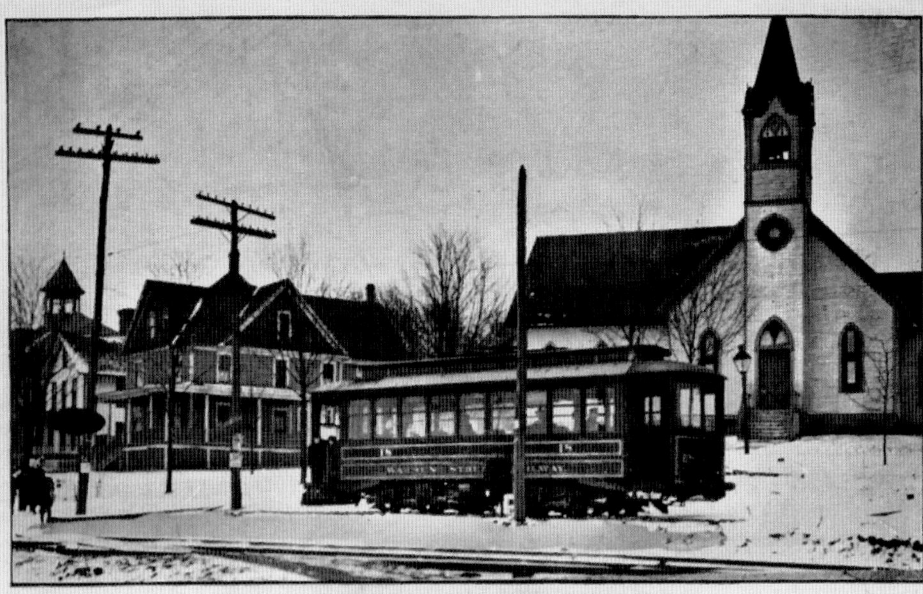

M. E. CHURCH AND PARSONAGE, SHEFFIELD, PA.

The 12-mile, rutted muddy road became a paved highway, U.S. Route 6, which paralleled the Warren and Sheffield Street Railway line from Warren to Sheffield. Passing by the Methodist Episcopal Church in Sheffield, the line linked Warren County to other communities by trolley. The last trolley operated on the Warren-Sheffield line on March 31, 1928.

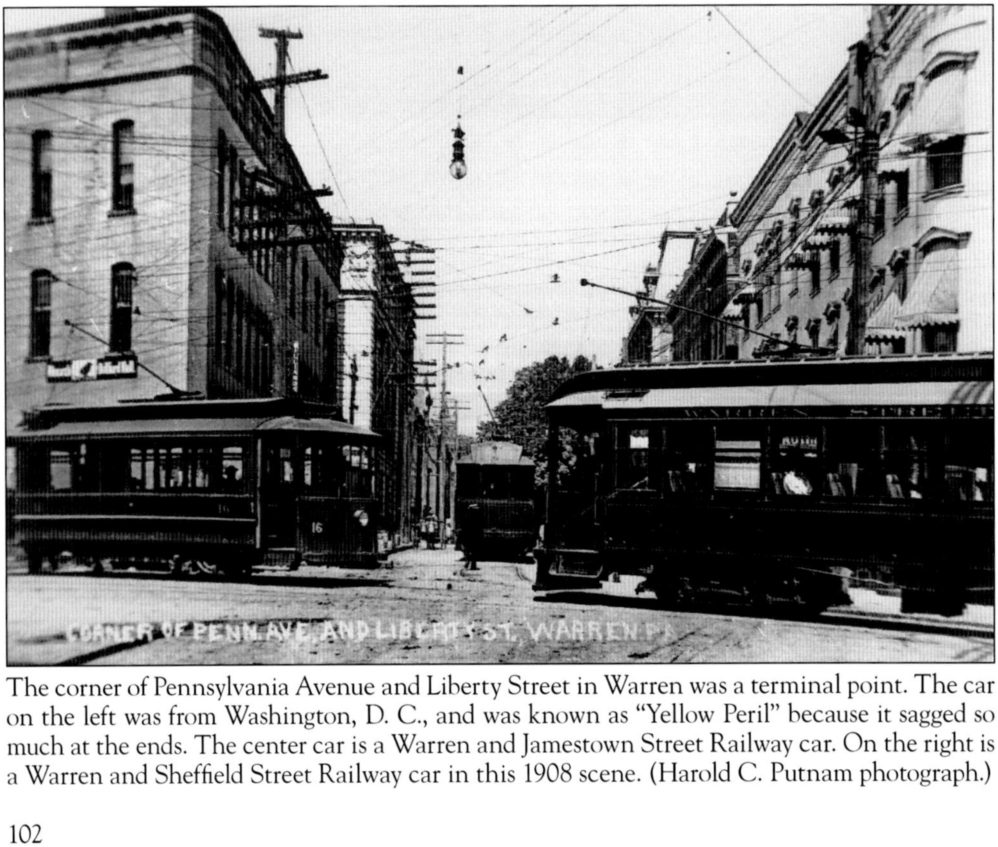

The corner of Pennsylvania Avenue and Liberty Street in Warren was a terminal point. The car on the left was from Washington, D. C., and was known as "Yellow Peril" because it sagged so much at the ends. The center car is a Warren and Jamestown Street Railway car. On the right is a Warren and Sheffield Street Railway car in this 1908 scene. (Harold C. Putnam photograph.)

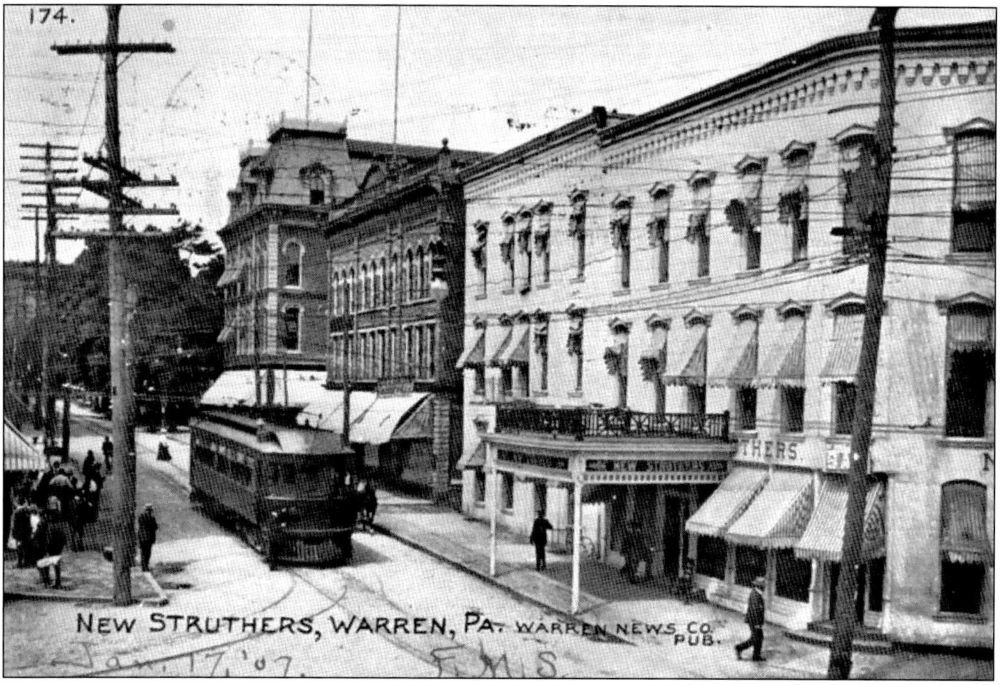

Pennsylvania Avenue in downtown Warren was the southern terminus of the Warren and Jamestown Street Railway line. The cars pictured here were number series 51 through 55 and were large, luxurious, heavy, and cumbersome. Trolley service was hourly with the first car leaving Warren at 6:00 a.m. An additional car provided service from this point to North Warren, resulting in a 30-minute headway on that portion of the line.

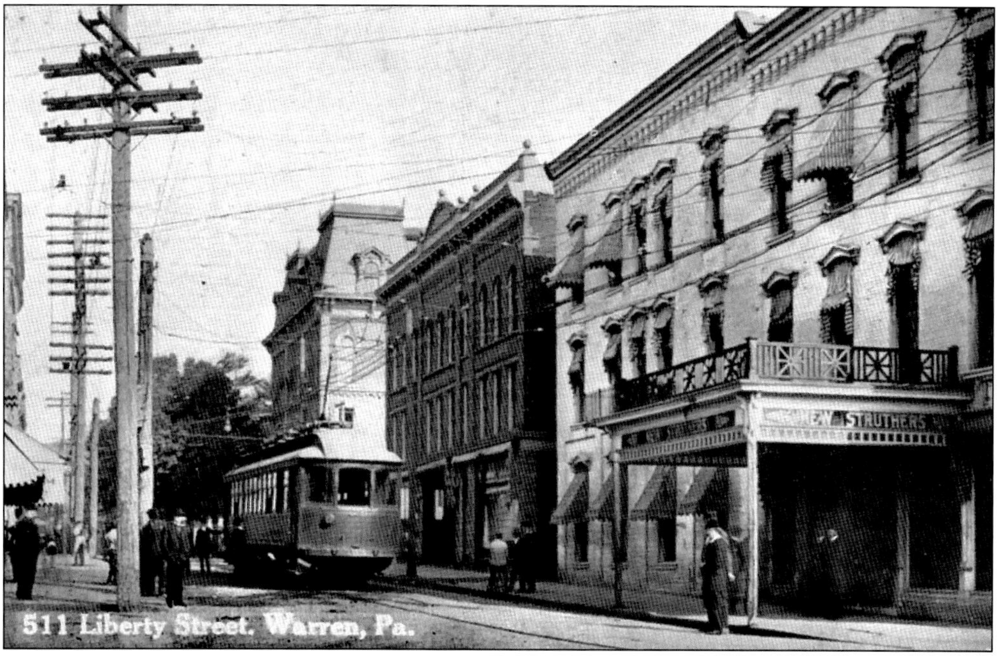

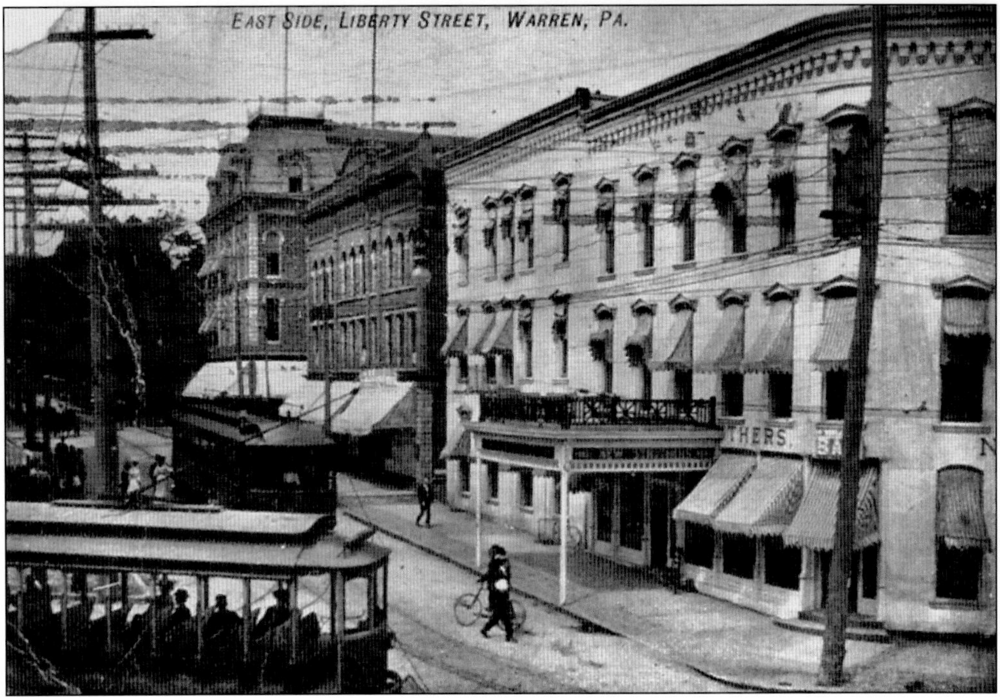

Pennsylvania Avenue and Liberty Street in Warren was the location for this Warren Street Railway open car on the left. The closed car is on Liberty Street on the Warren and Jamestown Street Railway. The McGraw Electric Directory 1924 showed 19 trolleys on the Warren Street Railway and 7 cars on the Warren and Jamestown Street Railway.

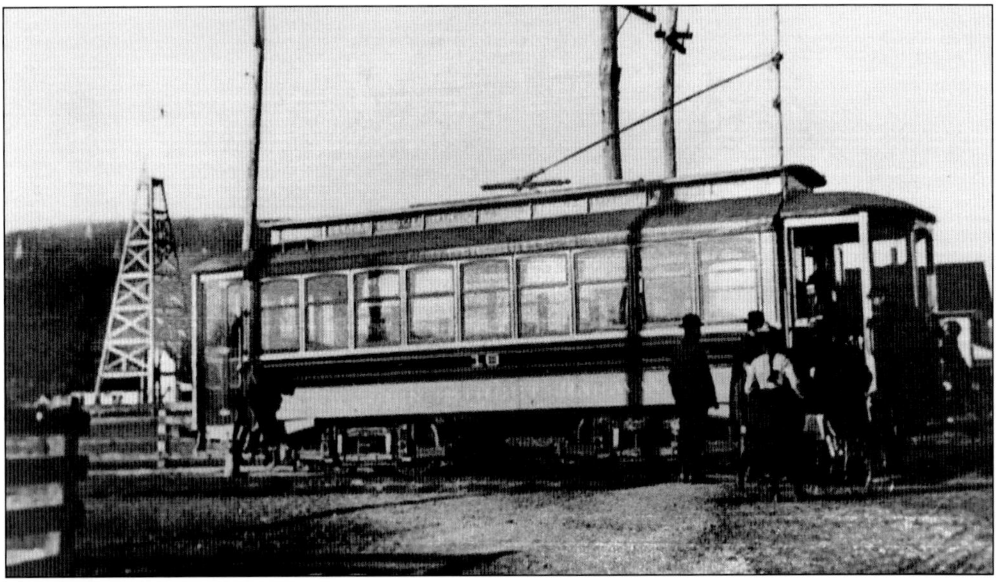

Warren and Sheffield Street Railway trolley No. 18 is at Tiona, Pennsylvania, about 1903. It was possible to go from Tiona to Erie by trolley using the Warren and Sheffield to Warren, the Warren and Jamestown to Jamestown, either the Chautauqua Traction or Jamestown, Westfield and Northwestern to Westfield, and the Buffalo and Lake Erie Traction Company to Erie. (Harold C. Putnam photograph.)

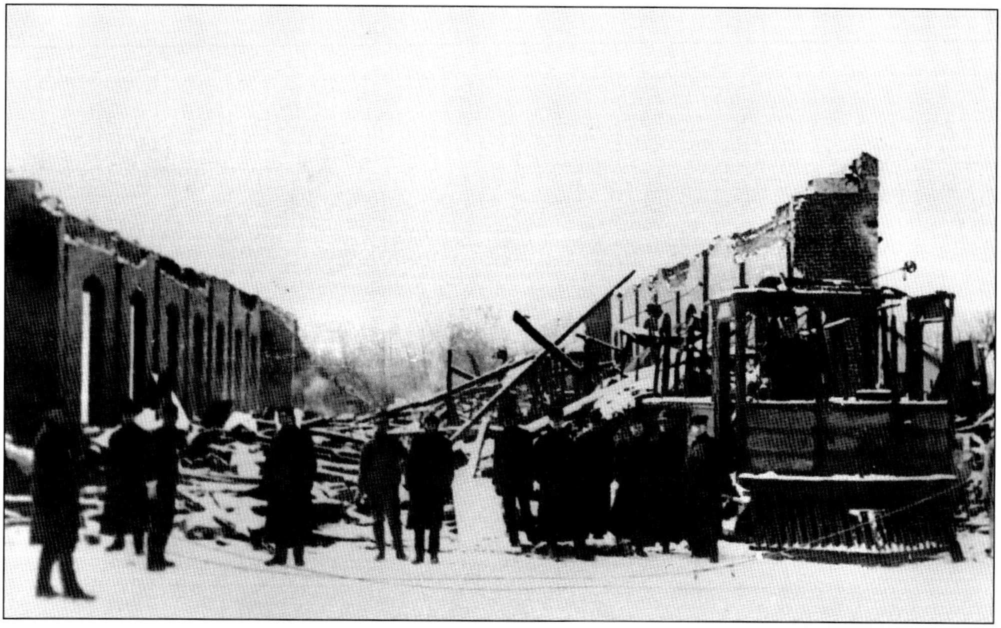

On February 24, 1907, a fire of unknown origin destroyed the trolley barn. The Warren Street Railway lost four trolleys and a snowplow. The Warren and Jamestown Street Railway lost two of their new passenger cars and a baggage car. Fortunately six summer cars were stored at Stoneham on the line to Sheffield, and there were two cars in service on the line to Jamestown. (Harold C. Putnam photograph.)

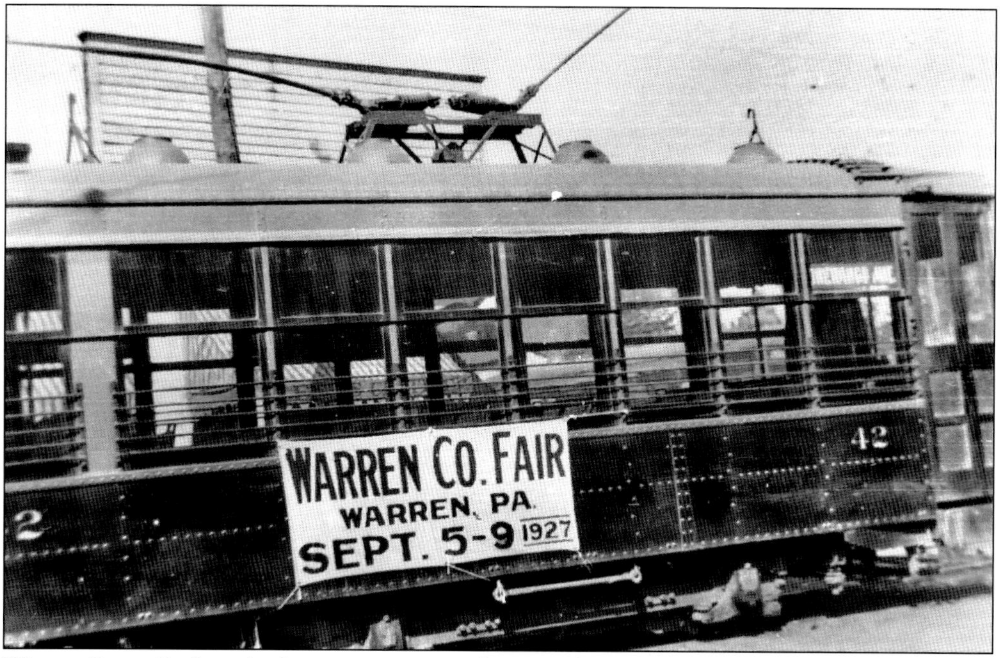

Warren Street Railway had one-man operated cars without a conductor, like No. 42, to reduce labor costs. This car is operating on the Conewango line in Warren. Ridership was decreasing on all the lines as more automobiles came on the scene. For example, the Warren and Jamestown ridership of 753,505 in 1920 declined to 333,357 in 1928. (Harold C. Putnam photograph.)

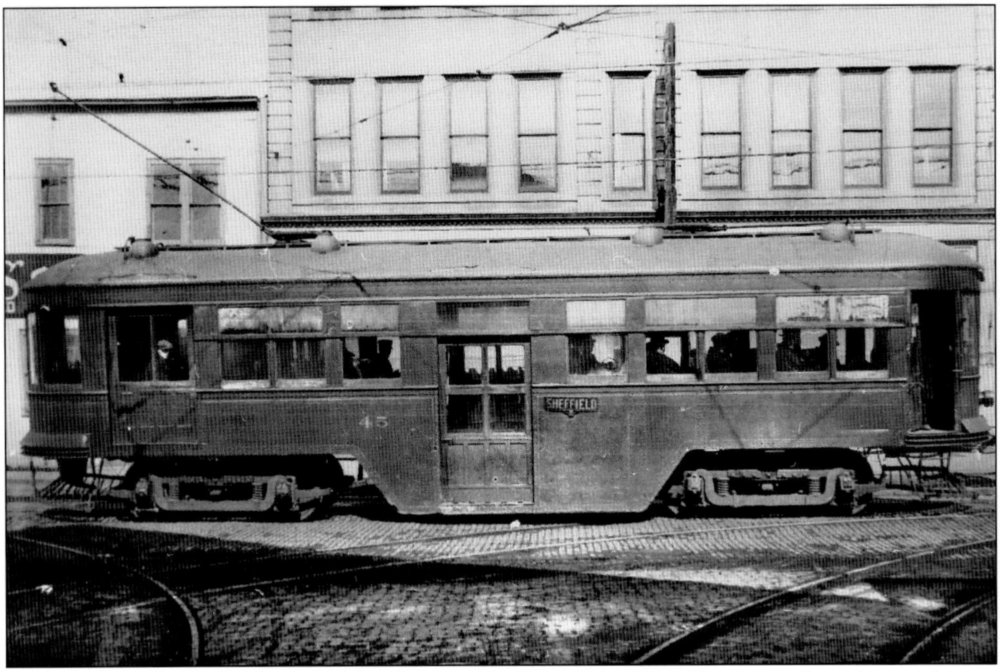

Warren and Sheffield Street Railway center-entrance car No. 45 is posed on Pennsylvania Avenue in Warren in front of the carbarn. The R. J. Schlossus Brass Foundry is the building on the left, and on the right is the Charles Hamm building, which later became Reliable Furniture. (Harold C. Putnam photograph.)

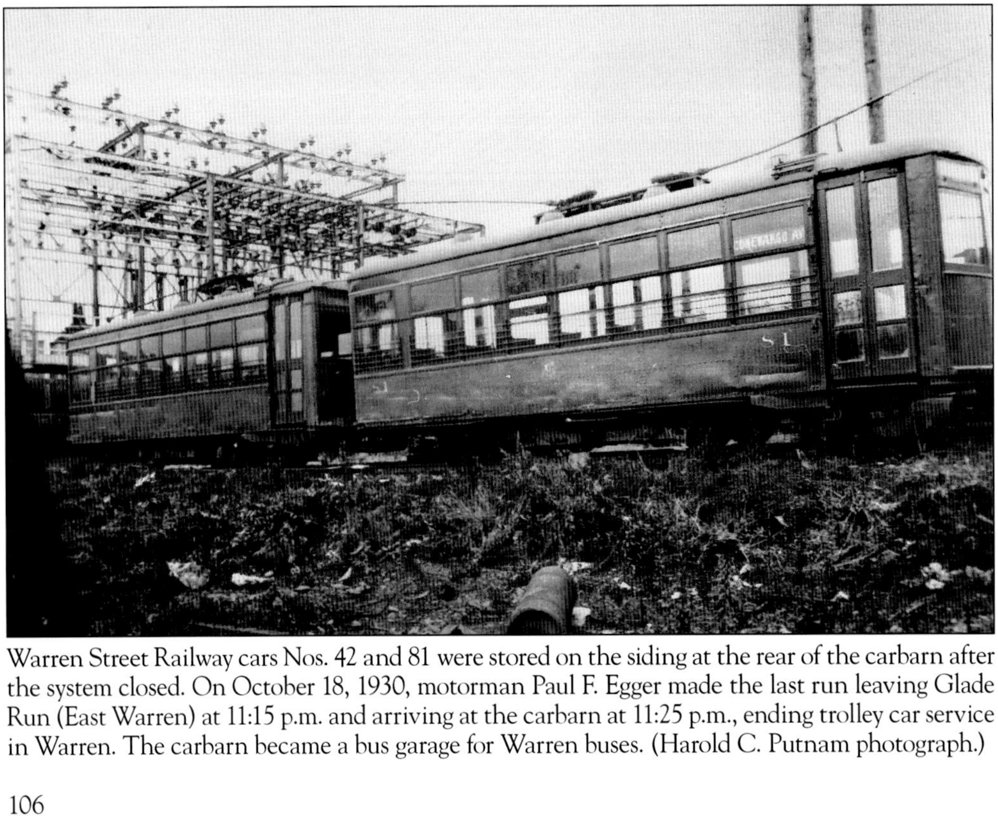

Warren Street Railway cars Nos. 42 and 81 were stored on the siding at the rear of the carbarn after the system closed. On October 18, 1930, motorman Paul F. Egger made the last run leaving Glade Run (East Warren) at 11:15 p.m. and arriving at the carbarn at 11:25 p.m., ending trolley car service in Warren. The carbarn became a bus garage for Warren buses. (Harold C. Putnam photograph.)

Seven

Corry and Titusville Trolleys

The charter of the Corry and Columbus Street Railway was placed on record December 17, 1895, and the first rails were laid in Corry during July 1906. Construction of the carbarn began on September 15, 1906. The carbarn, located on the west side of North Center Street, measured 30 feet by 130 feet and had a capacity of eight cars. The company had two open cars for summer weather and three closed cars for winter weather. Through the main part of the Corry Business district on Center Street, the line was double tracked. The rest of the line was single track with passing sidings at what are today Oakley Avenue and East Columbus Avenue. On August 27, 1923, a transformer burned out in the powerhouse, and service was discontinued.

The Titusville Electric Traction Company built a trolley line from Titusville to Pleasantville in 1898. In 1901, the line was extended from Titusville to Hydetown. The company wanted to build beyond Hydetown to Tryonville. However, the Pennsylvania Railroad would not let the trolley line cross the track, and a separate line was built from Hydetown to Mystic Park. Passengers from Pleasantville and Titusville headed for Mystic Park would take the trolley to Hydetown and walk across the Pennsylvania Railroad track to the car for Mystic Park. Construction continued beyond Mystic Park to a spot known as Canadea. From Hydetown to Pleasantville, the line operated through Titusville on West Spring Street, Diamond Street, East Central Avenue, East Main Street, and Plank Road. In Titusville, a city line operated north on Boulevard from East Main Street to Walnut Street, west on Walnut Street to Petroleum Street, north on Petroleum Street to East Spruce Street, west on Spruce Street to Third Street, and south on Third Street to West Spring Street. One car was assigned to this route, and it met the Hydetown-Pleasantville car at Boulevard and East Main Street as well as at Third and West Spring Streets. Climax siding on the east side of Titusville was the passing point for the two cars operating on the Hydetown-Pleasantville line. Twice a week, the trolley company operated a trolley freight car from the Pennsylvania Railroad station in Titusville to Pleasantville. There was trackage on Franklin Street from West Spring Street south to the Pennsylvania Railroad station to accomplish this. The company owned Mystic Park and leased Fieldmore Park, located one and three-fourths miles east of Titusville. Encountering financial problems, in August 1914, it was sold at foreclosure and was reorganized as the Titusville Traction Company. The once-busy trolley waiting station on Diamond and Martin Streets in downtown Titusville was seeing fewer passengers. Trolley service ended on December 31, 1924.

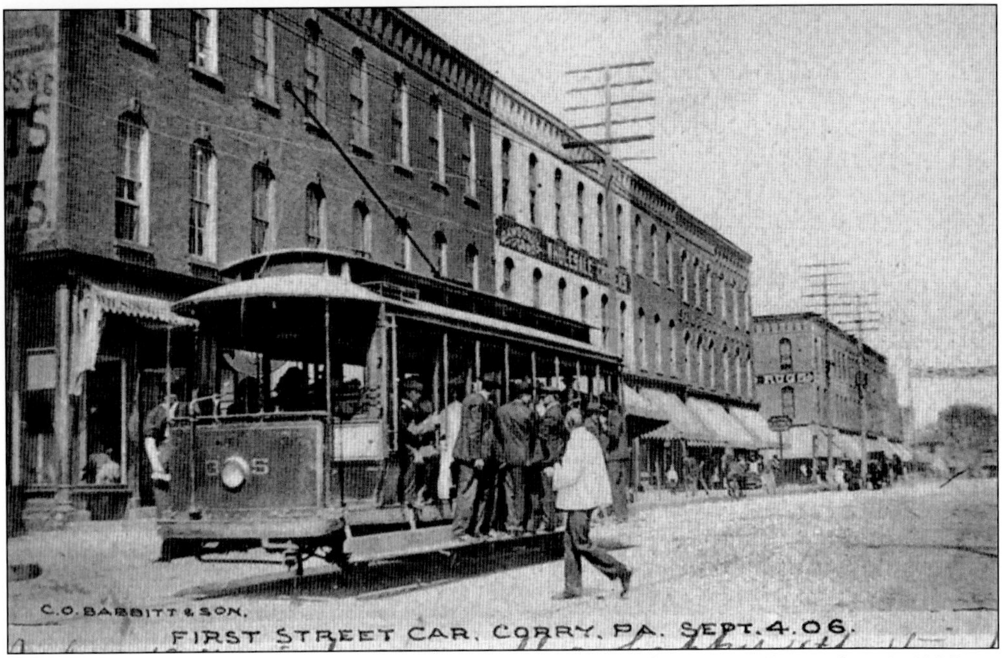

The Corry and Columbus Street Railway operated its first trolley car on September 4, 1906, on the four-mile line from Corry to Columbus, Pennsylvania. A charter had been secured from the Pennsylvania state legislature on December 6, 1901, to build a trolley line from Erie through Waterford, Mill Village, Cambridge Springs, Union City, and Corry, but that line was never built.

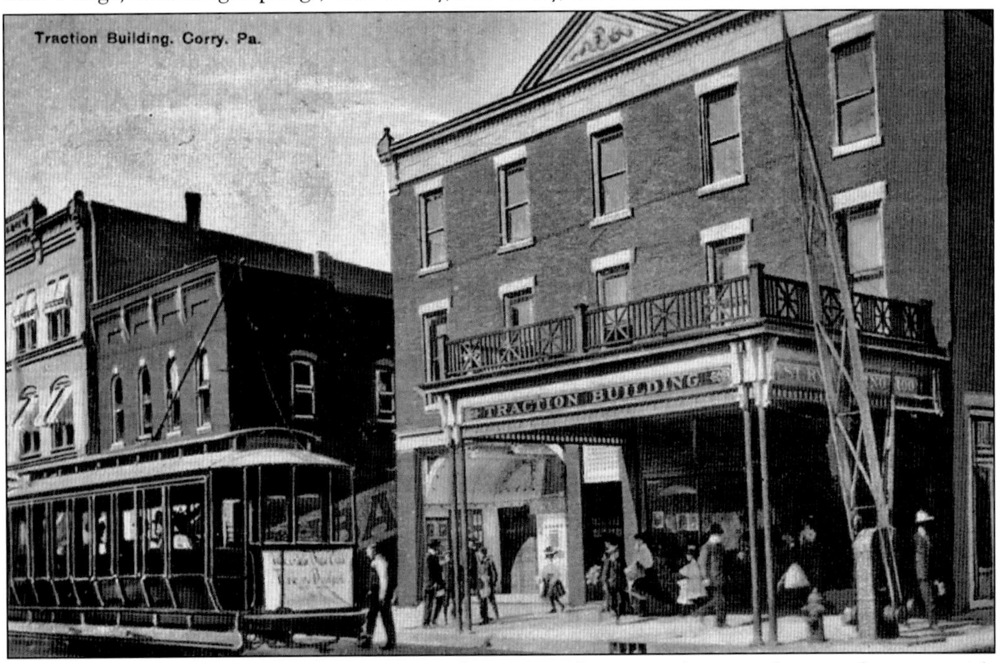

The Traction Building on Center Street in downtown Corry was busy in those early years, with trolley service from 7:00 a.m. to 11:00 p.m. The nearby Pennsylvania Railroad station and Erie Railroad station were served by numerous passenger trains, which provided Corry residents with a linkage to the rest of the country by rail.

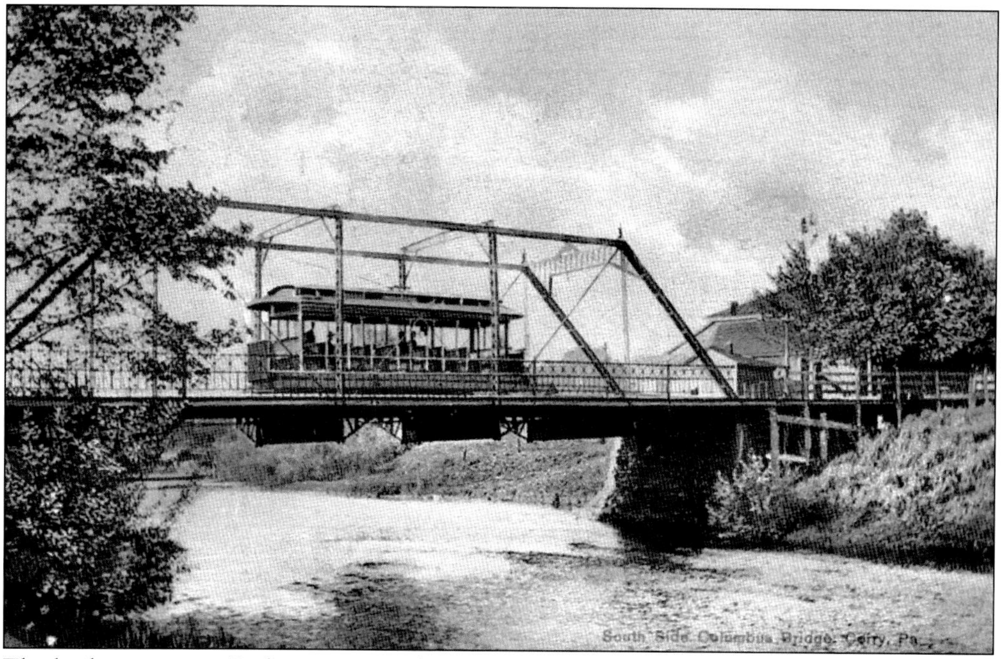

The bridge spanning Brokenstraw Creek in Columbus provided a pleasant view for Corry and Columbus Street Railway passengers. The line ended just east of the bridge, and the motorman would get out of the trolley and reverse poles for the return trip to Corry. From Columbus to Corry, the line followed what is today U.S. Highway 6.

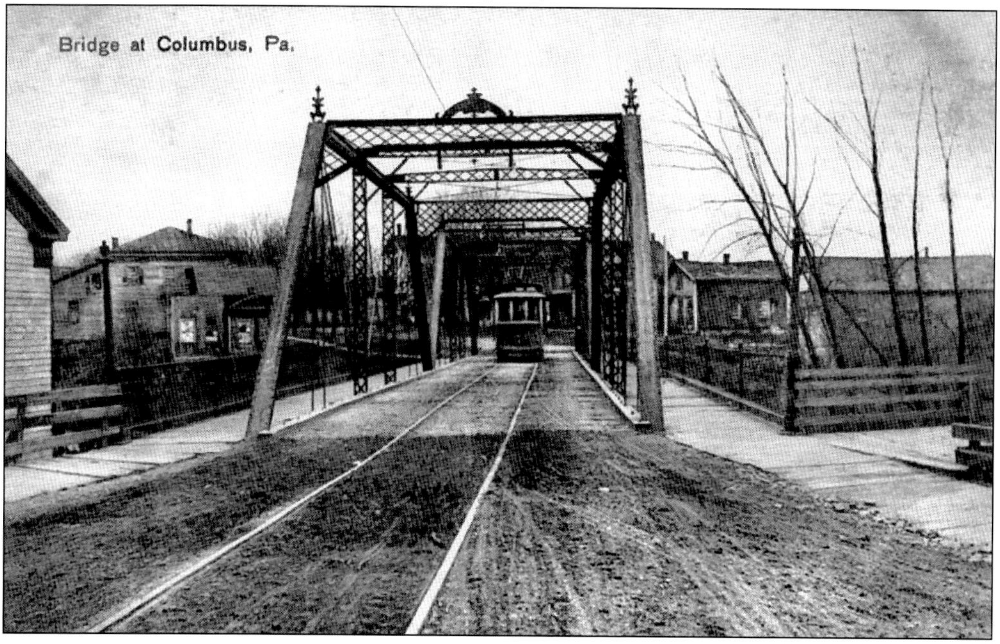

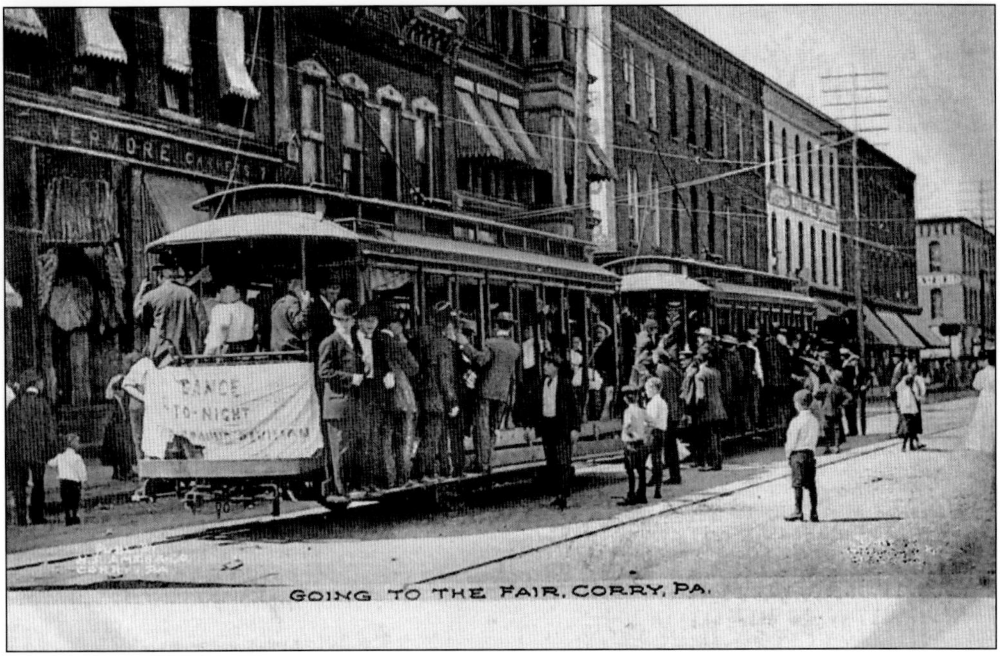

Advertising "Dance To-Night," every space was taken on the Corry and Columbus open car as it prepared to travel north on Center Street through the heart of the Corry business district. The four-mile line had a 5¢ fare from downtown Corry to the city limits, and the fare was an additional 5¢ to Columbus.

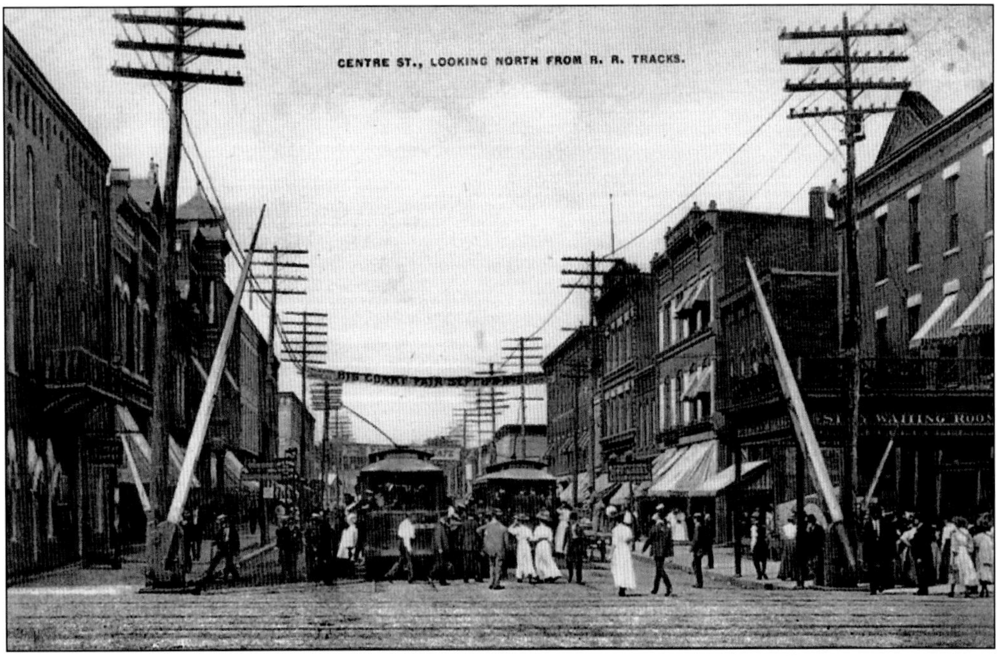

Throngs of people were coming to Corry by trolley for the big county fair of 1909. During 1909, the company planned an extension to Union City and another extension through Sugar Grove to connect with the Chautauqua Traction Company's line at Ashville, New York. None of these extensions were built, and the system would remain isolated from other trolley systems.

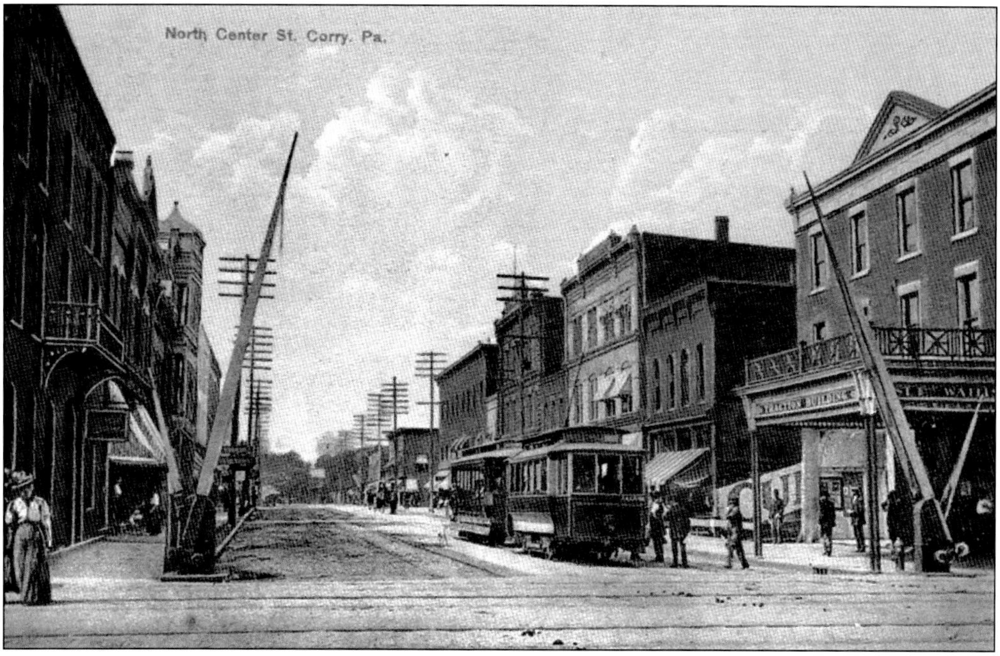

The Corry and Columbus Street Railway served a park at Columbus and in Corry served the fairgrounds, racetrack, and baseball park. For the summertime, the company's two open cars were popular, and the line brought riders into downtown Corry, which enhanced the vitality of the business district. In these postcard scenes, the trolley tracks end just north of the Pennsylvania Railroad track.

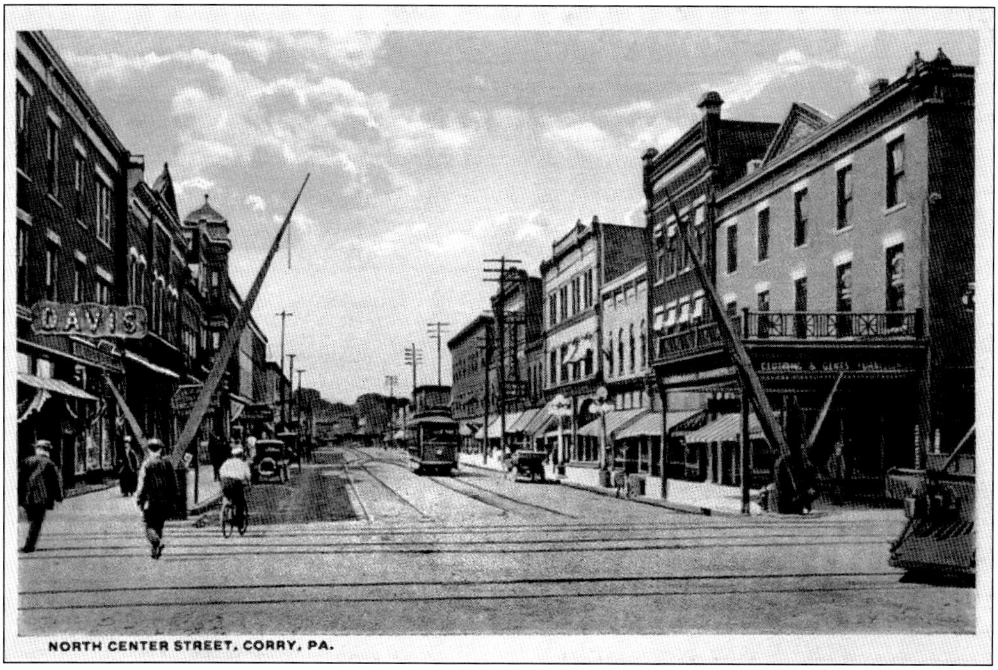

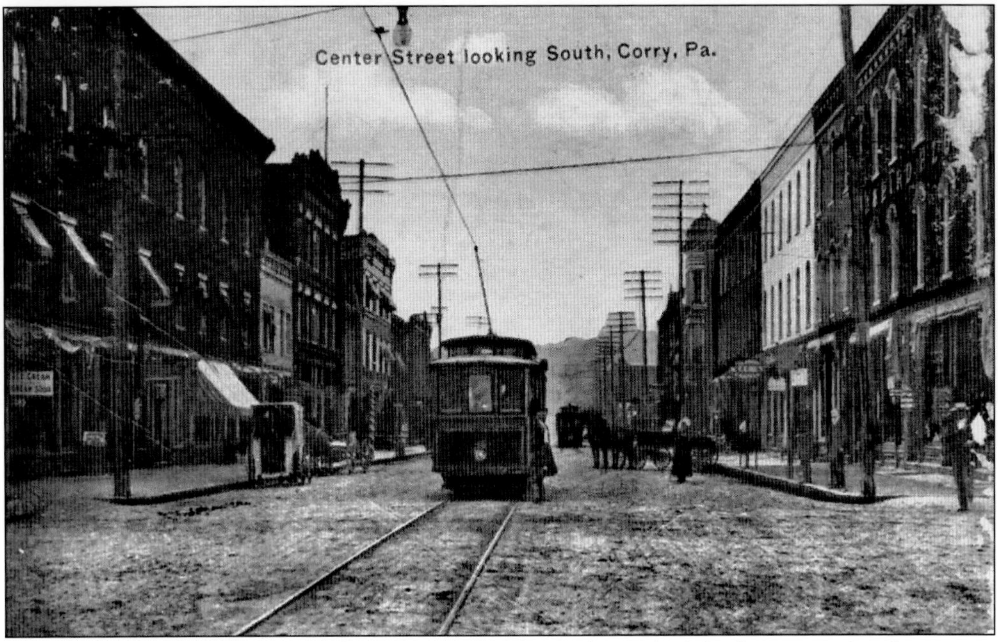

Center Street looking south in downtown Corry near the end of the line provides the setting for this Corry and Columbus Street Railway trolley. The company proposed to build a number of lines, including one from Corry to North East, Pennsylvania, but none of the lines were built. Corry was never connected to any other trolley line.

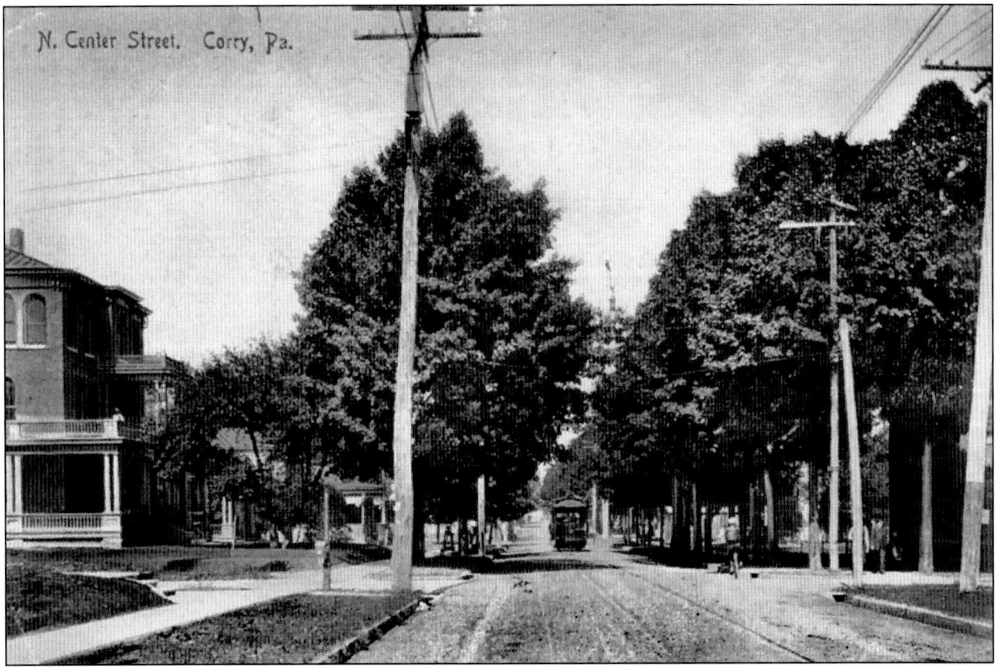

A Corry and Columbus Street Railway trolley passes through the residential area of North Center Street in Corry. This was the smallest trolley company in northwestern Pennsylvania. The McGraw Electric Railway List for August 1918 listed the following company officers: J. D. Woodward, president; Clifford Woodward, secretary; F. M. Raymond, treasurer; O. S. Fritz, chief engineer.

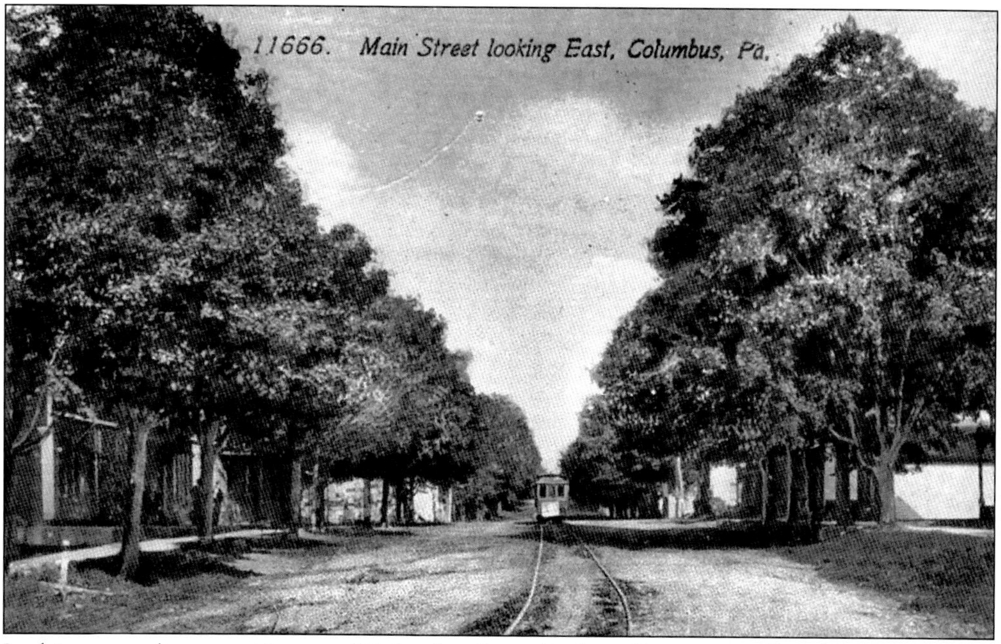

In this postcard scene, a Corry and Columbus Street Railway Company trolley clangs down Main Street in Columbus. Business never reached expectations, and the coming of the automobile siphoned off riders, which financially weakened the company. Service ended on August 27, 1923, when a transformer burned out in the powerhouse.

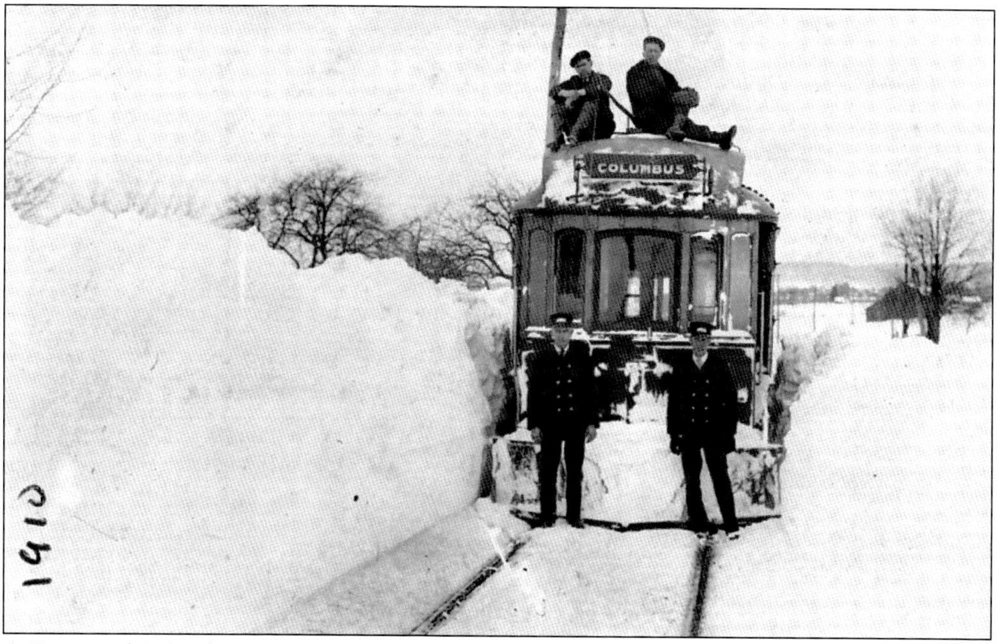

A Corry and Columbus Street Railway trolley is pictured amid a heavy winter snow accumulation in 1910. In the wintertime, the trolleys were fitted with snowplows. Traveling through Corry today during the winter makes one wonder how a trolley line could operate in this snowbelt region. It was possible because of the dependability and resourcefulness of the employees who did whatever was needed to maintain the service.

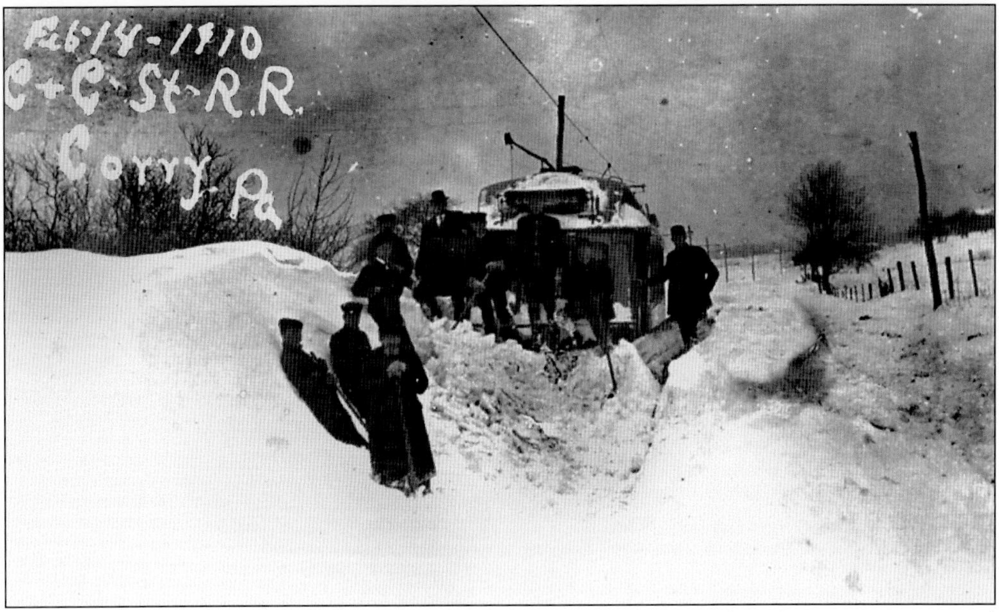

A Corry and Columbus Street Railway Company trolley is snowbound in this 1910 scene. Hand shoveling the snow was typical, particularly where it had drifted. According to the McGraw Electric Railway Directory for 1924 company officers were: Oscar S. Fritz, president and general manager; A. M. Howard, vice president; and D. J. Fritz, secretary and treasurer.

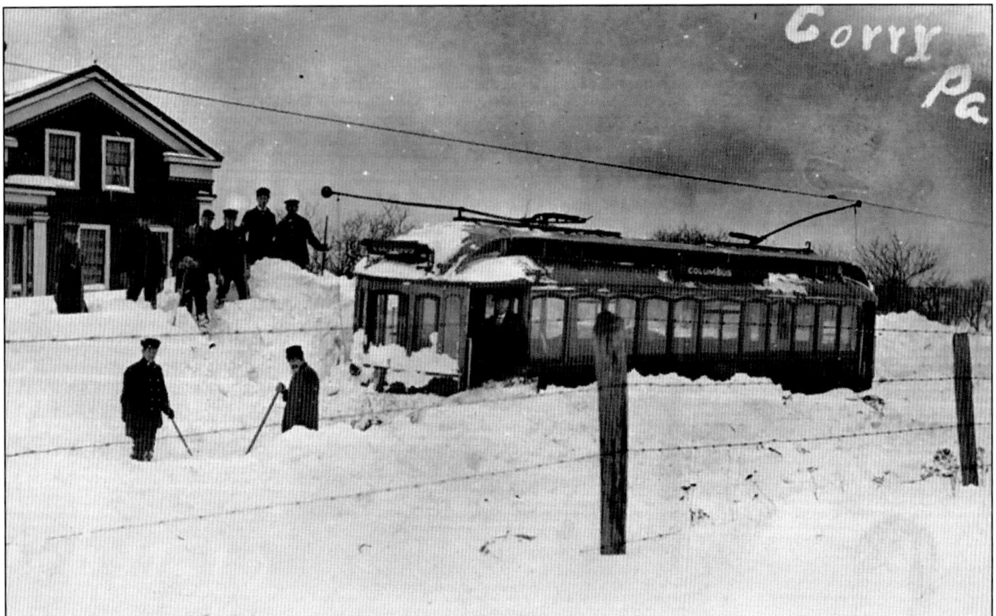

A snowbound Corry and Columbus Street Railway trolley car gives testimony to the severe winter weather facing the line. C. P. Northrup stands in the doorway of the car while Oscar Fritz, company president, stands second from the right on a snowbank. Heavy snow would delay service and contribute to financial problems with a loss of riders. (K. S. Durham collection.)

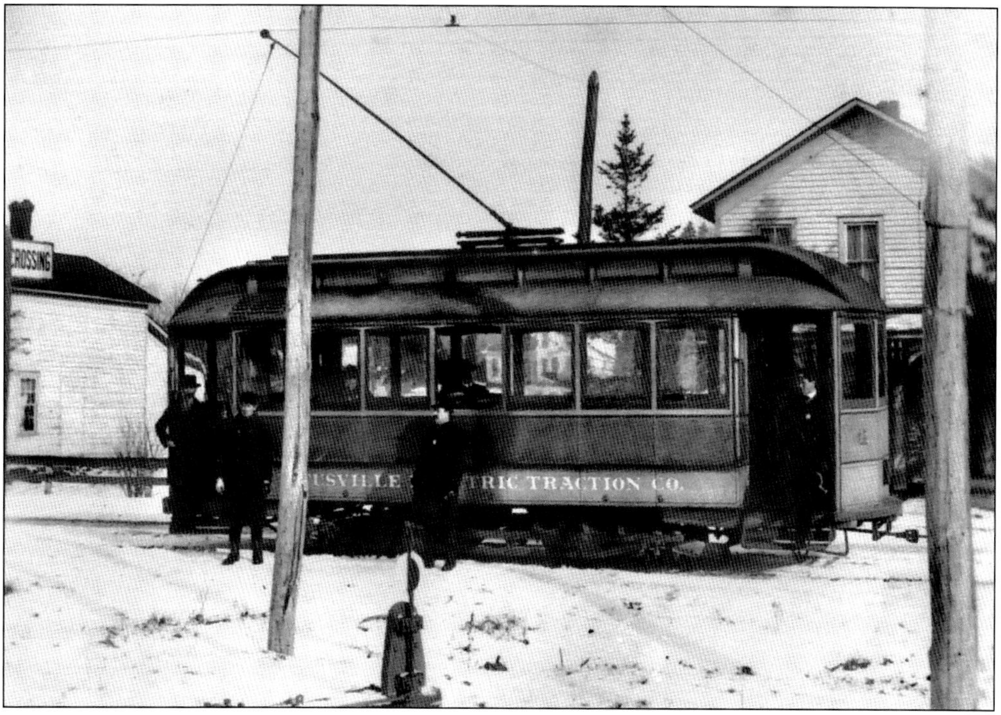

It was a cold winter day in 1910 that found Titusville Electric Traction Company car No. 4 and the crew waiting for more riders at Hydetown before beginning the trip to Pleasantville. Titusville was right in the center of the oil-producing region, and the line was built to handle future transportation needs. (Harry Ridgway photograph.)

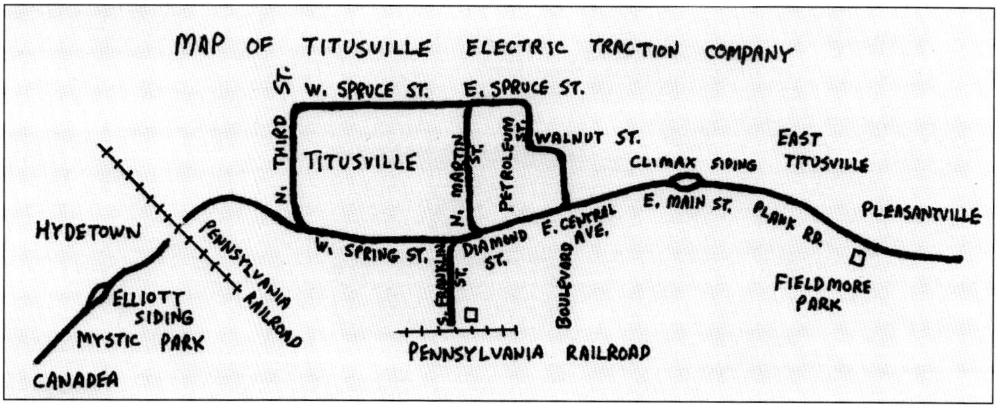

The main line through Titusville was via Spring Street and Diamond Street. In Titusville, a city line operated north on Boulevard from East Main Street to Walnut Street, west on Walnut to Petroleum Street, north on Petroleum to East Spruce Street, west on Spruce to Third Street, and south on Third to West Spring Street.

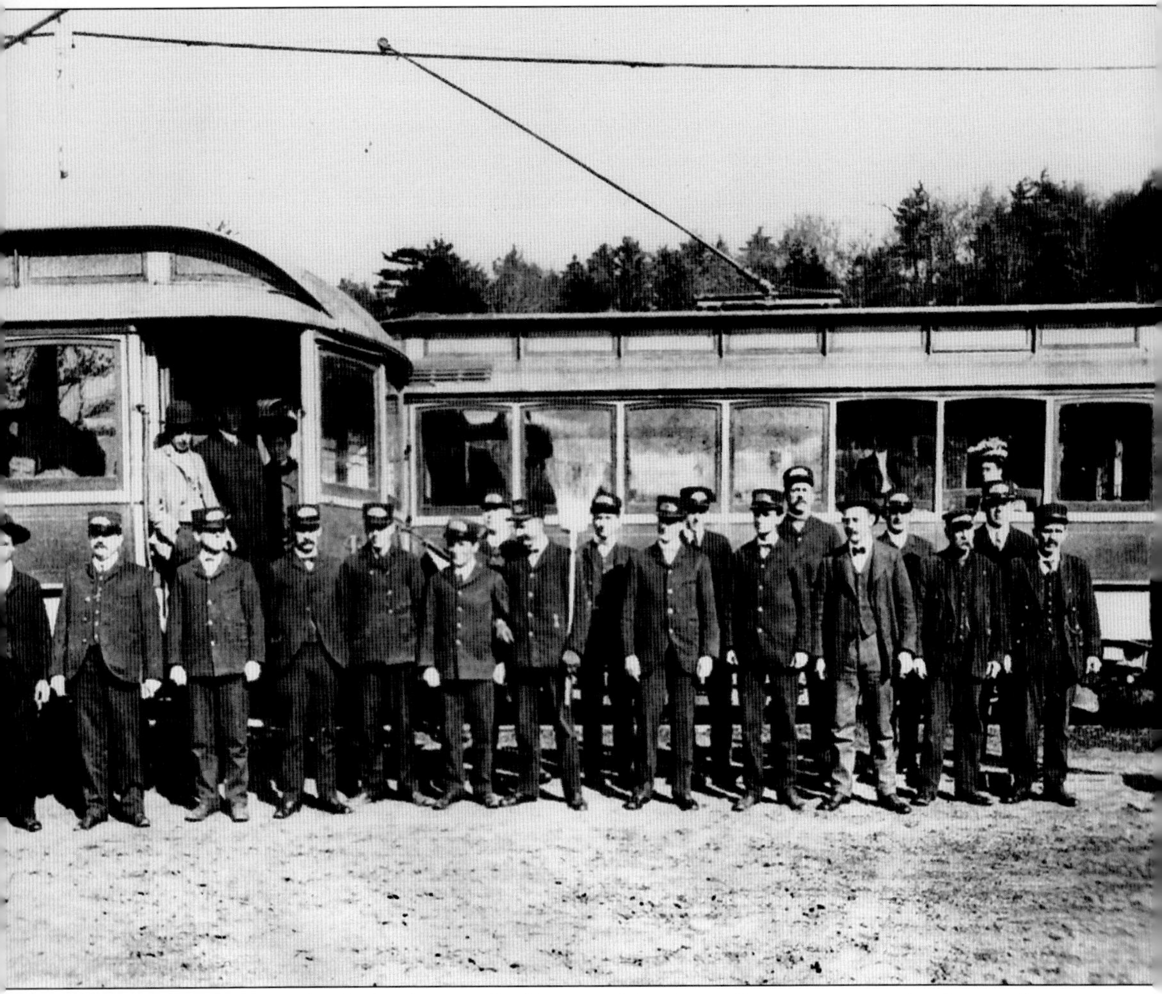

Operating personnel of the Titusville Electric Traction Company pose in front of cars No. 4 and No. 2 at the carbarn. The company operated 10 trolley cars on 16.71 miles of track. The McGraw Electric List for August 1918 listed the following officers: Frederick W. Gavin, president; George H. Dunham, vice president; Harry L. Moore, secretary and treasurer; Charles L. Beck, auditor; and J. A. Lamenskie, road master. McGraw Electric Directory for 1924 listed the following officers: Charles W. Benedict, president, general manager and purchasing agent; George H. Dunham, vice president; Frank Burton, secretary and treasurer; C. W. Hawbaker, electrical engineer; and J. A. Lamenskie, road master. (J. B. Stevenson photograph.)

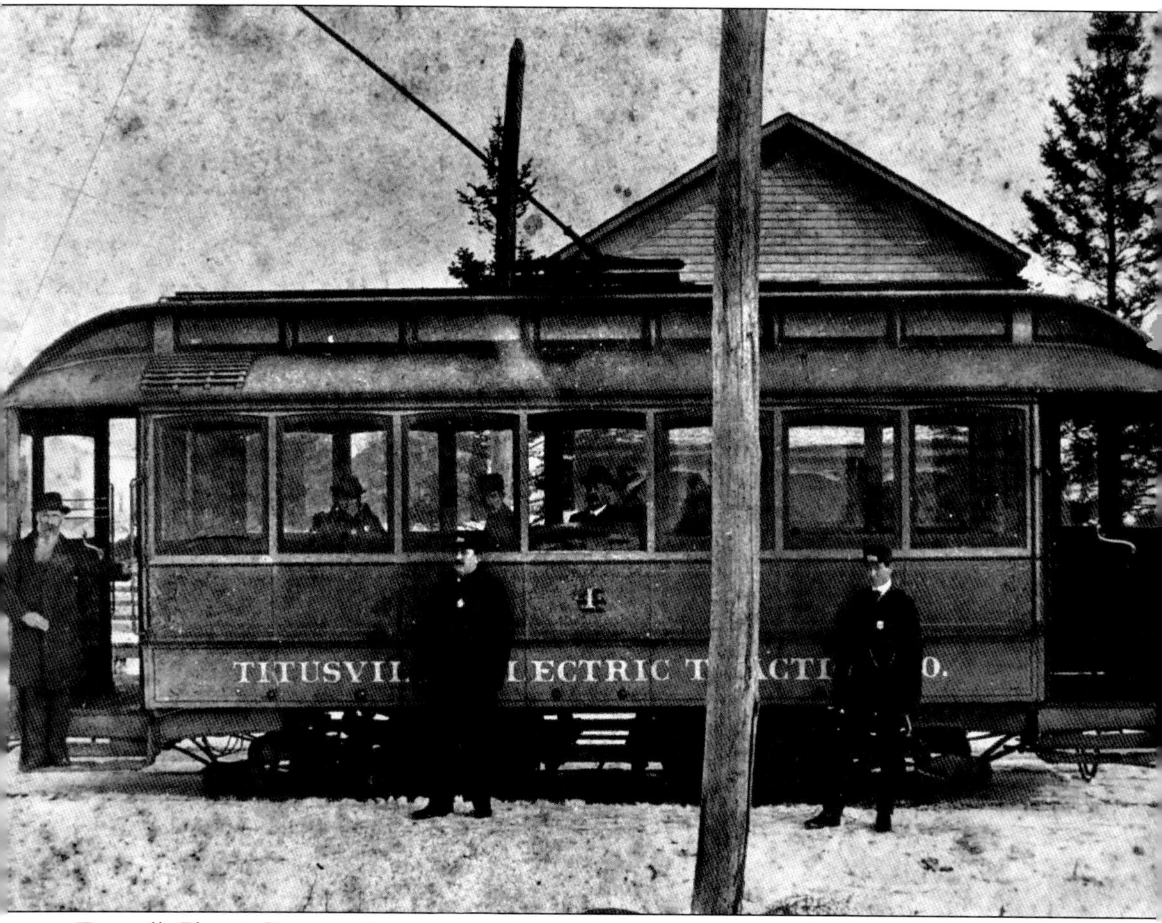

Titusville Electric Traction Company car No. 4 makes a brief photograph stop near Climax siding on the east side of Titusville, which was the halfway point on the Hydetown to Pleasantville line. Two trolley cars operated on this line, and they met at Climax siding. Service was hourly, and during the summer season, there was service every 30 minutes to Mystic Park and Fieldmore Park. (J. B. Stevenson photograph.)

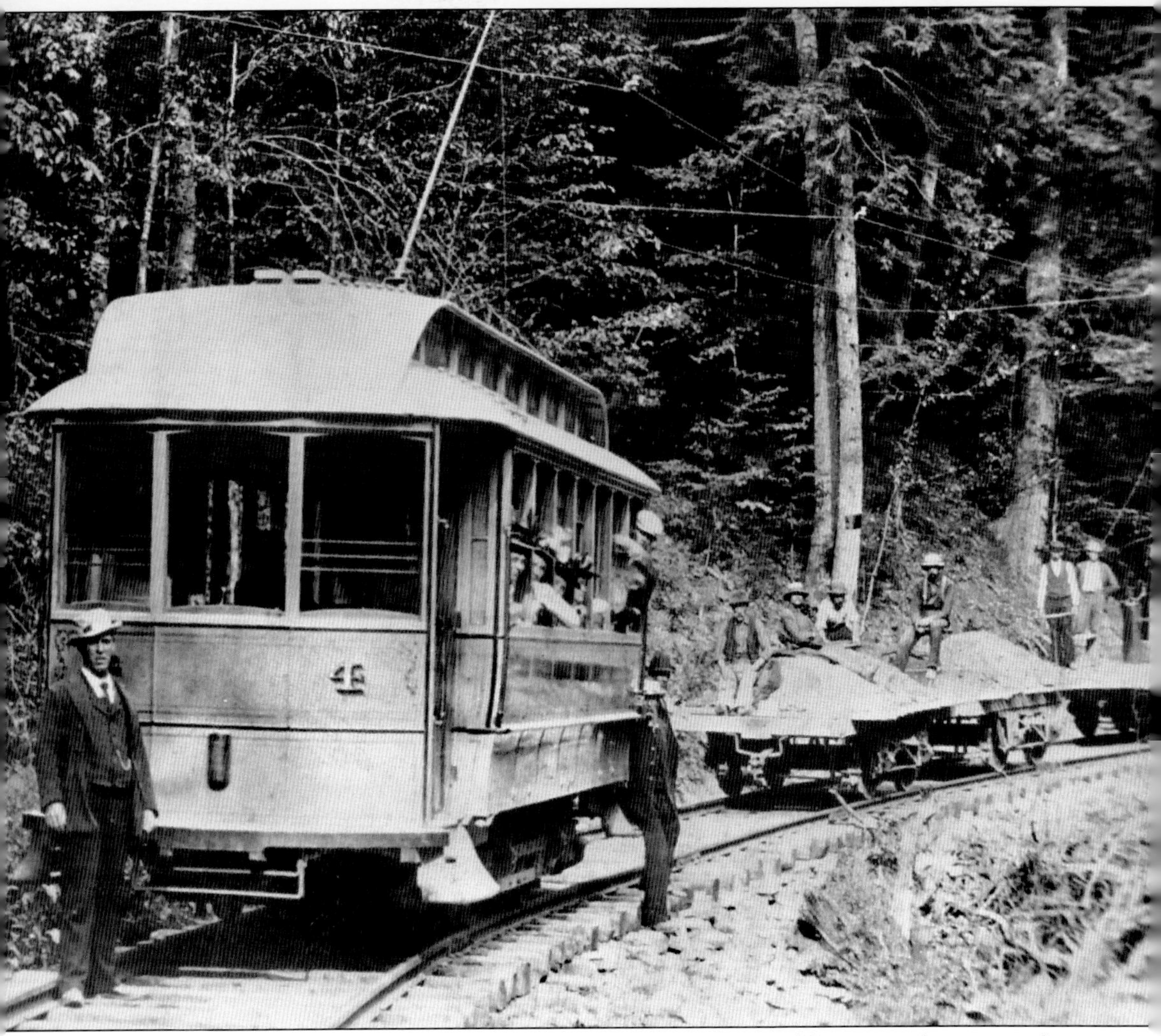

Titusville Electric Traction Company car No. 4 heads a procession of flatcars in this scene taken about 1910. The cars were painted a medium green and ivory with a Venetian red roof. A line was proposed from Titusville to Cambridge Springs, but it was never built, and the Titusville system remained isolated from other trolley lines. (J. B. Stevenson photograph.)

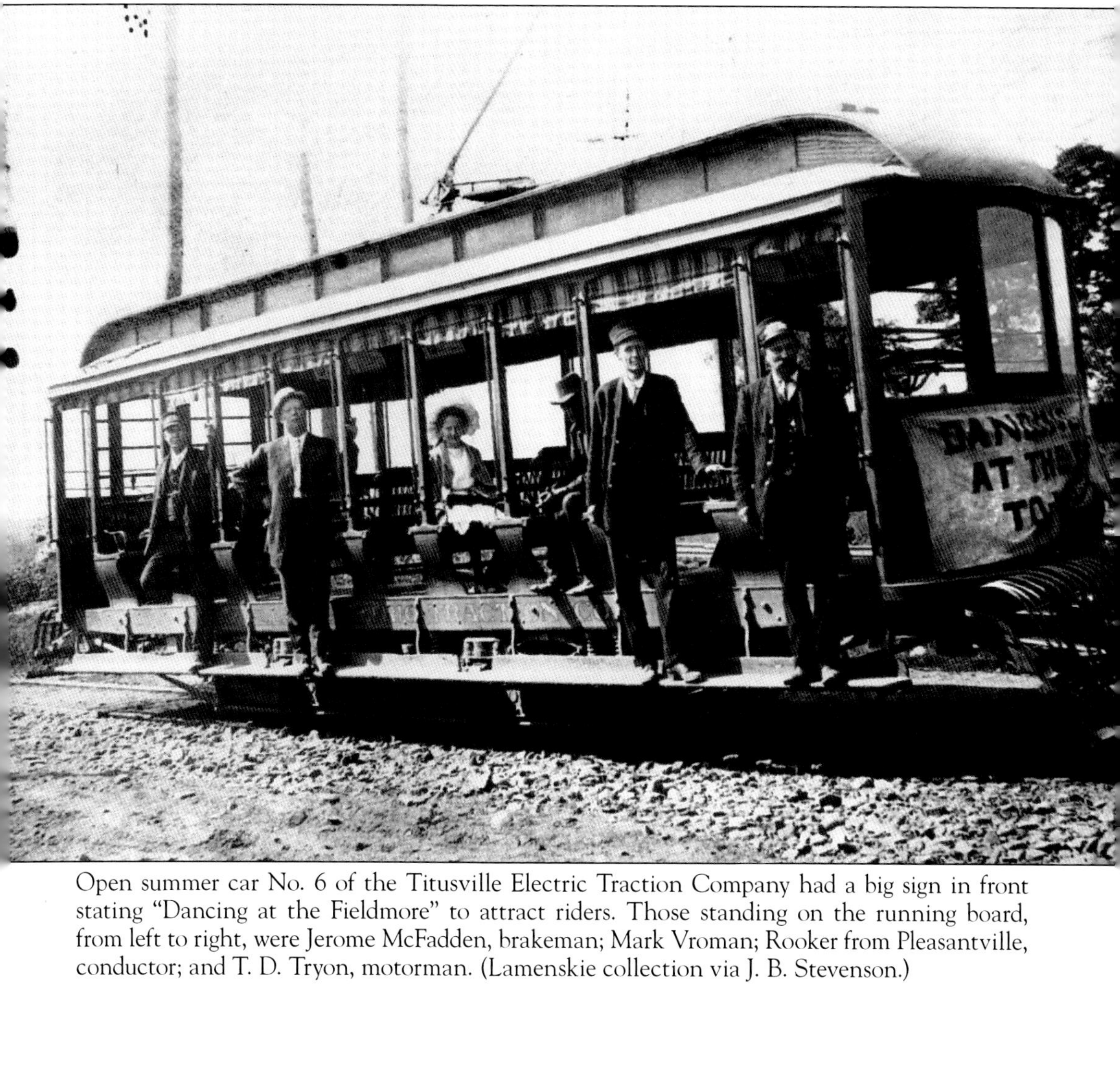

Open summer car No. 6 of the Titusville Electric Traction Company had a big sign in front stating "Dancing at the Fieldmore" to attract riders. Those standing on the running board, from left to right, were Jerome McFadden, brakeman; Mark Vroman; Rooker from Pleasantville, conductor; and T. D. Tryon, motorman. (Lamenskie collection via J. B. Stevenson.)

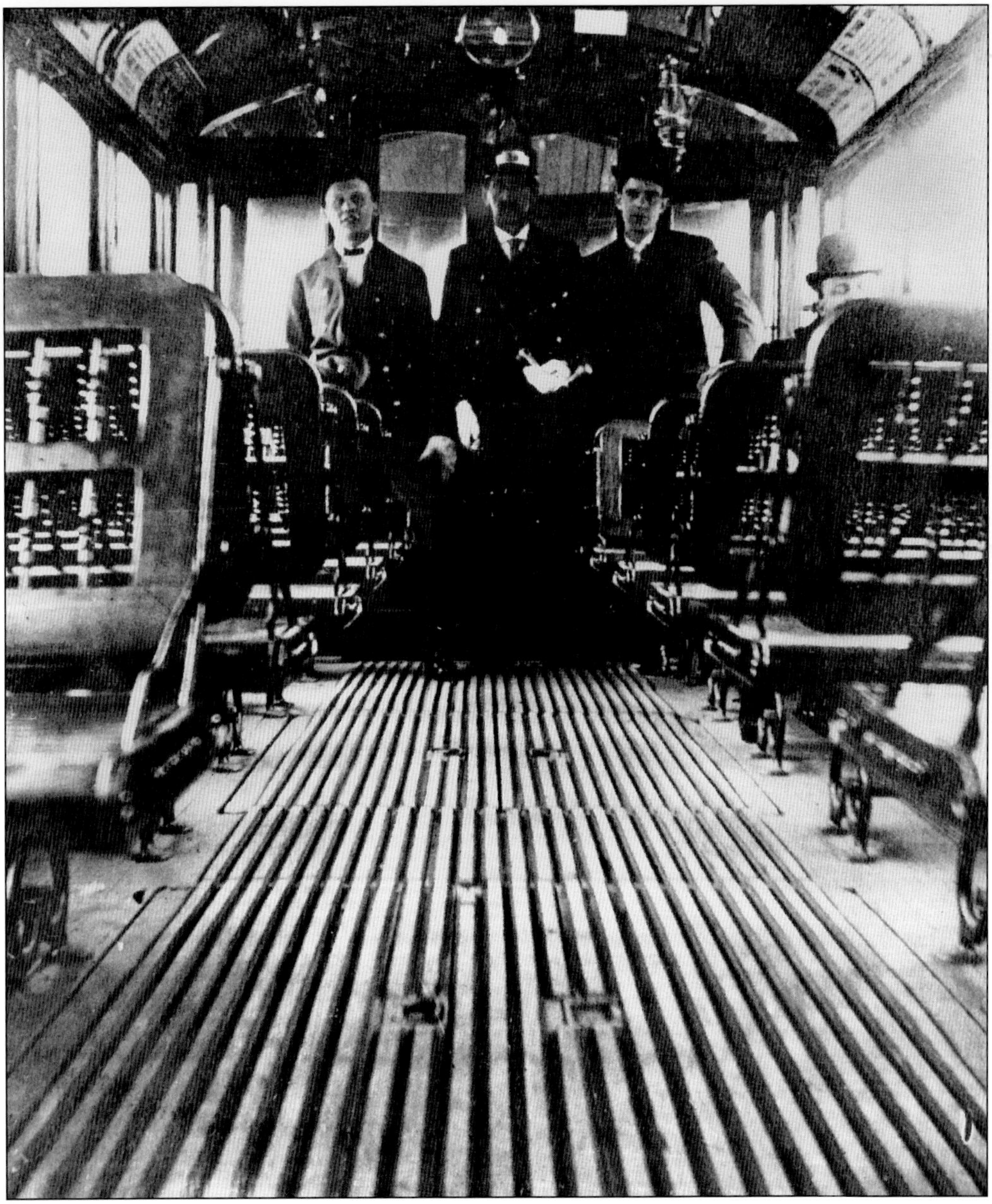

Interior view of Titusville Electric Traction Company car No. 6 shows the rattan seats, ornate lanterns, and car card advertising. There was a lot of pride in the system, and people had respect for property, which explains why a car in public service could have such fancy amenities. The carbarn and shop facilities were located at East Titusville. (J. B. Stevenson photograph.)

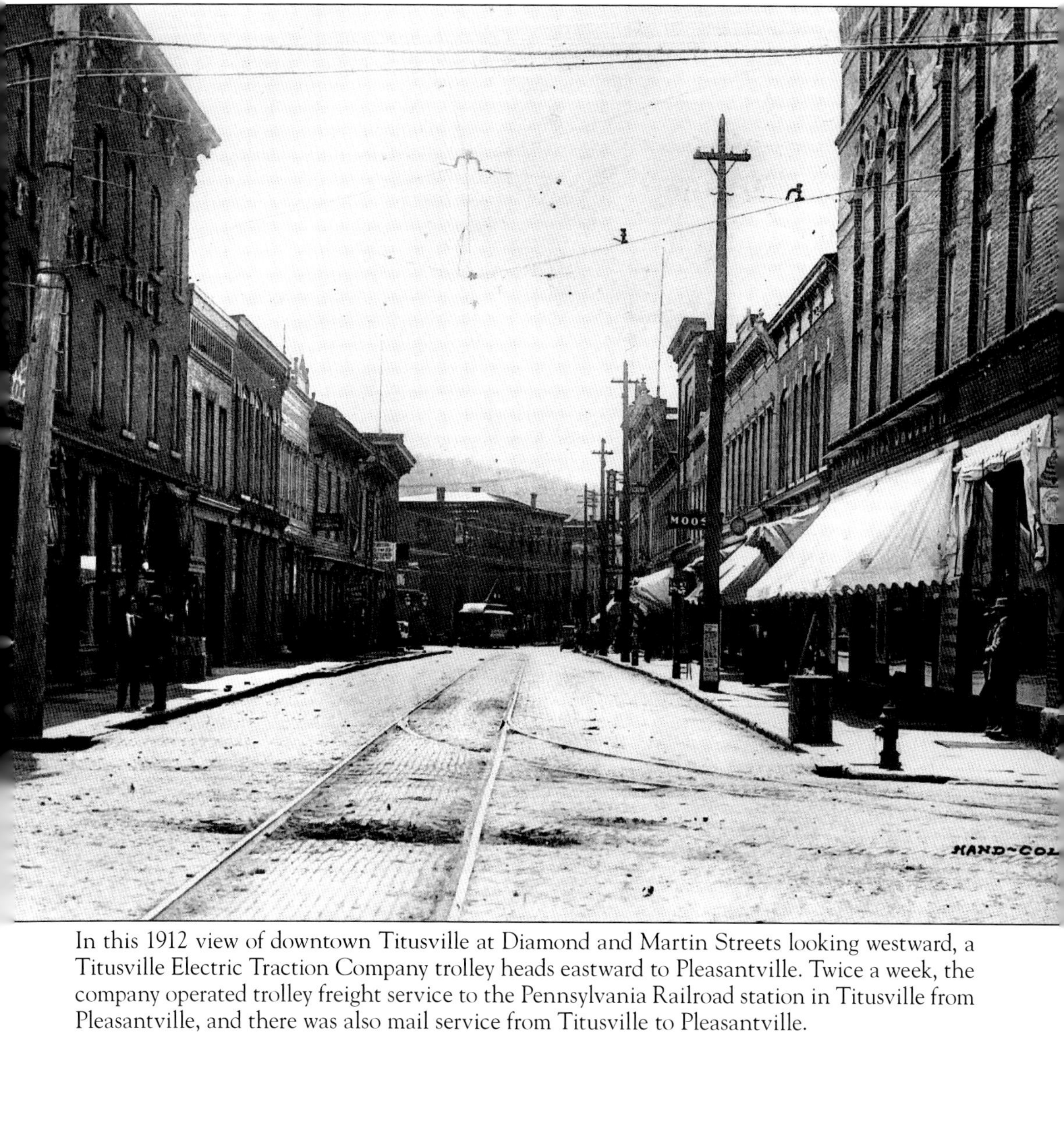

In this 1912 view of downtown Titusville at Diamond and Martin Streets looking westward, a Titusville Electric Traction Company trolley heads eastward to Pleasantville. Twice a week, the company operated trolley freight service to the Pennsylvania Railroad station in Titusville from Pleasantville, and there was also mail service from Titusville to Pleasantville.

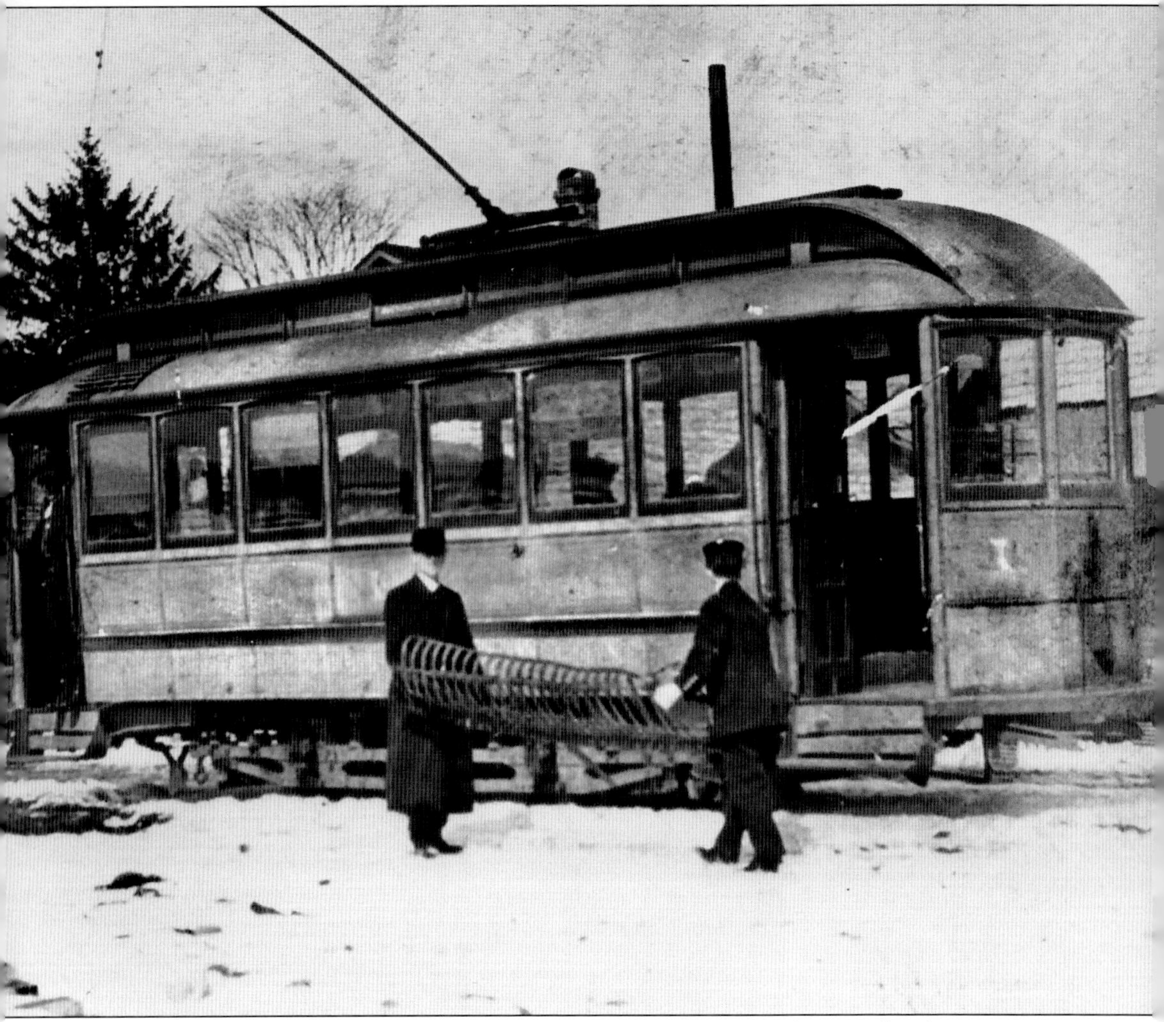

The motorman and conductor are taking the fender from one end of Titusville Electric Traction Company car No. 1 to the other end of the car at Hydetown for the return trip to Pleasantville. They would also have to reverse the pole before operating the car. The company had its own shop facilities at East Titusville, and sign painter John Dunn hand lettered the cars. (J. B. Stevenson photograph.)

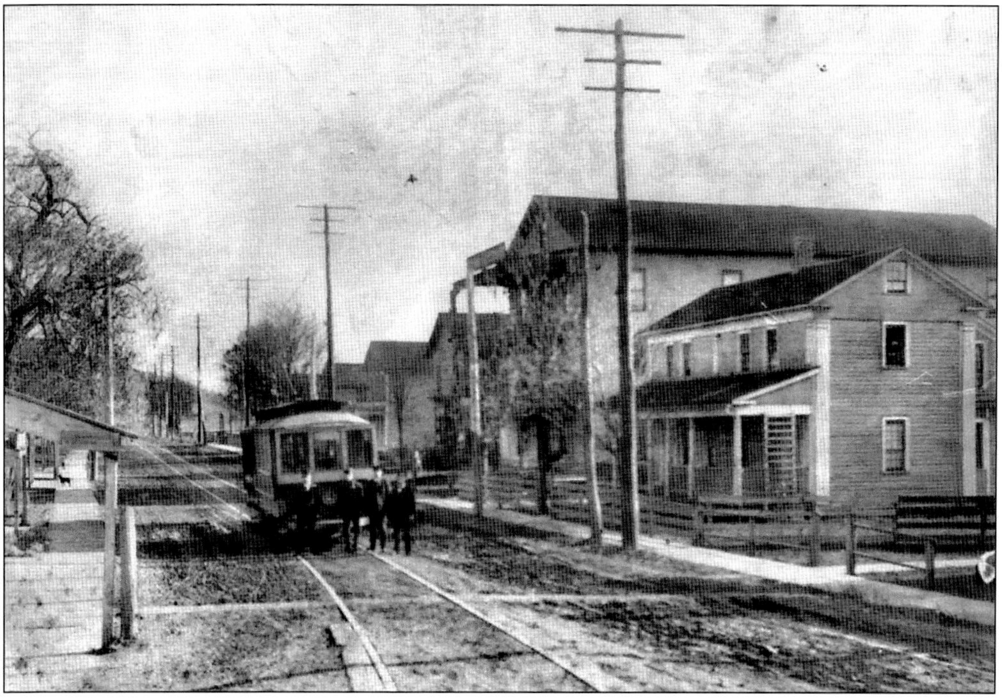

Titusville Electric Traction Company car No. 9 was ready to leave Hydetown for Mystic Park and Canadea. At Hydetown, passengers had to walk across the Pennsylvania Railroad track for a connecting car to Titusville and Pleasantville. The fare from Titusville to Pleasantville was 5¢ for a 20-minute ride. (Harry Ridgway photograph.)

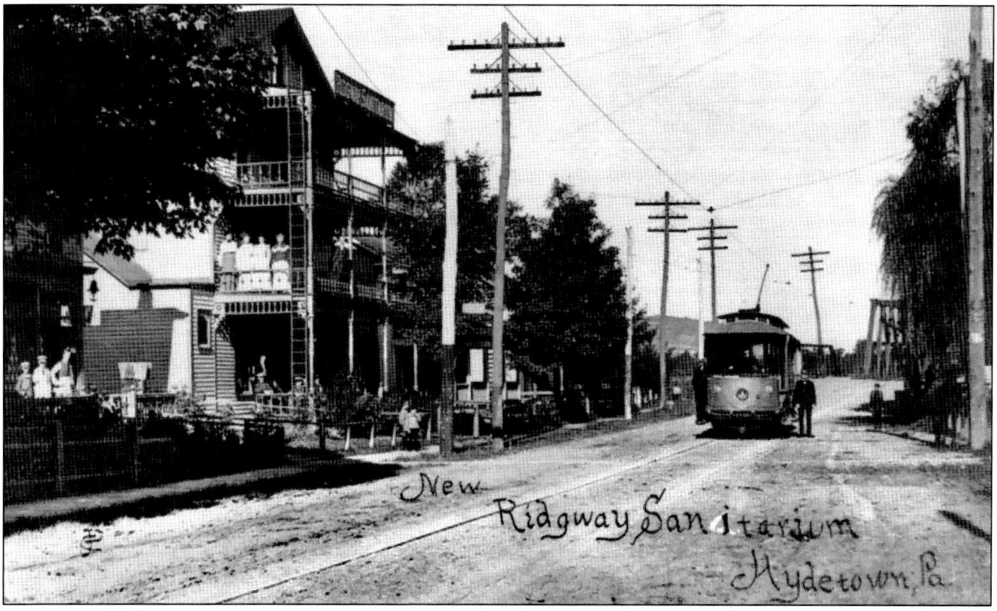

Car No. 8 was a half open–half closed car operating on the Hydetown-Canadea line of the Titusville Electric Traction Company. The car is shown at Hydetown. During October 1922, the Hydetown-Canadea line ended service. Jerome McFadden, who operated the first car 20 years earlier, made the last run. (Harry Ridgway photograph.)

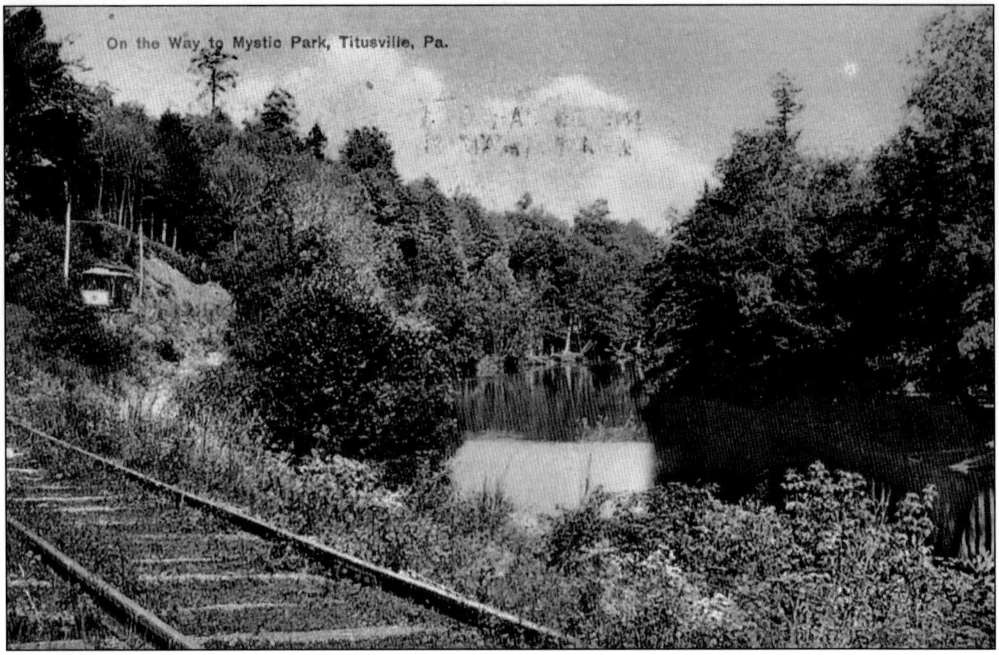

During the summertime, the Titusville Electric Traction Company operated trolley service every 30 minutes to Mystic Park and Fieldmore Park. When the Hydetown-Canadea line closed during October 1922, within a short time Mystic Park closed because the main purpose of the park was to generate ridership for the trolley line. In the picture below, car No. 9 arrives at Mystic Park.

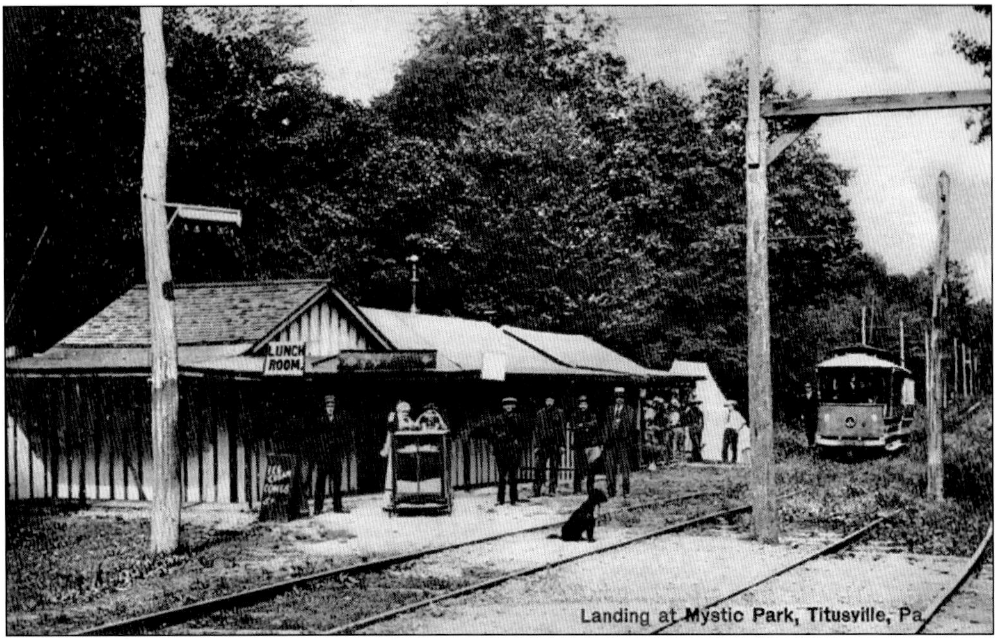

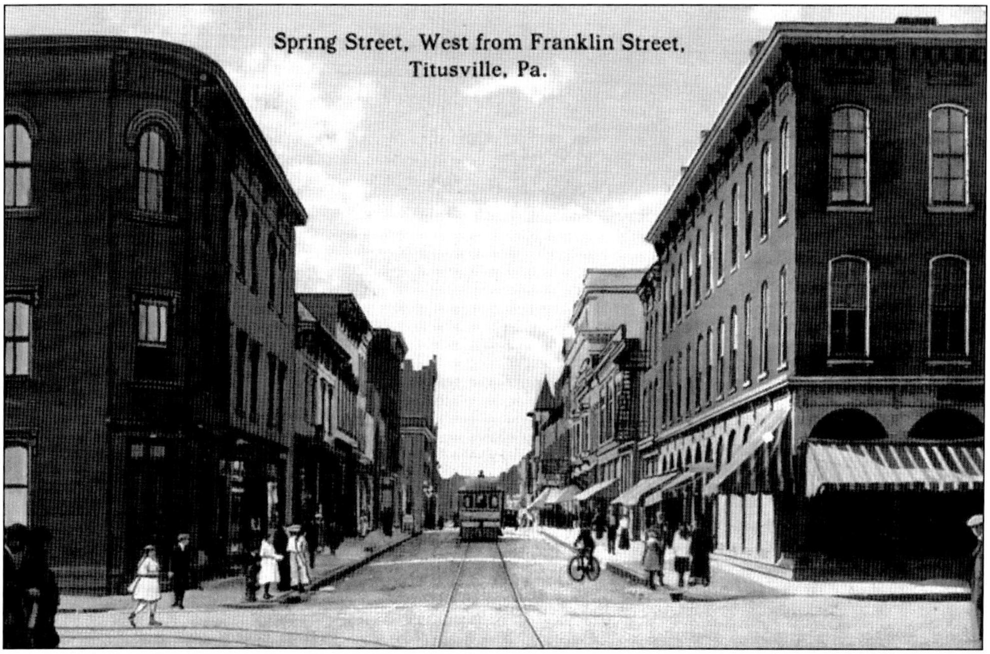

A Titusville Electric Traction Company trolley car was passing through downtown Titusville before the widespread use of the automobile. Spring Street west from Franklin Street shows the trackage that headed south on Franklin Street to the Pennsylvania Railroad Station in Titusville. This trackage was used twice a week by the trolley freight car, which operated from Titusville to Pleasantville.

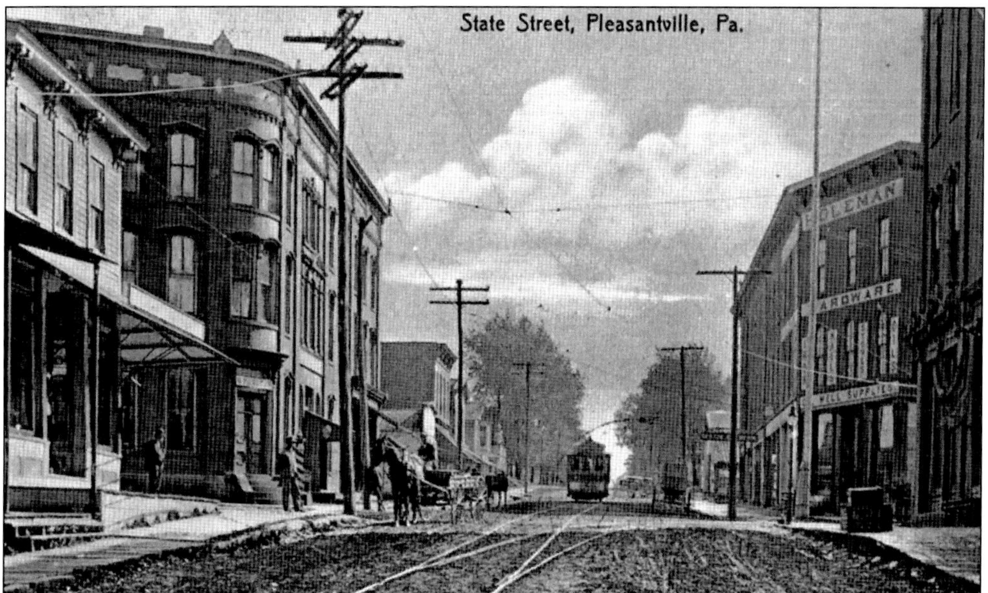

State Street in downtown Pleasantville is a dirt road as a Titusville Electric Traction Company trolley comes by without an automobile in sight. At this moment in time, Pleasantville was linked to the rest of the United States by trolley to Titusville, where connections could be made by the Pennsylvania Railroad to numerous cities.

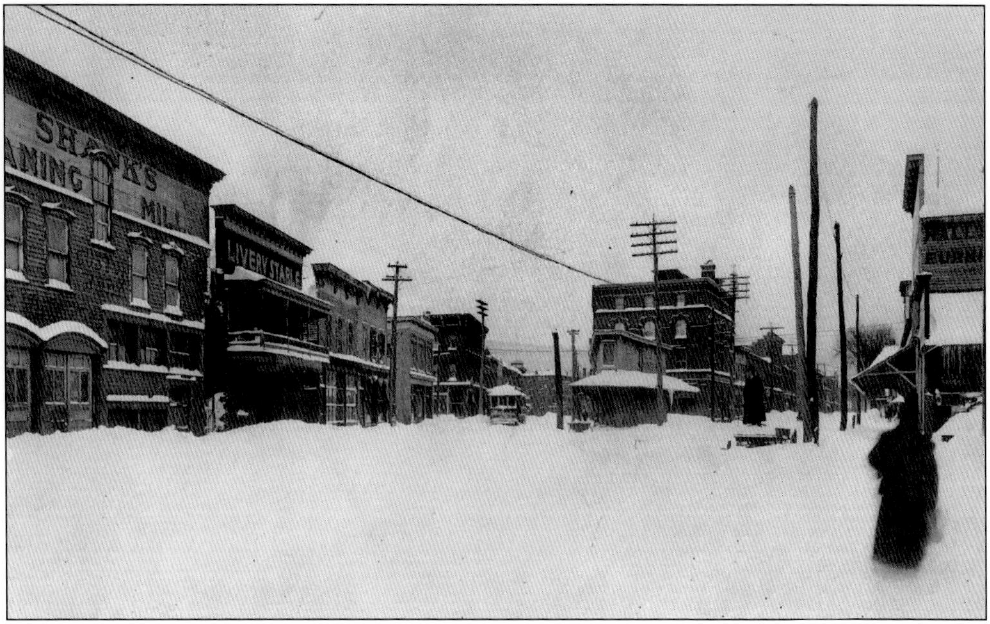

On Sunday, January 23, 1910, a Titusville Electric Traction Company trolley passes along Diamond Street looking east from Drake Street after a winter snow had blanketed the area. Winter snowfalls were a challenge to trolley companies in this region because the costs of snow removal impacted their lean budgets. (John Dunn photograph.)

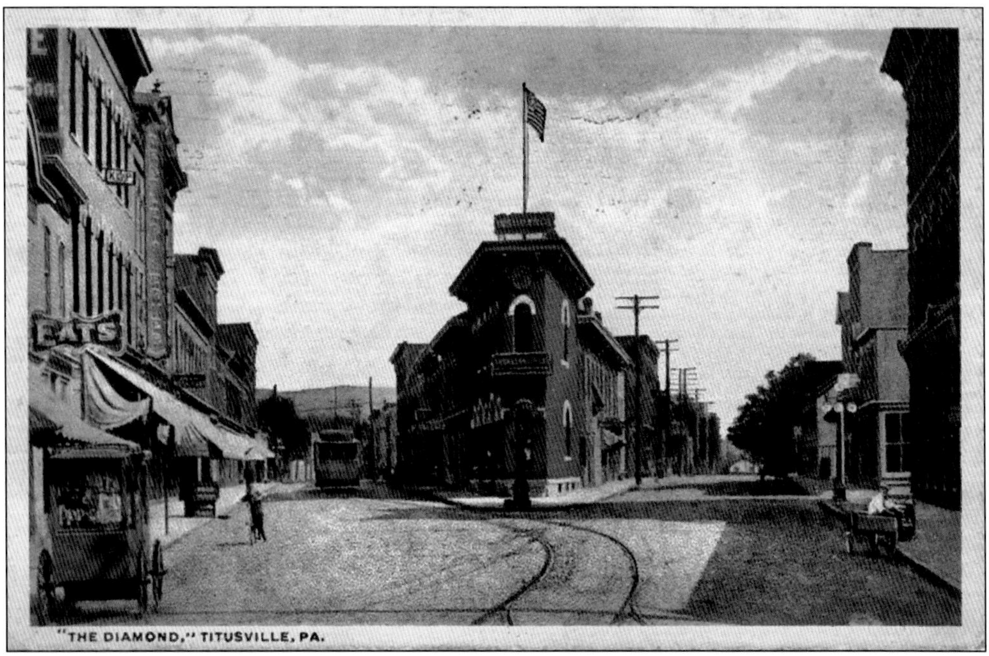

A Titusville Electric Traction Company trolley was passing by the Diamond in downtown Titusville. In spite of financial problems, the company endeavored to provide good service. For example, on Christmas Eve, December 24, 1923, a late car was operated from East Titusville at 11:30 p.m. into downtown Titusville to accommodate midnight churchgoers. The car stayed downtown and left for East Titusville after the church service was finished.

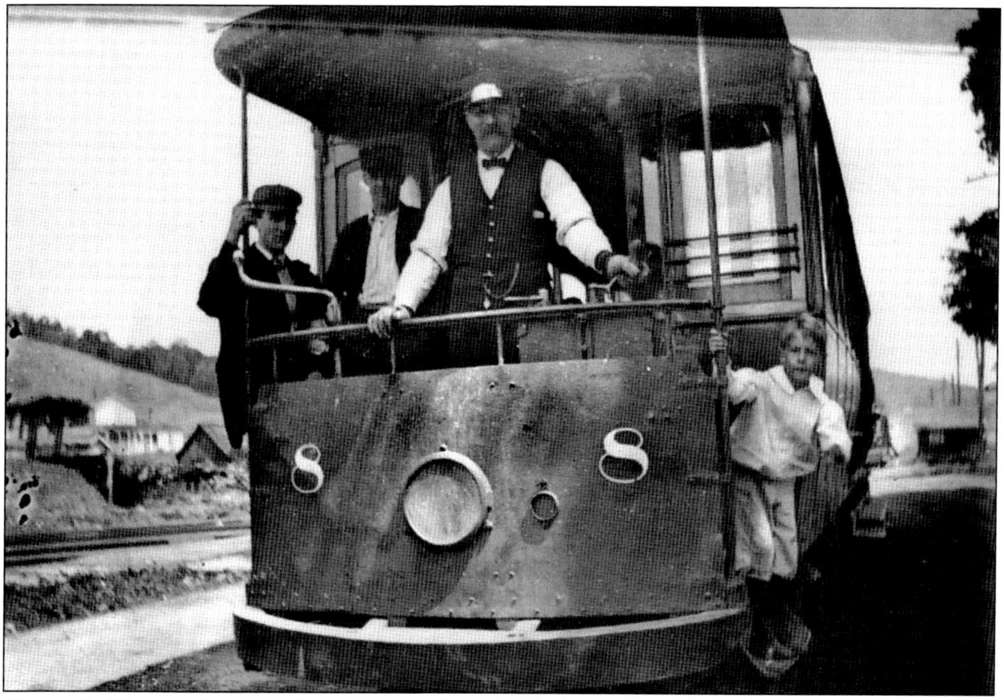

Titusville Electric Traction Company car No. 8, a half open and half closed car, was a popular way to travel in 1910 on the Hydetown-Canadea line. Before the advent of the automobile, people rode trolleys for the fun of it. The trolley car provided accessibility to the smaller communities of this region. (Harry Ridgway photograph.)

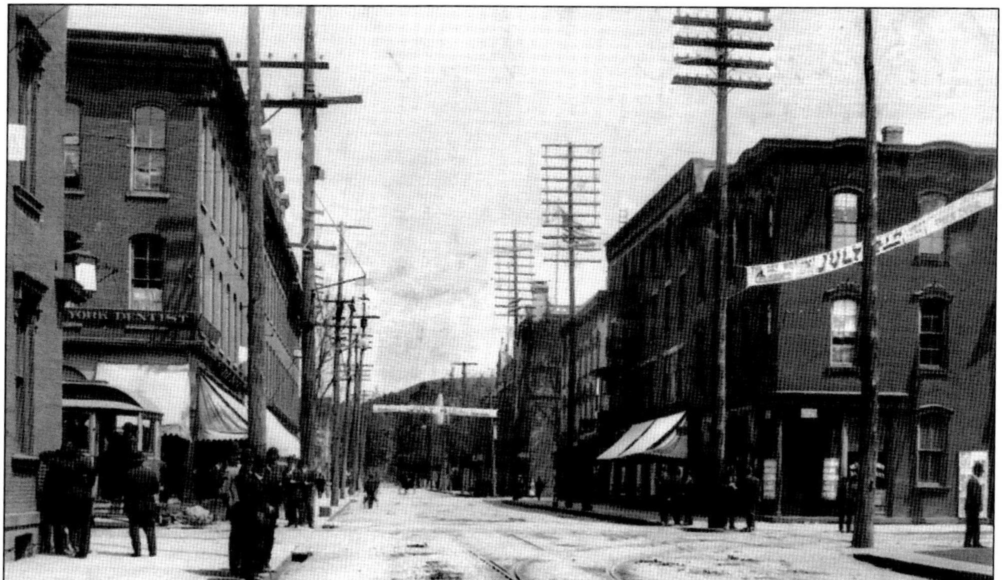

North Franklin Street in Titusville was used twice a week on the Titusville Electric Traction Company trolley freight run from the Pennsylvania Railroad station in Titusville to Pleasantville. The trolley company played an important role in the development of the region and strengthened downtown Titusville by bringing people to the shopping district. (John Dunn photograph.)

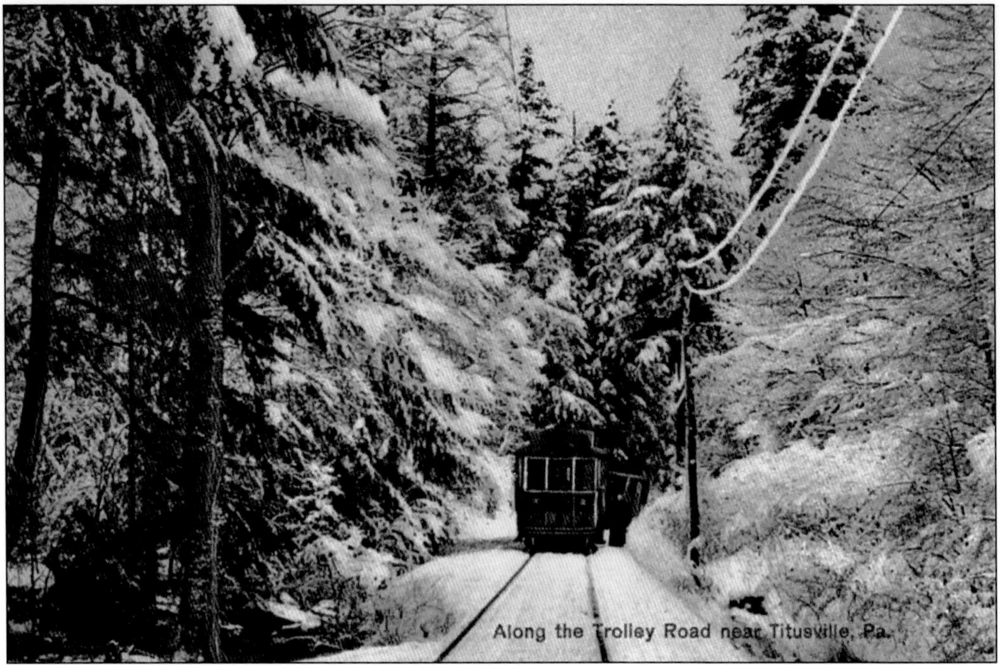

The Titusville Electric Traction Company trolley line to Mystic Park in the upper postcard view is a winter wonderland. In the scene below, a Titusville trolley was photographed in Pleasantville on February 15, 1910, in the winter snow. Although the trolley car had a brief history in this area, it has taken on a renewed life in the United States with a new name, light rail.

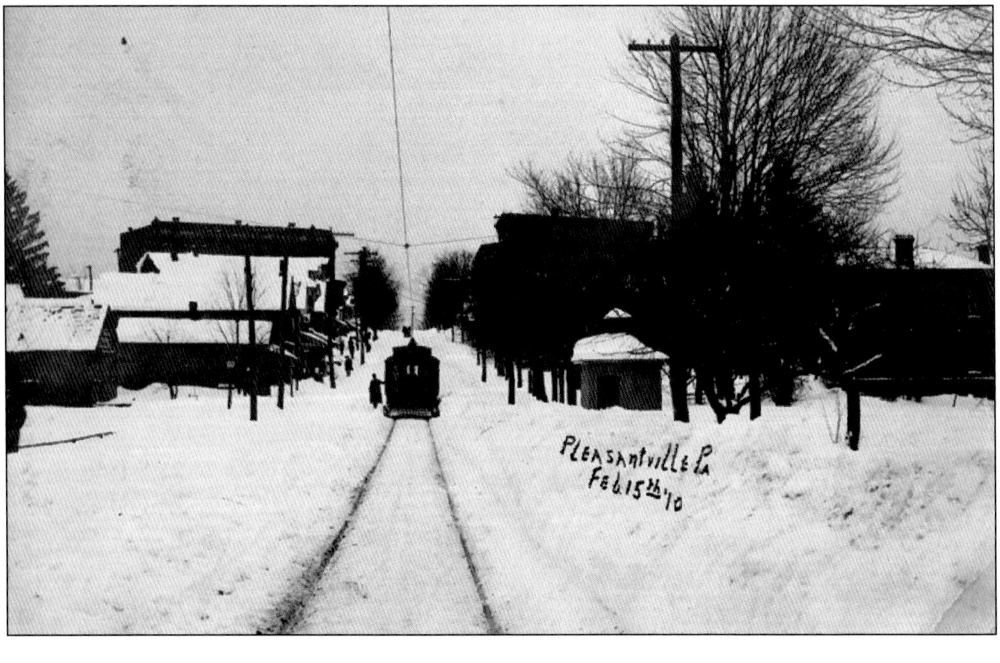